YANKEE
MAGAZINE'S
Ultimate
GUIDE TO
Autumn
IN
New England

YANKEE
MAGAZINE'S
Ultimate
GUIDE TO
Autumn
IN
New England

from
Yankee's Editors

Some of the material in this book may have previously appeared, before revision, in the *Yankee Traveler* newsletter, *Yankee Magazine's Travel Guide to New England,* and *Yankee* Magazine.

Text design by Jill Shaffer
Cover photo by Kindra Clineff

Library of Congress Cataloging-in-Publication Data is available.

ISBN 0-7627-0720-8
Co-published by Yankee Publishing Inc. and The Globe Pequot Press. Distributed to the trade by The Globe Pequot Press. Produced by Yankee Publishing Inc.

Printed in Canada.

First Edition
2 4 6 8 10 9 7 5 3 1 softcover

Contents

Don't miss this covered bridge, page 26.

Some of the old routes are best, page 116.

Not just any old tree, page 145.

*One off-road option,
page 180.*

Acknowledgments

I WOULD LIKE TO THANK my colleagues in the Travel Department: Mel Allen, editorial director, is a creative force in our department; his stories make a large contribution to this book. Carol Connare, senior associate editor, helped spearhead this project from its inception; her great ideas, energy, and writing have become a staple for the *Yankee* Travel group. Erica Bollerud, editorial assistant, provides us with good editorial judgment, sound fact-checking and photo research, and a lovely description of her trip on the Conway Scenic Railway during foliage. Big thanks go to Jean Camden for helping in so many ways — keeping the office running smoothly, acting as correspondence editor for the Travel Department, and keeping track of photos, payments, and mountains of mail. The newest member of the team, Katrina Yeager, has offered her fresh-from-college skills on all matters editorial, from fact-checking to dogged map research.

We are especially pleased with designer Jill Shaffer's work. She brings to this project 17 years of experience, which includes more than 50 titles. Her creativity and professionalism mark every page. Jamie Trowbridge, publishing director, has been a terrific source of support from the get-go. He knows foliage has been near and dear to the heart of *Yankee* Magazine for over 60 years, and he encouraged us to let the world know we are the authority on the subject.

Special thanks to our Production Department: Paul Belliveau, production director, juggles more schedules than any human should. He manages to keep everybody on deadline with a sense of humor (most of the time). Dave Ziarnowski, production manager, navigates his staff through the swift currents of desktop publishing, keeping pace with the growing technology. Special thanks to him for creating our useful maps. Lucille Rines, senior production artist, draws on 25 years of experience as a graphic designer; Yankee Publishing Inc. has had the good fortune to have her keen eye and expertise for most of her career. Thanks go to Rachel Kipka, also a senior production artist, for her technical skills and creativity. And through his illustrations, production assistant Brian Jenkins brings his fine artistic talent to these pages.

We are grateful to Lida Stinchfield and Stephanie McCusker for their excellent copyediting. Some might not consider this skill a craft, but copy editors are artisans, as far as we're concerned. Their attention to detail make this book eminently readable and useful.

Much gratitude goes to the editors and writers whose work we have included here. *Yankee* Magazine, *Yankee Magazine's Travel Guide to New England,* and our past travel books would not be as successful as they have been without the bright ideas and deft writing of these folks.

Yankee Magazine's Ultimate Guide to Autumn in New England is the third in a series of travel books co-published with the Globe Pequot Press. We extend a huge thanks to its capable staff for doing a great job distributing these books. Look for our other popular travel titles: *Yankee Magazine's Great Weekend Getaways in New England* and *Yankee Magazine's The New England We Love.*

Last but not least, we'd like to express our appreciation for Mother Nature. Without her clever and mysterious ways we would not have New England's briefest and best season of all: foliage.

– Polly Bannister
Managing Editor, Travel
Yankee *Magazine*

Introduction

N EW ENGLAND is my home. It hasn't always been. I was raised in the Midwest, but literally days after graduating from college, I left Indiana to settle in New England. There are lots of reasons why I came here; the enduring reason I stay is the seasons. Convention says we have four, but we know better.

There's winter with its snow, then the most welcome January thaw, and after that comes mud season, then spring with its fragrant flowers, followed by blackfly season. Then summer and salty beach days, followed by my favorite — fall. Bright blue skies, crisp apples, chilly nights, the first fires, and the bittersweet warmth of Indian-summer sun. This season's most generous gift, of course, is its flamboyant foliage display, unrivaled anywhere.

I know I am not alone in my love of autumn. During my years working for *Yankee* Magazine, I have talked to many readers about New England. They agree that what draws them to our region is the seasons — our dramatic, untamed, beautiful turning of nature's calendar. The conversation always ends with autumn, as if this is the grand finale, the last word on why seasons so nourish our spirit. Anyone who has witnessed New England's annual procession of fall color, even just one time, never forgets it.

The show starts with the burning red of the early swamp maples in Maine and in the mountains of Vermont and New Hampshire, and it continues throughout the region for more than a month. When the trees are nearly bare in the north, there remain the last colors on the southern coast of Connecticut. The palette: gold, bronze, orange, red, russet, copper, scarlet, peach, mahogany, and yellow. The pictures are postcard images: a church spire nestled in brilliant maples, a singular stand of white birches set off by yellow leaves, a picket fence against a backdrop of flaming red, and the classic Vermont hillside awash in color.

In *Yankee Magazine's Ultimate Guide to Autumn in New England* we give you these images, plus hundreds of recommendations and ideas on how to make the most of this brief but brilliant season. In this book you will find everything you need to know to enjoy fantastic foliage. Leaf peepers flock to see our color; knowing this, we have gone to great lengths to provide extensive lodging options. With this book in hand, you won't get caught without a room in October (and the room you end up with might even have a view to boot).

Since the inception of *Yankee* Magazine's Internet site, www.NewEngland.com, travelers from around the world have asked us for advice on how to catch the color. Year-round we receive foliage questions: When is peak? Where are the best views? What are *Yankee*'s favorite foliage driving tours? What do you do if you're stuck without lodging reservations? Beginning each August, the queries come flying at us through cyberspace. We've done our best here to answer these questions, as well as provide lots more essential information.

For each of our six states, we give you a driving tour that offers terrific vistas, off-the-beaten-path attractions, and lodging and dining suggestions. Knowing that there is hardly a prettier sight than foliage reflected in water, we tell you the locations of some of our most picturesque covered bridges (look for the "Covered Bridge Alert" icons). For first-person accounts, read our special feature, "Postcard From." And we've gone ahead to these tour destinations and asked town clerks, librarians, shopkeepers, and other locals for the places that make their towns unique (look for the "What the Locals Know" icons). As a special treat, we've connected the dots on these tours to create a two-week bonanza guaranteed to satisfy even the most die-hard foliage fanatic.

Two-Week Foliage Bonanza

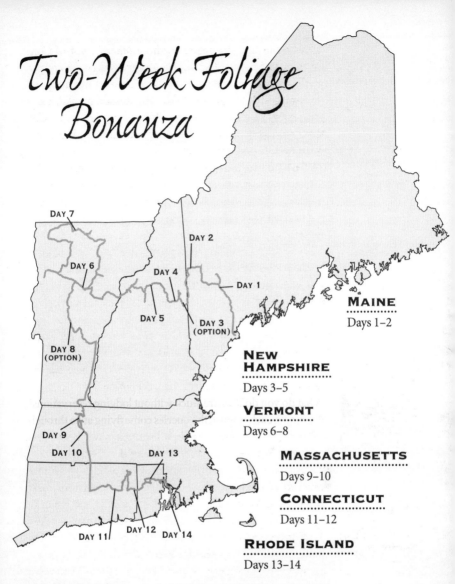

DAY 7

DAY 6

DAY 2

DAY 4

DAY 1

DAY 5

DAY 3
(OPTION)

DAY 8
(OPTION)

DAY 9

DAY 10

DAY 13

DAY 11

DAY 12

DAY 14

MAINE
Days 1–2

NEW HAMPSHIRE
Days 3–5

VERMONT
Days 6–8

MASSACHUSETTS
Days 9–10

CONNECTICUT
Days 11–12

RHODE ISLAND
Days 13–14

We tell you the stories behind New England's most scenic highways; where to find our champion trees; how to take foliage photographs as fine as any professional does; where you can drive for great summit views; and for the energetic, where to hike with the promise of a comfy inn at day's end. And if you're not a road warrior, there's a special chapter,

$ = most meals under $10

$$ = most meals $10-$16

$$$ = most meals $17-$23

$$$$ = most meals over $23

"Every Which Way but Pavement," devoted to other ways of catching the color — by canoe, kayak, windjammer, train, plane, and bike.

Practical information is included here, too, such as a chart of foliage zones with corresponding dates for peak color, current telephone numbers, admission fees, room rates, and restaurant prices. To the left you'll see a key that indicates what the dollar signs mean for meal prices.

For inspiration, we've added a color section, with photos from some of our favorite *Yankee* photographers. The bonus is a fold-out leaf poster — now you'll be able to tell a speckled alder from a quaking aspen.

In this book, we unlock New England's prettiest season for you and, in so doing, provide the *ultimate* guide to autumn. But more than that, consider this book an invitation to come share my favorite time of the year. The wonder of its beauty is just as impressive whether it's your first foliage season or your 50th.

– Polly Bannister
Managing Editor, Travel
Yankee *Magazine*

Behind the Wheel

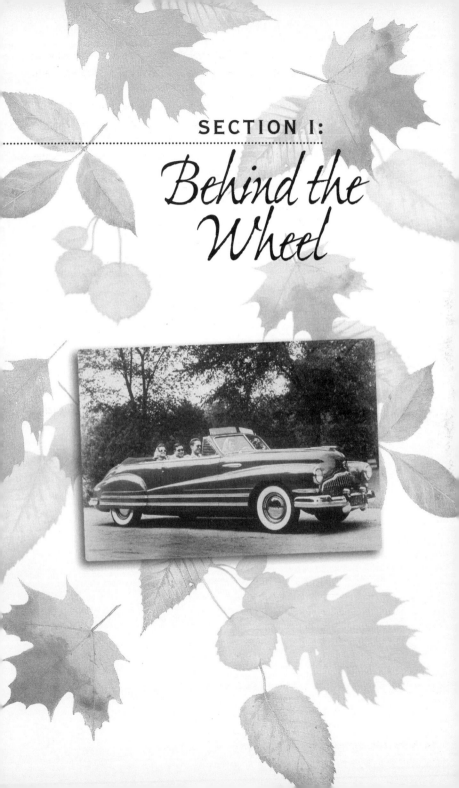

Maine WRIT LARGE
IN THE *Oxford Hills*

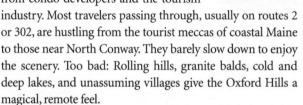

Pumpkins come in all sizes at Carter's Farm Market.

ORTUNATE QUIRKS of geography have saved both the region of western Maine from Bethel to Fryeburg and the area from the New Hampshire border to the Waterfords from condo developers and the tourism industry. Most travelers passing through, usually on routes 2 or 302, are hustling from the tourist meccas of coastal Maine to those near North Conway. They barely slow down to enjoy the scenery. Too bad: Rolling hills, granite balds, cold and deep lakes, and unassuming villages give the Oxford Hills a magical, remote feel.

Seeing the region doesn't require extended car travel — it's more a matter of getting there, then staying put or traveling about by foot. Try to visit during the world-famous (well, nearly) Fryeburg Fair in early October, a quintessential country fair of the highest order. If your timing doesn't work out, don't worry. The region's quiet attractions still hold plenty of allure.

This trip begins in Gray and concentrates on the Oxford Hills and Lakes region. We guarantee lots of vistas, a spectacular drive through Evans Notch, and the easiest hike with a real payoff at the top.

DAY ONE From the Maine Turnpike, take exit 11 to Gray and pick up Route 26, the sometimes scenic, sometimes not, traffic backbone of the area. If you are an animal lover or are traveling with children, don't miss the

Children pet deer at the Maine Wildlife Park.

Maine Wildlife Park. What started in 1931 as a farm to raise pheasants for release during bird-hunting season has evolved into a haven for orphaned and injured wildlife.

Run by the Maine Department of Inland Fisheries and Wildlife and a group of devoted volunteers, the park maintains both natural habitats for the animals as well as several nature trails, offers education programs, and has a gift shop run by the Maine Audubon Society. On our visit we saw bears, a big-antlered moose tucked safely in his hut, fishers, coyotes, peacocks, wild turkeys, a mountain lion, raccoons, and a wonderful selection of birds of prey, including barred and great horned owls, bald eagles, and kestrels. Many picnic tables are available under the shade of tall pines, and snacks are sold in the little shop. It is a good idea to bring dimes to buy food for the animals.

Harvesttime at the Sabbathday Lake Shaker Community.

The Sabbathday Lake Shaker Community and Museum is just eight miles north of Gray. At this, the last living Shaker community, harvest is the ideal time to visit. The air is filled with the sweet smell of their famous herbs drying in the autumn sun. Tours of the 17 white-clapboard buildings are available. You'll learn about the history of the Shakers and the English Ann Lee who founded this religious sect in 1775. We got a start on holiday shopping in the store that sells Shaker crafts (we doubt you'll be able to pass up the lovely oval boxes), furniture, herbs, baked goods, and fudge.

As you drive along Route 26 north, you'll see stretches dotted with mobile and modular homes, some rural poverty, and stunning views of foliage in the Oxford Hills. Agriculture is vital to this part of Maine, and the countryside reflects it with working farms and farm stands, where you'll find maple syrup, homemade ice cream, baked goods, cheeses, jams, and even bison meat.

If you're hungry, stop in at Hungry Hollow Country Store (on the right, six miles from Market Square in West Paris). Here homemade goodies abound; soups, sandwiches (lobster rolls always available through foliage season), baked beans, and Indian pudding are favorites. Eat in the six-seat store, at tables outside, or head up the road about one-half mile to the Snow Falls rest area on the left for a picnic. If a restaurant is more to your liking, we can recommend the River Restaurant across the street for excellent food at a good price.

Though you can't tell it from the road, the Oxford Hills hold an amazing diversity of minerals that have lured miners for generations. Perham's of West Paris is the largest attraction in the region. Nearly 100,000 people a year visit this world-class collection of gemstones. You'll see aquamarine, tourmaline, and amethyst among the many gemstones on display. The heart of the Maine selection was collected by Stan Perham, who founded the business with his wife, Hazel, in 1919. Their daughter, Jane Per-

Perham's of West Paris has been mining gems since the turn of the last century.

courtesy Perham's of West Paris

ham, a well-respected gemologist and author, runs it now. Part museum, part gift shop (fine jewelry, children's toys, crafts, and books), Perham's is an interesting stop even if you're not a rock hound. But if you are, ask for a map of Perham's local quarries and try your luck, at no charge. When we visited, a little boy had just turned up a watermelon tourmaline — but wouldn't disclose the quarry. (Bring your own hammer or pick, safety glasses, and bucket.)

One last great view before calling it a (full) day: Paris Hill. Backtrack on 26 to South Paris and look for the sign to Paris Hill, a road that climbs to a ridgetop. In the distance to the west, enjoy views of the White Mountains. Up close there are beautiful 19th-century buildings and the old stone Oxford County Jail, which now houses the Hamlin Memorial Library and Museum.

THE MAINE EXPERIENCE IS WRIT LARGE AT THE CENTER LOVELL INN.

One of Maine's leading crafts businesses, Christian Ridge Pottery, can be found a short distance away. From the center of town, take Lincoln Street to Christian Ridge Road (about ¼ mile on the right). In about a mile, you'll see Stock Farm Road on the right; follow signs to Christian Ridge Pottery. Their functional earthenware is sold across the country and in leading catalogs. Here you'll find pottery from $2 to $100 and great seconds, too. If your car is filled with apples from Hungry Hollow, consider buying a couple of apple-baking dishes — Christian Ridge has sold more than 700,000 of the ingenious things.

Some options for tonight's lodging follow. The Maine experience is writ large at the Center Lovell Inn, from the rustle of the white pines in the morning breeze to the call of the loon in the evening. In 1993, the former owners of the inn ran an essay contest, and out of 5,000 entries, Janice and Richard Cox won the contest and the inn. The Coxes, with the help of Janice's mom, Harriett Sage, and Harriett's husband, Earle, have received great reviews for their innkeeping and dinners. Some guest rooms are in the main house, and five are in the adjacent Harmon House. Dinner at the Center Lovell Inn (available to the public by reservation only) might include an appetizer of smoked pheasant ravioli in a wild mushroom cream sauce or baked brie in filo crust, and an entrée of fresh salmon, muscovy duck, veal piccata, or filet mignon.

Another good choice is the Waterford Inne, a classic country inn. Waterford, and especially the National Historic District known as Waterford Flat, is a pretty 19th-century period piece that shouldn't be missed. The Waterford Inne, a farmhouse complete with red barn and pond, is tucked away on a country lane surrounded by fields and woods. The atmosphere is warm and comfortable with a hint of elegance. The best part of all is that you don't have to leave for dinner — as long as you give them advance notice — and you'll find the meal delicious. (If you'd like wine with dinner, buy your bottle at nearby Springer's Store.)

You can also try the Kedarburn Inn, where you're guaranteed a restful night under a quilt handmade by owner Margaret Gibson. She and her husband, Derek, run their B&B from an 1858 Colonial on three acres set beside Kedar Brook in historic Waterford village. The first floor is a store with Maine-made crafts and Margaret's wonderful quilts (she takes custom orders). Peter and Emma Bodwell's popular restaurant, Peter's, is here, so relax once the car is parked — you can settle in for the night.

Earthenware being thrown at Christian Ridge Pottery.

courtesy Christian Ridge Pottery

If you're staying elsewhere, but want to visit Waterford, try having dinner at the Lake House. The food is elegant, and white linen and fresh flowers grace the tables. Don't hurry this experience, because chef Michael Myers is going to prepare your gourmet meal to order. He has eight rooms in the nicely restored inn, which was built in 1797 as the first tavern in Waterford.

Not far, at the junction of routes 5 and 35, travelers encounter one of New England's most famous road signs. Arrows indicate mileage to some exotic-sounding Maine towns: Norway, Paris, Denmark, Naples, Sweden, Mexico, Peru, and a few others. Nearby Tut's General Store serves up local gossip and good food.

WHAT THE LOCALS KNOW

The Good Earth

Folks in Oxford Hills know where to find the freshest local goods. Their hills are alive with working farms that welcome visitors, and each one has its own specialty. Here are some of our favorites.

Crestholm Farm Stand and Ice Cream, 207-539-2616. Rte. 26, Oxford. The hilltop view is irresistible from this farm that makes its own ice cream. Owned by Leslie, Suzanne, and Brian Hall, Crestholm is a Holstein dairy farm that sells honey, cheeses, and vegetables. Their free petting zoo includes ducks, goats, pigs, sheep, and calves. Open Mother's Day-

Halloween 10-6 (longer hours in summer).

Carter's Farm Market, 207-539-4848. Rte. 26, Oxford 04270. Run by the Carter family for 22 years, this market specializes in early cukes, sweet corn, tomatoes, homemade pickles and relish, pumpkins, winter squash, ornamental corn, and gourds. A part of the Maine Farm Bed-and-Breakfast Association, guests can stay here in two rooms ($60-$75, including full country breakfast) and enjoy the Little Androscoggin with their rented canoes and kayaks. Open year-round daily.

Crystal Spring Farm, 207-743- 6723. Rte. 26, Oxford;

halfway between Wal-Mart and Ames. The farm has been run by the Smedberg family, known throughout the area for their "one cow ice cream" (which is actually produced by more than a dozen Jerseys), for 34 years. Gayle and Roger offer "everything in its season," including bedding plants in the spring; sweet corn, fruits, and berries in the summer; and harvest vegetables, cheese, homemade bread, jams, homegrown beef and pork, and wreaths at Christmas. Open year-round daily 9-5; longer summer hours.

Hill and Gully Llamas, 207-527-2319. 15 Dunn Rd., North Norway. Hillary Ware raises llamas and educates people about these versatile animals that have been domesticated

DAY TWO Head north on Route 5/35 toward Bethel, the well-known ski town that is home to Sunday River. Today's views include Evans Notch, one of the region's most dramatic mountain passes. If you're getting anxious for a covered bridge, drive about five miles north to Newry. Spanning the Sunday River is Artist's Covered Bridge, so named because of its attraction by many 19th-century landscape painters.

From Bethel, drive west on Route 2 to Gilead. We stopped at G&T Country Store for inexpensive sandwiches: egg salad, grilled cheese, and tuna. We passed up the freshly made lemon meringue pie and regretted it all afternoon. They also sell homemade biscuits. This local lunch counter is the spot to

for 6,000 years. Llamas are good pack animals, and their soft fiber can be spun into warm hats and sweaters. Her herd numbers 19, and she welcomes visitors (for an up-close encounter with this gentle, graceful animal) by appointment. Open year-round.

Beech Hill Farm and Bison Ranch, 207-583-2515. Rte. 35, North Waterford. This ranch offers bison steaks, sausage, and jerky, as well as an on-site trading post (they sell everything bison here, from robes, skulls, and mounts to cookie cutters). Call ahead to arrange a hayride that offers great mountain views. Open year-round by appointment or by chance.

Hungry Hollow Country Store, 207-674-3012. Rte. 26,

Bethel Rd., West Paris. At this 32-acre orchard you can pick your own apples, pears, plums, peaches, and seasonal vegetables and flowers (antique roses). The farm is located just up the hill from the country store, where the specialty is old-fashioned all-meat chicken pie. But that is only the beginning of a large and delicious inventory that includes breads, pies, cookies, baked beans, Indian pudding, wheel cheese, homemade jams, maple syrup, and Maine crafts. Create your own gift baskets. Open year-round daily 7-5:30.

Cooper Farms, 207-674-2200. Rte. 26, West Paris. Located across the street from Hungry Hollow, this

courtesy Hungry Hollow

Delicious baked goods at Hungry Hollow Country Store.

farm stand sells fresh fruit and vegetables, Vermont cheese, homemade baked goods, apples, and maple syrup. Open July 4-November daily 9-6.

stock up on water, snacks, and juice before heading into the White Mountain National Forest.

Today is devoted to a hike in the White Mountain foothills. Hikes can range from a half-hour stroll along a river to a demanding nine-hour march up and across rugged granite ridges. If you are not in the mood for a strenuous day, just find a pull-off, safe from logging trucks, and pick your way along the big rocks along the Wild River. (We could have spent all day in the shallow riverbed.)

The region's best hiking is along the northern stretch of Route 113, which bisects the Evans Notch area of the White Mountain National Forest (road closed during the winter). These leafy woodlands along the valley floor are uncommonly well-endowed with streams and tumbling waterfalls. The ridges, which run to about 3,000 feet (less than half Mount Washington's height), afford remarkable views stretching from Lake Sebago to the towering Presidential Range, which is often dusted with snow by early autumn.

One terrific hiking trip of medium difficulty, suitable for both novices and experienced hikers, is East Royce Mountain. The round-trip requires two to three hours, depending on your vigor and inclination to dawdle streamside along the way.

Heading south on 113, the East Royce trailhead will be on your right (marked with a small U.S. Forest Service sign fronting an unpaved 20-car parking lot). The 1.3-mile hike (one-way) begins with a gentle ramble along Royce Brook then heads upward, becoming more strenuous as you approach the summit. The trail is well-marked but rugged in spots. The best views of the notch — and

WHAT THE LOCALS KNOW

Where to Find Great Ice Cream

We heard about the Corner Store in Stow from a *Yankee* subscriber who wrote:

I want to share a wonderful, small eating place that has lots of local color. There is a bakery, deli, and ice-cream counter that is small (only four stools). Folks stand around here to chat and enjoy the huge and scrumptious homemade sandwiches, baked goods, and enormous ice-cream cones. When we visited, the line reached out the door.

– sent to Yankee *Magazine by Wilma Horton*

Stow Corner Store & Bakery, 207-697-2943. Rte. 113, Stow. Open in summer daily 7 A.M.-9 P.M.; off-season 7-7. *Editor's note: I checked this place out, and it is great. Linda and Alfred Wright have been running the business for nearly 20 years, and they know just what people want: fresh coffee, home-baked goods, sandwiches, pizzas, beverages (including wine), and giant ice-cream cones. A great place to buy picnic supplies.*

the entire eastern range of the White Mountains — open up on a series of ledges about a quarter mile below the summit. Enjoy a picnic lunch, then retrace your steps back to your car.

Several other excellent hikes, including those in the wild Caribou-Speckled Wilderness Area, are easily accessible from Route 113. They're detailed in a free list of area hikes published by the White Mountain National Forest. Revive yourself with ice cream and baked goods at the Stow Corner Store & Bakery.

Prepare to slow way down as you drive through East Fryeburg. Pretty farms give way to rolling hills in a land that reveals why this area was settled long before other parts of Maine. Known to locals as the intervale, rich soil in this floodplain produces bountiful crops of potatoes, sweet and field corn, beans, and squash. *Now* it makes sense that the state's largest agricultural fair is held in Fryeberg.

Apart from the fair, Fryeburg doesn't wear its attractions on its sleeve. This town of 2,700 boasts a few small stores and a well-regarded preparatory school but hasn't gussied itself up much. Although Fryeburgers drive to the malls of North Conway (New Hampshire) for groceries and supplies (avoiding Maine's 6 percent sales tax), the town still has the brisk, prosperous feel of a former center of commerce that has aged with dignity.

If you can manage, plan your trip to include the Fryeburg Fair (it is always held Sunday to Sunday and includes the first Wednesday in October). The fairgrounds are on Route 5 North, but don't worry about finding it; just follow the traffic. The fair, with 300,000 in annual attendance, is an unvarnished New England classic. It's held by and for people who take livestock, vegetables, and fresh-baked pies seriously. *Very* seriously.

Take plenty of time to wander the fairgrounds. Small arenas, both indoors and out, are typically filled with Mainers who wear their best American Gothic expressions when watching the goat judging and horse pulls. About the only sign of gentrification is the presence of llamas, which, like pigs and cattle, are judged with a critical eye.

Permanent expo halls are arrayed with produce and baked goods, all awaiting the sharp eye of the judges. Zucchinis the

IF YOU CAN MANAGE, PLAN YOUR TRIP TO INCLUDE THE FRYEBURG FAIR.

Hemlock Covered Bridge is one of Fryeburg's many attractions.

size of a leg occupy some tables; jars of pickles and extraordinary pies bedeck others. For city dwellers, the most intriguing exhibit may be the poultry, which come in an exotic variety of remarkable plumages.

For lunch: fried dough, of course, dusted with powdered sugar. For just this one day, forget everything your doctor told you about fats.

If your tolerance for crowds is thin or you're visiting when the fairgrounds are vacant, consider an afternoon canoe trip on the Saco River. The Saco winds lazily through farmlands and pine forests from the White Mountains to the Maine coast. The segment from just west of Fryeburg to northeast of town — a peaceful stretch with prominent sandbars for picnicking — is among the most crowded on midsummer weekends. By fall, however, the hordes (and the insects) have departed and views of vibrant distant hills are unrivaled. Saco River Canoe & Kayak, Inc., rents out canoes and can arrange a shuttle back to your car. Reservations are essential during the foliage season.

Ready to call it a day? Depending on your budget and inclination, choose accommodations in Fryeburg, or for lake views, Bridgton or Naples.

In Fryeburg, the Admiral Peary House is off the main drag on a quiet, leafy street. The B&B is named for famed Arctic explorer Robert E. Peary, who lived here from 1877 to 1879 while working as a land surveyor. (He reached the Pole 30 years later.) The sturdy farmhouse has been well restored by Ed and Nancy Greenberg (the four guest rooms are in a converted, attached barn) and has been modernized with a clay tennis court, hot tub, and fine flower gardens.

The Oxford House Inn on Main Street offers five rooms in a 1913 Edwardian run by John and Phyllis Morris. The gardens are lovely, and the mountain view from the breakfast room can't be beat. Dine (on what might be called "country haute cuisine") at their popular restaurant, which is open to the public. The Morrises know food, and it shows. We had a delicious breakfast prepared by Phyllis: fresh-from-the-oven scones, pancakes with wild Maine blueberries, eggs, crisp bacon, and very good coffee.

At Acres of Austria you might be greeted by goats before your hosts, Candice and Franz Redl, welcome you to their private B&B. Located on a remote 65 acres of river, meadow, and pine grove, the atmosphere is decidedly Austrian, and with advance notice Franz will cook his hearty dinner specialties: *jaeger schnitzel, kas'nockn',* and *schweinsbraten.*

In Bridgton, the Noble House, run by Jane and Dick Staret, has nine guest rooms furnished with antiques. Across the road they have a private beach on Highland Lake, where a canoe awaits. If you are an antiques buff, don't miss Bridgton. In the past few years, the town has attracted numerous shops. If antiques aren't what you're looking for, try one of our favorite shops, Craftworks, in the Upper Village. Their extensive inventory (pottery, clothes, books, toys, and local crafts) fills a former church and two other buildings.

Two Beautiful Bridges

Hemlock Covered Bridge, built in 1857 of post-and-beam construction with a granite block foundation, is in East Fryeburg, a little west of Kezar Pond. From the junction of routes 5 and 302, take 302 east 5½ miles to Hemlock Bridge Road. Turn left and drive for about three miles on paved, then dirt, roads. The 116-foot-long bridge is well worth a visit.

Drive south toward the Ossipee River, and the 183-foot **Porter Covered Bridge** straddles Oxford and York counties. From Fryeburg, take Route 5/113 to East Brownfield; here take Route 160 to Porter. The bridge links the towns of Porter and Parsonsfield.

GET YOUR BLOOD MOVING WITH A SHORT HIKE UP JOCKEY CAP.

In Naples, the Augustus Bove House is an 1820 Colonial that was Hotel Naples from 1850 to 1939. The guest register includes opera star Enrico Caruso, Joseph P. Kennedy, and Howard Hughes. Here you'll find nice views of Long Lake.

Another fine B&B is Lamb's Mill Inn, an 1890s farmhouse on 20 acres; fields, woods, and perennial gardens surround this treasure.

Today the tour moves into New Hampshire, but before leaving the area, get your blood moving with a short hike up Jockey Cap. This climb to the top takes about ten minutes and affords breathtaking views of the White Mountains and local lakes. Look for the Jockey Cap Motel on Route 302; tucked between this and a small general store, there is a little white wooden arch. This is the entrance to the path; take the right fork, then left. If children are with you, be sure to leave time to scramble on the huge boulders at the head of the trail. At the rocky summit, a bronze marker designed by Arctic explorer Admiral Peary identifies the view.

If you are continuing our foliage bonanza, head west on Route 302 into New Hampshire.

– Wayne Curtis

ESSENTIALS

Oxford Hills Chamber of Commerce, 207-743-2281. P.O. Box 167, South Paris, ME 04281.

Bridgton-Lakes Region Chamber of Commerce, 207-647-3472. Box 236, Bridgton, ME 04009.

Fryeburg Information Center, 207-935-3639. Rte. 302, Fryeburg, ME 04037.

Maine Wildlife Park, 207-657-4977. Rte. 26, Gray. Open mid-April to Veterans Day daily 9:30-5:30 (gates close at 4 P.M.). $3.50, seniors $2.50, children 4-12 $2, under 3 free. (www.state.me.us/ifw/wildlifepark.htm)

The Sabbathday Lake Shaker Community and Museum, 207-926-4597. Rte. 26, New Gloucester. Open Memorial Day-Columbus Day Monday-Saturday 10-4:30. $6, children 6-12 $2.

The River Restaurant, 207-743-7816. Rte. 26, Norway. Open Tuesday-Sunday for lunch ($) and dinner ($$-$$$).

Perham's of West Paris, 800-371-4367, 207-674-2341. Rte. 26, West Paris. Open year-round daily (except Thanksgiving and Christmas) 9-5.

Hamlin Memorial Library and Museum, 207-743-2980. Off Rte. 26, Paris Hill. Open year-round Tuesday-Friday 11:30-5:30.

Christian Ridge Pottery, 207-743-8419. 210 Stock Farm Rd., South Paris. Open year-round (call ahead in February) Monday-Saturday 10-5.

Center Lovell Inn, 800-777-2698, 207-925-1575. Rte. 5, Center Lovell, ME 04016. Open all months except November and April. Ten rooms. $97-$290, depending on room and meal plan. (www.centerlovellinn.com)

The Waterford Inne, 207-583-4037. Box 149 Chadbourne Rd., Waterford, ME 04088. Open year-round. Eight rooms, one suite. $75-$105, including breakfast. ($$-$$$) Dinner available with advance reservations. (www.innbook.com/water.html)

Kedarburn Inn, 207-583-6182. Rte. 35, Waterford, ME 04088. Open year-round. Seven rooms. $75-$125, including breakfast.

Peter's Restaurant, 207-583-6265. Located in the Kedarburn Inn. ($$-$$$) Open May-Columbus Day weekend.

Lake House, 800-223-4182, 207-583-4182. Rtes. 35 and 37, Waterford, ME 04088. Open year-round. Eight rooms. $95-$150 (B&B), $150-$205 (MAP). ($$$) Open for dinner July-August daily; May, June, September, and October Tuesday-Sunday; closed November and April; in winter only weekends. (www.lakehousemaine.com)

Tut's General Store, 800-281-4437. Rte. 35, Waterford. Open daily at 6 A.M.

G&T Country Store, 207-836-6036. Corner of Rte. 2 and Flat Rd., West Bethel. Open Monday-Thursday 6 A.M.-8 P.M., Friday-Saturday 6 A.M.-9 P.M., Sunday 8-6.

White Mountain National Forest Hikes, available from Evans Notch Ranger Station, RFD 2, Box 2270, Bethel, ME 04217.

Fryeburg Fair, 207-935-3268. Fairgrounds Rte. 5 North, Fryeburg. Always held Sunday to Sunday, and includes the first Wednesday in October. Weekends $5, weekdays $4; under 13 free; parking $2.

Saco River Canoe & Kayak, Inc., 207-935-2369. 188 Main St., Fryeburg. Open May to mid-October. Shuttle $9-$11, canoe rentals $25.50-$28, kayaks $20. (www.sacorivercanoe.com)

The Admiral Peary House, 800-237-8080, 207-935-3365. 9 Elm St., Fryeburg, ME 04037. Open year-round. Six rooms. $98-$128, including breakfast. No smoking. (www.mountwashingtonvalley.com/admiralpearyhouse)

The Oxford House Inn, 800-261-7206, 207-935-3442. 105 Main St., Fryeburg, ME 04037.

Open year-round. Five rooms. $75-$125, including breakfast. ($$$) Gourmet dinner 6-9 P.M. (mountwashington valley.com/oxfordhouse)

Acres of Austria, 800-988-4391, 207-925-6547. RR 1, Box 177, Fryeburg, ME 04037. Open year-round. Four rooms. $75-$105, including breakfast. (www.bbhost.com/acresofaustria)

The Noble House, 207-647-3733. Box 180, Bridgton, ME 04009. Open year-round. Nine rooms. $78-$125, including breakfast.

Augustus Bove House, 207-693-6365. Corner rtes. 302 and 114, RR 1 Box 501, Naples, ME 04055. Open year-round. Six rooms. $79-$175, including breakfast. (www.maineguide.com/naples/augustus)

Lamb's Mill Inn, 207-693-6253. Lamb's Mill Rd., RR 1 Box 676, Naples, ME 04055. Open year-round. Six rooms. $85-$105, including breakfast.

New Hampshire's
WHITE MOUNTAIN *Glory*

Cannon Mountain is the site of America's first aerial tramway.

Y OU DON'T HAVE to be a hiker to enjoy New Hampshire's majestic White Mountains, where roads lead into the heart of New England's most renowned peaks. Make this drive and along the way you can visit inns and eateries with broad views of Mount Washington (New England's highest peak at 6,288 feet) and the Presidential Range. After a few hours you may come to expect mountain views at every turn, but it's unlikely you'll tire of them. The mountains change — cloaked with fog in early morning and often razor sharp by midday; their forms take shape around the winding roads like a well-turned tale.

Begin this tour in North Conway, take in some of the area's best attractions, enjoy knock-your-socks-off mountain views, and sleep in New Hampshire's prettiest towns. Most of the trip is on scenic 302, the route that will take us into Vermont for the next driving trip — *Yankee*'s famous all-time-best foliage tour.

DAY ONE Route 302 joins Route 16 North in North Conway, where almost any hour of the day you'll find traffic comparable to rush hour. The name of the game here is shopping. Longtime favorite stops are Yield

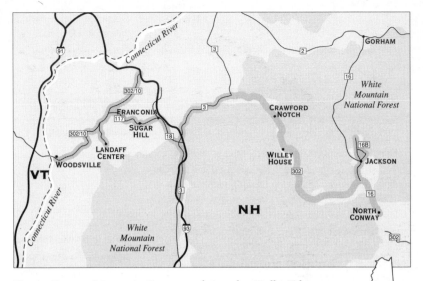

House, Eastern Mountain Sports, and Annalee Dolls. Take your pick of outlets; most are located in Settlers' Green Outlet Village Plus (over 50 stores, including Gap Clearance Store, Nike, Dockers, Orvis, and others) or in the Tanger Outlet Centers, with Polo/Ralph Lauren, L.L. Bean Factory Store, and (in the Red Barn Center) Jones New York, Factory Finale, and many, many more. (Both outlet areas are on Route 16.)

If you tire of name brands and long to see something handmade, stop at the League of New Hampshire Craftsmen. Then there is also Zeb's. A little removed from the outlets, this store stocks only goods made in New England. Named after a Martha's Vineyard sea captain, Zeb's is a "new" general store full of toys, food, baskets, and — yes — bag balm.

Though we don't recommend it, there are enough stores in the area to spend the entire foliage season shopping. If you find you've shopped till you're about to drop, please see our suggestions for lodging in North Conway. But when we've come just for shopping, our favorite excursion ends not in North Conway, but a little south, away from the commotion. Eaton Center, with its idyllic setting on Crystal Lake, is just 15 minutes south on Route 153. We reserve a room at the Inn at Crystal Lake, an 11-bedroom 1884 Victorian that is the centerpiece of the village. Relax in the evening with a walk along

Some Good Places to Drop, When You've Shopped North Conway

White Mountain Hotel and Resort, 800-533-6301, 603-356-7100. West Side Rd. at Hale's Location, North Conway, NH 03860. The dramatic stone face of White Horse Ledge rises behind this good-sized hotel. Amenities include a nine-hole golf course, fitness center, and year-round outdoor pool. The best place to view the foliage is out the windows of the Ledges dining room, where guests can gaze out upon Mount Cranmore during any meal. Open year-round. 80 rooms. $69-$179, including breakfast — only in winter and in spring midweek. Ledges dining room open for breakfast, lunch ($$), and dinner ($$$). (www.whitemountainhotel.com)

Cranmore Inn, 603-356-5502. Kearsarge St., North Conway, NH 03860. The oldest continuously operating inn in the valley, just one block from North Conway's main drag. Open year-round. 18 rooms, including three mini-suites. $54-$94, including breakfast. (www.cranmoreinn.com)

Stonehurst Manor, 800-525-9100, 603-356-3113. Rte. 16, North Conway, NH 03860. ($$-$$$) Dinner is a real treat here: Staff serve up Continental extravagances (beef Wellington, veal Oscar) or wood-fired, stone-oven pizzas. You'll feel like royalty in this three-story, English-style villa punctuated with fine wood and stonework and rooms that are accented with antiques. Open year-round. 24 rooms. $86-$216, including breakfast and dinner. (www.stonehurstmanor.com)

The 1785 Inn and Restaurant, 800-421-1785, 603-356-9025. Rte. 16, North Conway, NH 03860. Come for the mountain views but savor the history: This Revolutionary-era home has original hand-hewn beams and 215-year-old original fireplaces. ($$$) Study the wine list (over 200 labels) sitting by the fire before a gourmet dinner. Open year-round. 17 rooms. $99-$209, including breakfast. (www.the1785inn.com)

Nereledge Inn, 603-356-2831. River Rd., North Conway, NH 03860. Just a short walk from the village. You might not make it beyond the porch rockers of this 1787 Colonial farmhouse boasting views of Cathedral Ledge and the Moat Mountains. The fireplaced sitting room is an

the lake and a game of billiards by the fire. Just a bit east in Snowville, another wonderful choice is the Snowvillage Inn. Built as a summer home in 1916, the inn has sweeping views of the Presidential Range, including Mount Washington. The inn's restaurant is recognized for its elegant country dining. (Nothing like a four-course candlelit dinner to revive you after a day of shopping.)

For those hearty travelers and nonshoppers who want some action, the Conway Scenic Railroad in North Conway offers round-trip train rides through some of the finest evening draw, with games and darts. Open year-round. 11 rooms. $59-$139, including breakfast. (www.nereledgeinn.com)

Oxen Yoke, 800-862-1600, 603-356-6321. Kearsarge St., North Conway. This cozy inn is owned and operated by the much larger Eastern Slope Inn, which anchors downtown North Conway. Just a few blocks from the village, this circa-1900 Victorian offers a quieter alternative with mountain views. Best of all, guests may use all the amenities at Eastern Slope. Open year-round. 21 rooms. $58-$177, including breakfast only on weekends. (www.easternslopeinn.com)

The Victorian Harvest Inn Bed & Breakfast, 800-642-0749. 603-356-3548. 28 Locust Lane, North Conway, 03860. Peace and quiet reign at this smaller-scale 1850 Victorian. Some rooms have gas fireplaces and many have mountain views. Open year-round. Six rooms. $70-$130, including breakfast. (www.victorianharvest inn.com)

Wyatt House Country Inn, 800-527-7978, 603-356-7977. Main St., North Conway, NH 03860. How best to relax after a day of shopping? Book a room at this 1893 Victorian set on the banks of the Saco River with a panoramic view of the Moat Mountains. Open year-round. Seven rooms. $60-$189, including a candlelight gourmet breakfast served on English Wedgwood and Irish lace. (www.wyatthouse.com)

Fox Ridge Motor Inn, 800-343-1804, 603-356-3151. Rte. 16, North Conway, NH 03860. Here's a welcome departure from North Conway's plethora of motels on "the strip." This gem sits high on a hill on 300 acres and is virtu-

ally invisible from the main road. Its perch affords great mountain views and a peaceful setting. Most rooms have private patios. After a long day of shopping, the indoor and outdoor swimming pool and whirlpool are a godsend. Open May-November. 136 rooms. $65-$150. Breakfast available (not included) in dining room off lobby. (www.foxridge@ redjacketinns.com)

Green Granite Inn, 800-468-3666, 603-356-6901. Rte. 16, North Conway, NH 03860. This inn is family owned and is one of the most attractive and hospitable places in the Mount Washington Valley. Newly renovated, it has indoor and outdoor pools, an exercise room, and sauna. Open year-round. 91 rooms. $59-$199, including continental breakfast. (www.greengranite.com)

scenery in the Northeast. Choose between two Valley Excursions or the longer Notch Trip.

Families will enjoy Heritage New Hampshire (adjacent to Story Land in Glen), which presents 300 years of Granite State history. We enjoyed the visit here as much as our ten-year-old. More than 100,000 New Hampshire fourth-graders have experienced "time travel" since Heritage opened its doors 20 years ago.

Admission books a visitor's passage on a 17th-century sailing ship that arrives in the New World in 1635. Explore early woodlands, see how Native Americans lived, watch a replica of a circa-1725 printing press roll off the daily news, gaze at an awesome 35½-inch diameter white pine mast tree, hear President George Washington give a speech in Portsmouth, visit an 1850s kitchen, and hop aboard for a simulated train ride through Crawford Notch during foliage. Heritage New Hampshire is operated, along with Story Land, by the Morrell Family.

Though the area along routes 16 and 302 is packed with inns, B&Bs, resorts, and motels, you'll want to reserve ahead at this time of the year. Here is a handful of good choices.

POSTCARD From

Conway Scenic Railway

We boarded the "Notch train" and soon departed. As the train picked up speed, each of the cars rocked back and forth like hammocks strung end to end between the engine and the caboose viewing platform. We settled in for a 5½-hour round-trip ride through famed Crawford Notch. The guide's burly voice crackled over the loudspeaker with a steady stream of history and lore — tales of the railroad's varied past. He directed our attention to railside attractions such as the foundations of old houses, rare stands of trees, and the confluence of rivers: "It is not every day that you see a confluence, so take a good look."

Trundling through intersections and backyards, we observed the phenomenon of

people waving at trains, and we all waved back. We were lulled by the rocking cars, the stories, the crisp weather, and of course the trees, which increased in number and vividness as we neared the peaks of Mount Washington and the Presidential Range. The train paused over the especially impressive parts, allowing us to drink in the vistas. We craned our necks to see up the slopes of Mount Wally, and down into the deep valleys

of trees spreading below towering train trestles. At the apex of the trip, we arrived at Fabyan Station and disembarked to stretch our legs. There were few trees at this elevation, and the station was mainly populated by hikers of the Appalachian Trail, busily putting on extra layers. We didn't envy them: We were just a few minutes away from a cup of hot cocoa, more stories, and the colorful return trip.

– Erica Bollerud

Conway Scenic Railway, 800-232-5251, 603-356-5251. Rte. 16, North Conway Railroad Station. Open shoulder seasons only weekends; mid-May to the end of October daily. Lunch and dinner served July 4 through foliage. Prices vary according to excursion but average (with train fare) $20-$45. (www.conwayscenic.com)

Les MacDonald/courtesy Conway Scenic Railway

In Glen, the Bernerhof, a turreted Victorian inn has long been known for its wonderful Swiss cuisine. But you'd never guess what luxury awaits in some of the guest rooms: hot tubs à deux under skylights or stained glass. The inn also hosts a Taste of the Mountains Cooking School and Prince Place, a premier restaurant.

In Jackson: Carter Notch Inn is an elegant, late-1800s country cottage with a wraparound porch where wicker abounds. The Ellis River House is an 1893 Colonial with a recent addition (20 rooms total), outside heated pool, some suites, a sauna, spectacular mountain views, and river frontage. A Victorian designed in 1902 by Stanford White for the Baldwin family (of piano fame) houses the Inn at Jackson. Here you'll find an outdoor Jacuzzi, large rooms (many with fireplaces), and good views of the village and mountains. The Inn at Thorn Hill, another White-designed summerhouse, makes an ideal retreat. Among several buildings are 19 bedrooms, and guests usually have designs on the dining room, where gourmet fare and an award-winning wine list will wow even the most sophisticated diner. Another good option is the Village House, an 1860 Colonial on six riverfront acres, with a wraparound porch, tennis court, and outdoor Jacuzzi. If you're an animal lover, you'll find lots to talk about with innkeeper Robin Crocker, who raises service dogs and is involved in the NEADS puppy-raiser program.

Conway's Two Bridges

West Side Road is a scenic route that runs from Conway to North Conway. By taking this, you can avoid the traffic of busy Route 16 *and* see two covered bridges along the way. The **Conway-Saco River Bridge,** the third bridge on this site, was built in 1890 and is 244 feet long. To visit: From 16 in Conway Village, turn west on West Side Road; bear right to go through the bridge. The **Conway-Swift River Bridge** was rebuilt in 1869 after a flood destroyed the original circa-1850s bridge. Now only for foot traffic, the paddleford truss bridge is 128 feet long and 21 feet wide. This bridge was restored in 1991. To visit: From 16 in Conway Village, turn west on West Side Road; bear left; the bridge will be on your right.

DAY TWO   On today's itinerary you'll be deep in the mountains, not just looking out at them. Since the Kancamagus Highway (Route 112) can be overcrowded at this time of year, we suggest that you take a less-traveled scenic loop through Jackson (if you didn't already do this last night to find your sleeping quarters). Follow Route 16

The Mount Washington Hotel sits at the foot of the Presidential Range.

north to Route 16B and drive across a covered bridge into Jackson, a pocket-size town. Stay right on 16B up a steep hill. This rural five-mile circuit takes you past some beautiful old hillside farmhouses and offers mountain vistas. On the right looms the Eagle Mountain Resort, a majestic old hotel that has been completely updated without losing its grand flavor.

As you come back into Jackson village, turn left at the community church. Don't miss this rewarding short walk: Park your car downtown and follow the sidewalk alongside Route 16B, which winds along Jackson Falls. This stretch of the Wildcat River begs to be admired. In the low water of fall, you can pick your way among the boulders and imagine how threatening this is during spring runoff. At the Jackson Falls sign you can walk out on the wooden footbridge.

As you head south out of town, turn left after the Wildcat Inn & Tavern; this back-road loop will take you to Route 16A, which passes all the little inns in Intervale. Then follow Route 302 northwest. Soon the mountains will close in and you'll follow the Saco River into the White Mountain National Forest and Crawford Notch State Park. Historic Willey House, a gift shop, is on the left, and across the street there is a good spot to stretch your legs with a stroll over the river via footbridge. We stopped here, bought a handful of fish food from the dispenser, and enjoyed tossing it to the lively fish below.

Back on the road, seven miles later you'll come to the Mount Washington Hotel, a stately white edifice with a red

TODAY YOU'LL BE DEEP IN THE MOUNTAINS, NOT JUST LOOKING OUT AT THEM.

roof. For nearly 100 years, this grand hotel has fringed the foot of Mount Washington like a bride's petticoat. A columned veranda, an octagonal dining room, and newly renovated rooms spell luxury. A good stop for lunch is the hotel's downstairs café. Stroll around the building on the immense open porches to appreciate the incredible scale of this complex built by a wealthy railroad magnate in 1902. Presidents, royalty, and scores of celebrities have stayed here, and as many as 57 trains arrived daily during the resort's heyday.

Just past the hotel you'll see the turnoff for the Mount Washington Cog Railway — the means for a journey to the summit of Mount Washington on the second-steepest railway track in the world. This was the world's first mountain-climbing cog railway; it opened in 1869, and it still ascends the highest peak in the Northeast under steam locomotion. No matter what the temperature, bring a sweater. Mount Washington is notorious for changeable conditions.

After you've seen the sights from on high, take Route 3 south to the Franconia Parkway (Route 93 south). Few drives in New England are more dramatic than this sinuous squeeze past craggy cliffs, including the Old Man of the Mountain. Many fail to glimpse the boulder face profile from the road. To see the outline clearly, get out of your car and follow the 800-foot walkway to Profile Lake (once called the Old Man's Washbowl).

The Mount Washington Cog Railway is one of the few steam-powered trains in the country.

Jim McElholm/Single Source Photography

The Flume Gorge

We parked at the Visitor Center, a giant lodge that serves as access for a two-mile loop through the Flume. My daughter, husband, and I were excited to finally visit this natural gorge, an 800-foot-long corridor of granite. We hiked the dirt path slowly and soon got to the good part — wooden walkways suspended from 70-foot-high walls. A cool mist hung in the air and the Flume Brook barreled noisily underfoot. Our knees grew weak when we looked down. I was grateful for an excuse to slow down and steady my legs; nobody should rush the Flume. The father of a family of boys asked me to snap their portrait. They lined up against a wooden railing, smiling, more at the view than at the camera. In the background we heard constant "ooohs and ahhhs" above rushing water. It felt like we were in a rain forest where mist rises and settles on brilliant green mosses and ferns. I'd seen places this magical in Hawaii, but I was awed by this natural beauty so close to home. We stopped at an overlook to gaze at a scenic pool with a handful of other admirers. I commented to a woman nearby that this was our first visit. She replied that the Flume is an annual tradition for her family, and I thought to myself that we

Waterfall at the Flume, an 800-foot-long corridor of granite.

should make it so, too.

– *Polly Bannister*

Flume Gorge, 603-745-8391. Exit 1 off I-93, Lincoln. Open mid-May to late October. $7, children $5.

⋯⋯⋯⋯⋯⋯⋯⋯⋯⋯⋯⋯⋯⋯⋯⋯⋯⋯⋯⋯⋯⋯⋯⋯⋯⋯⋯⋯⋯⋯⋯⋯⋯⋯⋯⋯⋯⋯

While you're here, take a five-minute ride on the Cannon Mountain Aerial Tramway to the 4,200-foot summit. In 1938 the first passenger aerial tramway operated from this site, and you can stand inside it at the New England Ski Museum next door. Five miles south lies one of the region's most awesome natural wonders — the Flume Gorge.

You'll sleep well tonight in the quiet of Sugar Hill, a hilltop town named for its abundance of sugar maples. Drive north on I-93, turn onto Route 18 north then left onto Route 117. A handful of inns dot the landscape. Every one of the six rooms at Foxglove, A Country Inn, looks like a set from a romantic movie. The Hilltop Inn offers spectacular mountain views, handmade quilts, and a delicious buffet breakfast prepared by caterers/innkeepers Mike and Meri Hern. At the Sugar Hill

Inn, Bette Davis always stayed in the room overlooking mountains and fields of lupine (Sugar Hill is home to an annual lupine festival each June). You can dine in on weekends and choose from entrées such as rack of lamb or cranberry-glazed duck. The Homestead Inn was founded by Moses and Sarah Aldrich, Sugar Hill's first permanent settlers on the original King's Grant, and has been handed down through seven generations. Next door, visit the converted 90-foot-long barn called Sugar Hill Sampler, which houses a museum with family artifacts, heirlooms, photos, tools, and crafts and a gift shop featuring miniatures, pottery, jams, candy, quilts, and antiques. Views don't get any better than those from Sunset Hill Road. At the end, you'll find Sunset Hill House; with 29 rooms, it is the largest lodging establishment in town. From their ridgetop location, you can see the Green Mountains to the west and the Whites to the east.

Start the day with breakfast at Polly's Pancake Parlor on Route 117 in Sugar Hill, a must for its no-sugar pancakes topped with pure maple syrup. They grind their own grains for six different pancake mixes, and all the baking is done on the premises. Also, they have been charting peak foliage for more than 40 years (you can buy a copy of these records). After breakfast, follow signs from Main Street to routes 302 and 10 south to Lisbon.

Stop in Bath and walk through the longest covered bridge in New Hampshire and one of the oldest in America, built in 1832. The Brick Store claims to be America's oldest general store. Don't worry if this is true, just enjoy the extensive inventory, slowly strolling wide

Best View: Landaff Center

Approximately 300 people live in this hamlet nestled between the White Mountains and the Connecticut River. What they know is that they live among the most picturesque scenery in the area and that a surefire foliage photo opportunity is the view from their town hall. They also know things might have been very different if Governor John Wentworth had gotten his way in 1770 when he solicited to have Landaff become the site of Dartmouth College. I asked a few residents what they thought of this, and all agreed they were pleased Hanover had been selected instead. Their views would not be the peaceful ones we see today.

Landaff Center: Heading south from Lisbon, turn left on Landaff Road, drive about 1.5 miles to Jockey Hill, bear left, and it is about another 1.5 miles to Landaff Center. For a scenic loop, turn right in Landaff on Center Hill Road, then take another right on Mill Brook Road, which ends at Route 302 a little west of Lisbon.

The Brick Store calls itself America's oldest general store.

David Voorhis

floorboards that creak from hundreds of years of use. We had ice cream at the Hop, a 1950s-style parlor next door. The walls are decorated with records, movie bills, and concert posters, including some rare and valuable Beatles memorabilia.

The Connecticut River divides New Hampshire and Vermont, winding through what are known as the Upper Valley towns, the last of which is Woodsville. If Polly's pancakes are beginning to wear off, try Chalet Schaefer for lunch. During foliage, it offers fowl and game dishes that feature venison, wild boar, rabbit, bison, pheasant, and duck, but its specialty for more than 20 years has been a German menu with wieners, homemade sauerkraut, and other authentic treats.

If you'd like to wait for lunch until you are in Vermont or have heard of the famous P&H Truck Stop, you're only a few miles away from homemade food that has lured hungry folks round the clock for years. The tour continues on Route 302 into a very scenic stretch of Vermont farmland.

– Polly Bannister

Oldest and Longest Bridges

The **Bath Covered Bridge** is the longest in New Hampshire (the one in Cornish is longer, but its western part lies in Vermont) at 374 feet 6 inches long. It was built around 1832 of old hewed arches and has new overlapping arches that were added when the bridge was raised over the railroad. To visit: The bridge is west of Route 302 in Bath Village, next to the Brick Store. Not far away is another, the **Bath-Haverhill bridge,** on the route between Haverhill and Bath, which were larger and more influential than Woodsville, where it is actually located. Built in 1832 to span the Ammonoosuc River, it is the oldest authenticated covered bridge in the state. To visit: The bridge is on Route 135, ¼ mile north of Route 302 in Woodsville.

ESSENTIALS

Mount Washington Valley Chamber of Commerce & Visitors Bureau, 800-367-3364, 603-356-3171. P.O. Box 2300, North Conway, NH 03860; Visitor Center is across from the railroad station. Open year-round. (www.4seasonresort.com)

White Mountains Attractions Association, 800-346-3687, 603-745-8720. P.O. Box 10, Rte. 112, North Woodstock, NH 03262. (www.visitwhitemountains.com)

Conway Village Chamber of Commerce, 603-447-2639. Seasonal information booth is located south of town on Rte. 16.

Franconia-Easton-Sugar Hill Chamber of Commerce, 800-237-9007, 603-823-5661. Box 780, Main St., Franconia, NH 03580. Visitor information booth open through foliage. (www.franconianotch.org)

Twin Mountain Chamber of Commerce, 800-245-8946, 603-846-5407. Box 194, Twin Mountain, NH 03595.

Settlers' Green Outlet Village Plus, 603-356-7031. Rte. 16 and Settlers Dr., North Conway. Open Monday-Saturday 10-9, Sunday 10-6. (www.settlersgreen.com)

Tanger Outlet Centers, 800-407-4078. Rte. 16, North Conway. Open Monday-Saturday 9-9, Sunday 10-6. (www.tangeroutlet.com)

League of New Hampshire Craftsmen, 603-356-2441. 2526 Main St. (Rte. 16), North Conway. Open daily 10-5; summer and foliage season 9-6. (www.nhcrafts.com)

Zeb's, 800-676-9294, 603-356-9294. 2675 White Mountain Hwy. (Main St.), village of North Conway. Open year-round daily 9 A.M.-10 P.M. (www.zebs.com)

Inn at Crystal Lake, 800-343-7336, 603-447-2120. Rte. 153, Eaton Center, NH 03832. Open year-round. 11 rooms. $70-$140, including breakfast. (www.innatcrystallake.com)

Heritage New Hampshire, 603-383-9776. Rte. 16, Glen. Open Memorial Day-late June only weekends 10-5; late June to mid-October daily 9-5. $10, children 6-12 $4.50, under age 6 free. (www.heritagenh.com)

Story Land, 603-383-4186. Rte. 16, Glen. Open Memorial Day-late June only weekends, 10-5; late June-Labor Day, daily 9-6; Labor Day-Columbus Day only weekends 9-5. (www.storylandnh.com)

Bernerhof, 800-548-8007, 603-383-9132. Rte. 302, Glen,

NH 03838. Open year-round. Nine rooms. $75-$150, including breakfast. ($$-$$$) Dinner available here (for guests, $25 in addition to room price). (www.bernerhofinn.com)

Carter Notch Inn, 800-794-9434, 603-383-9630. Carter Notch Rd., Jackson, NH 03846. Open year-round. Seven rooms. $49-$119, including breakfast. (www.journeysnorth.com)

Ellis River House, 800-233-8309, 603-383-9339. Rte. 16, Jackson, NH 03846. Open year-round. 20 rooms. $79-$229, including breakfast. ($$-$$$) Dinner for guests, with advance notice. (www.erhinn.com)

Inn at Jackson, 800-289-8600, 603-383-4321. Main St. and Thorn Hill Rd., Jackson, NH 03846. Open year-round. 14 rooms. $69-$189, including breakfast. (www.innatjackson.com)

The Inn at Thorn Hill, 800-289-8990, 603-383-4242. Thorn Hill Rd., Jackson, NH 03846. Open year-round. 19 rooms. $160-$300, including breakfast and dinner. ($$-$$$) Dining room open nightly 6-9 P.M. (www.innatthornhill.com)

The Village House, 800-972-8343, 603-383-6666. Rte. 16A, Jackson, NH 03846. Open year-round. 14 rooms. $65-$135, including breakfast. (www.villagehouse.com)

Eagle Mountain House, 800-966-5779, 603-383-9111. Carter Notch Rd., Jackson, NH 03846. Open year-round. 93 rooms and suites. $70-$170, including breakfast in some packages. Breakfast ($) and dinner ($$$) available in Highfields restaurant. (www.eaglemt.com)

Mount Washington Hotel & Resort, 800-258-0330, 603-278-1000. Rte. 302, Bretton Woods, NH 03575. Open year-round. 200 rooms. $185-$400. ($$-$$$$) Lunch and dinner daily. (www.mount washing-tonhotel.com)

Mount Washington Cog Railway, 800-922-8825, 603-846-5406. Off Rte. 302, Bretton Woods. Open May-late June only weekends; July-November daily; excursions depart hourly 8-5. $44, seniors $40, children 6-12 $30. (www.cograilway.com)

Cannon Mountain Aerial Tramway, 603-823-5563. Exit 2 off I-93, Franconia. Open mid-May to late October. $9, children $5, under 6 free.

Foxglove, A Country Inn, 888-343-2220, 603-823-8840.

Rte. 117 at Lovers Ln., Sugar Hill, NH 03585. Open year-round. Six rooms. $85-$165, including breakfast.

Hilltop Inn, 800-770-5695, 603-823-5695. Main St., Sugar Hill, NH 03585. Open year-round. Six rooms and suites, plus cottage. $80-$175, including breakfast.

Sugar Hill Inn, 800-548-4748, 603-823-5621. Rte. 117, Sugar Hill, NH 03585. Open year-round, except months of November and April. 16 rooms and suites. $95-$250, including breakfast; during foliage $225-$325, including breakfast and four-course dinner. Dinner open to public ($35 prix fixe); reservations required. (www.sugarhillinn.com)

Homestead Inn, 800-823-5564, 603-823-5564. Junction of Sunset Hill Rd. and Rte. 117, Sugar Hill, NH 03585. Open year-round. 19 rooms. $60-$115, including three-course breakfast. (www.the homestead1802.com)

Sunset Hill House, 800-786-4455, 603-823-5522. Sugar Hill Rd., Sugar Hill, NH 03585. Open year-round. 27 rooms, five of which are suites. $80-$150, including breakfast. ($$-$$$) Dinner only by reservation.

Enjoy pancakes galore and views at Polly's Pancake Parlor.

Polly's Pancake Parlor, 603-823-5575. Rte. 117, Sugar Hill. Open April only weekends 7-2; the week after Mother's Day to the week after Columbus Day daily 7-3; Columbus Day week to Thanksgiving only weekends 7-2. A mail-order catalog featuring maple syrup, other maple products, and pancake mixes is available by calling 800-432-8972.

Chalet Schaefer, 603-747-2071. 85 Central St., Woodsville. ($-$$) Open Monday-Friday 11:30-5, Tuesday-Saturday 5-9 P.M. Dinner reservations recommended.

P&H Truck Stop, 802-429-2141. Exit 17 off I-91, Wells River, Vermont. Open 24 hours a day, seven days a week.

THE
Best Vermont
FOLIAGE TOUR
WE'VE *Ever Found*

THIS ITINERARY covers a big chunk of Vermont's northwestern corner, some of the most unvarnished and underpopulated nooks in the land o' leaves. Compared with any other New England state, Vermont has more designated scenic highways (highways made more beautiful by the lack of billboards, which Vermonters have outlawed). The Green Mountain State offers beautiful farms, quiet country roads, pristine villages, and sophisticated inns with gourmet dining. In the fall, millions of acres of deciduous trees turn brilliant shades of red, gold, and orange for a foliage show unrivaled anywhere. Remember, though, that autumn is a

A classic farm in Montpelier.

courtesy Vermont Department of Tourism and Marketing

mighty popular time to visit, so be sure to have your lodging reservations in hand before setting out, especially if you are traveling on the weekend.

This tour begins at the Vermont-New Hampshire border in Wells River on Route 302, heading toward Barre. Over the next two days you'll see miles of colorful vistas, the world's largest granite quarry, the country's smallest state capital, and Vermont's first National Park.

DAY ONE Wells River is the start of the Bayley-Hazen Military Road, built during the years 1776 to 1779 by General Jacob Bayley and General Moses Hazen. Ordered by George Washington, it was constructed from the

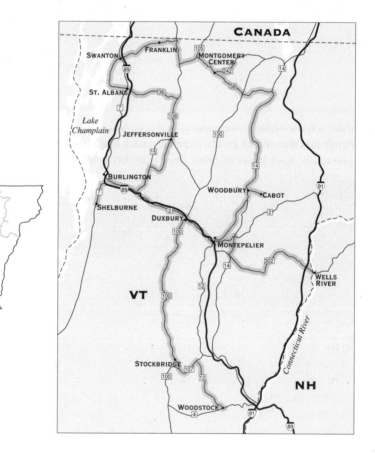

upper Connecticut River to St. Francis, Quebec, and was intended to serve as a military route should the Revolutionary War spread to the northern border. Today the roadbed is still visible as it rises at the north end of the Route 5 bridge across the Wells River and disappears over a crest on Bible Hill. We like to stretch our legs on the first couple of miles of this historic road. Starting at the granite marker at the end of Main Street, we continue to a clearing above Tickle Naked Pond in Boltonville for rewarding views of the White Mountains. ("Tickle Naked" comes from the Algonquin name *Tickenecket* meaning "place of some little beavers.")

Homemade bread is a specialty at the P&H Truck Stop.

Any time of the day or night you can find warm food and an equally warm welcome at the P&H Truck Stop in Wells River. Owner Nelson Baker says he has kept the restaurant open for so long (24 hours a day, seven days a week) that he doesn't think he could find the keys if he tried. If it is a weekend, the parking lot will be full, with more family cars than trucks. Inside, you enter smack into a bakery case of big, fresh loaves of bread (they bake 300 a day) and plates full of 20 different flavors of pie. Talk to a trucker anywhere in the country, and he'll recommend the maple cream pie at P&H. You'll be seated quickly. In the air you're likely to hear the murmur of English and French conversation, while music drifts from jukeboxes. The mood is light, the food is good; what more could you ask for?

Return to 302, where southeast of Barre lie the famous granite quarries. Here in the lush hills of Vermont is a lode of granite so vast and deep that it could last forever. Beginning 200 years ago, men from all over the world came here to work. In the decades that followed, quarrying of local granite grew into an industry of such prominence that by the 1960s the stoneworkers could boast there was a piece of Barre in every city in the nation.

The Rock of Ages Visitor Center is located in Graniteville. At the green in Barre, turn south on Route 14 and follow the

Quarry workers at the Boutwell, Milne & Varnum quarry, circa 1900.

Aldrich Public Library

signs. Though this may not be Vermont's number-one tourist stop (Ben & Jerry's is), it is a dramatic attraction. A path behind the center leads to one of the state's oldest quarries, and tours (in an open bus) to the working quarries are also available. Don't miss the intricate and moving memorials in Mount Hope Cemetery on Route 14 north of Barre. Here stonecutters have painstakingly carved sculptures for themselves and their families. We spent an hour quietly walking the roads here, reading epitaphs and international names, marveling at the art and love reflected in stone.

Take Route 14 north to Route 2 in East Montpelier. From here we are going to head west to Shelburne (just a little south of Burlington). In Montpelier, you can choose between I-89 or Route 2; both will lead to Burlington, and both offer good views. Route 2 will be slower, as it passes through more villages. On the interstate, allow about a half hour. (Don't think we are ignoring Montpelier; we're coming back this way!)

Next stop is Shelburne Farms. It is located at the intersection of Bay and

WHAT THE LOCALS KNOW

Where to See the Foliage Twice

Follow Route 302, and just west of the village of Groton, you'll find the junction with Route 232. Head north on 232, and in about 1½ miles you'll see the southern end of Ricker Pond. In less than a mile, enter Groton State Forest, and on the right you'll see the entrance to Groton Lake, a state beach popular for swimming and picnics. The glimpses of foliage across the lake are beautiful, but continue on. Drive north, and on the right look for Owl's Head. Take this gravel road to a parking area. From here, take the easy hike to cliffs that offer great vistas. See the foliage twice — once pointing skyward and again reflected perfectly in the water.

Owls Head trail, about 5.2 miles north from the junction of routes 302 and 232.

Shelburne Farms

We stopped first in the gift shop at Shelburne Farms, an unassuming little building with a great selection of gifts — gourmet foods, English china, gardening books, and farm and animal toys. Our daughter, Sara, dropped to her knees at the kids' books, smiling sweetly at pictures of baby animals. There she stayed while my husband and I tried to avoid multiple trips to the

called it "the Farm Barn." Shelburne Farms is a 1,400-acre working farm, a National Historic Site, and a nonprofit education center. But really it is a place of dreams. Seward and Lila (Vanderbilt) Webb amassed nearly six square miles of the Lake Champlain Valley and through the late 1880s created the ideal farm. The centerpiece is the grandest barn ever to be built in this country.

courtesy Shelburne Farms

This Queen Anne-style mansion is now the Inn at Shelburne Farms.

cheese sampling counter. Little cubes of Shelburne Farms' award-winning cheddar (mild, medium, sharp, and smoked) beckoned. We bought tickets for a 90-minute tour and watched a 15-minute video on the history of the farm before hopping on an open-air bus.

The gravel driveway wound around a bend, and there amid a manicured stretch of green stood a huge castlelike building, complete with turrets and courtyard. I caught my breath as the guide

Then there is the house, sitting on a knoll above the shore of Lake Champlain. Our tour included seeing a few rooms of the Webbs' former country home. It is now an exclusive inn and restaurant. Many of the furnishings are original to the house. Most everyone snapped pictures outside in the flower garden. I suspect, too, that most everyone (the grown-ups) secretly imagined this was their home. If only for a day, we'd like to experience the grandeur. Sara, though,

wanted only the barn and the promise of milking a cow.

At the children's farmyard she petted piglets, goats, calves, and patiently waited her turn to milk a gentle Brown Swiss from the farm's herd of 150. Outside, parents watched their children squat and waddle after ducks and chickens. Once in a while we'd lift our heads and take in the landscape. Sara gently clutched a baby chick in her hand and looked at us with a pleading expression that said, "Can I take it home?" Shelburne Farms holds magic for all ages, and no visitor leaves without wanting to take home a piece of this heaven.

– Polly Bannister

Shelburne Farms, 802-985-8686. 1611 Harbor Rd., Shelburne. Farm Store and Visitors Center open year-round 10-5; late May to mid-October, guided tours offered daily at 9:30 and 11:30 A.M., and 12:30, 2, and 3:30 P.M. $5, seniors $4, children $3.

The Inn at Shelburne Farms, 802-985-8498. Open mid-May to mid-October. 24 rooms. $95-$185 (shared bath), $195-$350 (private bath). ($$$-$$$$) Open nightly for dinner. (www.shelburnefarms.org)

Harbor roads, off Route 7 (take I-189 from I-89) in Shelburne. Originally designed as a model agricultural estate in 1886 by Dr. William Seward Webb and Lila Vanderbilt Webb,

Harriet W. Riggs

Shelburne Farms has magnificent 19th-century buildings in the most pastoral setting imaginable.

Retrace your route and take Route 2 (Williston Road) east from Burlington, stopping for snacks at Cheese Traders and Wine Sellers. In 10,000 square feet there is a huge inventory of cheeses, over 3,000 wines, and every Vermont microbrew you could want. Another good deli stop is the Cheese Outlet located downtown (if you're looking for an excuse to go into town). You'll be in the country when you reach Richmond, 12 miles away. Our route calls for a left at Richmond's only intersection, but if you want to see the famous Round Church, turn right, cross the bridge, and look to the

Richmond's Old Round Church, a rare architectural gem, has 16 sides and was built circa 1812-1814.

left. The church, built in 1813, actually has 16 sides.

Turn back to Richmond, head north on Jericho Road, and continue five miles to Jericho Center. The marker on the green commemorates Wilson "Snowflake" Bentley, a turn-of-the-century Jericho farmer who took the first photographs of snowflake crystals. Continue beyond Jericho Center on Brown's Trace Road for three miles to Route 15, then turn right. Ahead and a bit to the right stands Mount Mansfield — that's the chin of the mountain's illustrious profile farthest to the left (north); the nose and forehead lie farther south. (Use your imagination.)

Stay on Route 15 for half a mile, then bear right and continue three miles to Underhill Center. Head straight through town to Pleasant Valley Road, watching for a sign (a mile north) for Underhill State Park, where some of the best Mount Mansfield hiking trails begin. Although there are signs, your best bet is to carry a copy of the Green Mountain Club's *Long Trail Guide*. A ramble along the old CCC Road or

Cantilever Rock Trail offers a way to see the colors at less than highway speed.

Return to Pleasant Valley Road and follow this rolling byway north through woodlands and meadows, bearing right at the fork six miles ahead onto Upper Valley Road, which delivers you to Jeffersonville by way of dairy farms and some fine views of the Lamoille River valley. If you're ready to call it a day, on the corner of Route 108 and Upper Valley Road you'll find Historic Smugglers Notch Inn. This 18th-century village inn has been hosting guests long before skiers descended on the area. Innkeepers Cynthia Barber and Jon Day are enthusiastic hikers and cyclists who happily share their favorite outdoor routes with guests. They serve dinner in their large dining room, or you can choose from a handful of family restaurants in town. Don't miss a stroll down Main Street in Jeffersonville. This charming rural town has a well-known bakery (Windridge) and some lovely galleries, including the Mary Bryan Memorial Art Gallery, known for its landscape paintings.

If you are interested in more action, take a detour south about 15 miles on Route 108 to Stowe. Here you will find shops, movies, après-ski entertainment, and an abundance of lodging and dinner choices. Edson Hill Manor and Ten Acres Lodge, located in Stowe and owned by Jane and Eric Lande, are inns that consistently receive rave reviews for their dining, which is open to the public. You can take a gondola ride up Mount Mansfield to the Cliff House. For an overnight in Austrian style, book a room at the mountaintop Trapp Family Lodge. Closer to Jeffersonville on Route 108 is Smugglers' Notch Resort, where both formal and informal dining choices abound.

DAY TWO In the morning, drive north from Jeffersonville on Route 108. At Bakersfield, the blip in the road ten miles north, turn left opposite the cemetery onto Route 36. Two and a half miles west is East Fairfield, where you can take a side trip to visit the reconstruction of President Arthur's boyhood home, known as the President Chester A. Arthur State Historic Site. Here you will get an idea

Don't miss Jeffersonville, one of Vermont's most charming villages.

WHAT THE LOCALS KNOW

The Best Little Gift Shop Around

We received this note from a *Yankee* reader recently:

I am writing to tell you about the "best-kept secret" the west coast of New England has to offer. One-half mile west of Route 7 in Georgia, Vermont, snuggled in the corner at the bend in the road, is the best little gift shop in the area. "Weeds 'n Things" is an unassuming establishment surrounded by gardens. After you ring the doorbell and step through the outer door, a golden gate awaits you. Pass through the gate and you'll hear the sound of a waterfall. Inside lies an enchanted place with wonderful things — from Victorian elegance, to casual country, to antiques, to one-of-a-kind dried flower arrangements (the owner, Pauline Nye, and her daughter, Sara Nye Vester, grow all the flowers for drying on three acres here), floral scents, and a wall of ribbons to delight any shopper.

– sent to Yankee *Magazine by Bonnie Mae King*

Weeds 'n Things, 802-524-2826. 586 Plains Rd., Georgia (a few miles south of St. Albans). Follow signs for shop located ½ mile off Ethan Allen Hwy. (Rte. 7). Open year-round Monday-Saturday 9-5; from Thanksgiving to Christmas also Sundays 10-4.

....

of what a wilderness this was in 1830. It still is. To get there, turn right at Lyn's Market onto New Street, then go to a fork and bear left onto Dodd Road. Continue to the next intersection, where you'll see signs for the Arthur Site. Turn right; the site is a half mile down the road. To return (views on the way back are terrific), retrace your steps to Route 36, stay on this through East Fairfield, and in five miles you'll enter Fairfield. Here you can pick up a sandwich, a maple-white chocolate scone, or a whole pie at Chester's in the Square, where everything is homemade.

When you crest a hill six miles west of Fairfield, you may have trouble paying attention to the road. The view that suddenly spreads before you takes in a vast swath of the upper Champlain valley, with St. Albans in the foreground, Lake Champlain in the middle distance, and New York's Adirondacks as a backdrop for it all. St. Albans is a redbrick period piece: A century ago it was northern New England's rail capital, and during the Civil War it was the site of the conflict's northernmost action, when Confederate raiders robbed the town's banks and made off into Canada. Stop to appreciate the handsomely preserved Victorian facades on Main Street and the stately public buildings facing the park on Church Street. One of these houses is the St. Albans Historical Museum, with an eclectic trove ranging from railroadiana to an old-time doctor's office. If you're hungry, try Jeff's Maine Seafood.

Head west out of town for three miles on Route 36 (Lake Street) to St. Albans Bay. Turn right and follow Route 36 for ten miles along Lake Champlain to Swanton, gateway to the waterfowl-rich Missisquoi National Wildlife Refuge, west of town via Route 78, and a good place to stretch your legs. Continue your itinerary on Route 78 east and drive five miles to Highgate Center (intersection with Route 207). Stay on 78 east out of Highgate Center, and after about 1.5 miles, the road will fork. There's a long red barn on the left; just past the barn, at another fork, bear left onto Franklin Road, which will take you through five miles of dairy country. Franklin County is Vermont's milk-producing leader; the local St. Albans Co-Op is the supplier of much of the cream that goes into Ben & Jerry's ice cream. Follow the road through Franklin, which, if everyone sneezed at once, would be in Quebec. When the road comes to a T, turn left and follow Route 120 north. Ahead and a little to the right, you'll see the summit of Jay Peak, with its cantilevered aerial tramway station. On your right, a few miles farther, Lake Carmi reflects the colors of the surrounding hills. Stay on Route 120 through East Franklin, then take Route 108 south to the junction with Route 105. Turn left and head east along the Missisquoi River to East Berkshire, where you take Route 118 south to Montgomery Center, a dining and lodging focus for the year-round resort at Jay Peak.

Though this is not an official breaking point in the tour, we would be remiss not to mention the following establishments in the area. They are nice enough to make you want to stay a while. Montgomery's Black Lantern Inn has ten rooms in an 1803 brick house and six suites in an adjacent house. A mile down 118 to Montgomery Center is the Inn on Trout River with its cheery Victorian rooms. The inn's restaurant, Lemoine's,

Not Just One but Five Covered Bridges

Between North and East Montpelier on Route 14, **Coburn Bridge** passes over the Winooski River. This 69-foot-long bridge was built in 1851. To view: Heading south on 14, turn left on Coburn Road and the bridge will appear in about seven miles.

Off Route 12 south from Montpelier you'll find four more, all within a few miles of Northfield Falls. On Cox Brook Road, there are the **Upper** and **Lower Cox Brook bridges**. The former is 52 feet long and was built in 1899; the latter spans 57 feet and was built in 1872. **Northfield Falls Bridge** is near the junction of Cox Brook Road and Route 12. Built in 1872, it spans the Dog River for 137 feet. Just a bit farther south on 12 is the **Slaughter House Bridge**, also spanning Dog River (for 60 feet); it was built in 1872.

specializes in grilled meats and seafood. Another dinner option is the eclectic and eccentric Zack's on the Rocks, where the crispy duckling and tournedos béarnaise are as much of a draw as the hanging-gardens dining room.

For the last word in foliage panoramas, take Route 242 from Montgomery Center to the Jay Peak Resort & Aerial Tramway. Trams run every half hour. You can have lunch back in Montgomery Center at Kilgore's, where they will build you a hearty sandwich on fresh-baked bread and ladle out an honest bowl of soup. For an afternoon encounter with the leaves, head east from Montgomery Center through Hazen's Notch on Route 58, a gravel road through deep woods ablaze with the yellow foliage of birches. Where the Long Trail crosses the road, you find that the Green Mountain Club's Hazen's Notch Camp is a good hiking and picnic destination six-tenths of a mile north of the road.

After ten miles, Route 58 crosses Route 100 (and turns to blacktop) at Lowell; continue for eight miles to Irasburg, looking north along the way for some of the best long-distance views. Just before Irasburg, you'll come to a T intersection; turn right onto Route 14, which you'll follow through town and to points south. Route 14 out of Irasburg follows the Black River, which flows north into Lake Memphremagog. As you drive south through the valley's pastures and hay fields, you'll notice left-hand turnoffs for the secondary roads through the Albanys and the Craftsburys, each town with elegant inns and restaurants that could seduce you to extend your trip. But don't let Laura Ashley fool you — this is still wild country. (Near Lake Elligo, which hugs Route 14 in Craftsbury, researchers recently identified scat proving the long-debated existence of mountain lions in Vermont.)

Stay on Route 14 through Hardwick, 24 miles south of Irasburg, and continue for 19 miles of lake-strewn, wooded country to East Montpelier. En route, detour to Cabot (left turn at Woodbury) for a tour of Cabot Creamery.

At East Montpelier, pick up Route 2 west for the seven miles into Montpelier. Note the golden dome of the state capitol rising before you. By now, you should know why it's topped with a statue of Ceres — the Roman goddess of agri-

Lodging Picks Along Route 100

The Black Locust Inn, 800-366-5592, 802-244-7490. Box 715, Rte. 100, Waterbury Center, VT 05677. Find views of Green Mountains from this three-gabled 1832 farmhouse. Hosts Len, Nancy, and Valerie Vignola will assure your comfort with down pillows, complimentary wine and appetizers, and a hot three-course breakfast. Open year-round. Six rooms. $89-$135. (www.blacklocustinn.com)

Old Stagecoach Inn, 800-262-2206, 802-244-5056. 18 N. Main St., Waterbury, VT 05676. Run by father and son Jack and John Barwick, this 1826 Federal/Queen Anne house is beautifully restored. There's stained glass, wood paneling, Oriental carpets, antiques throughout, and a full bar in the library. Open year-round. 11 rooms. $45-$130, including breakfast.

Inn at Blush Hill, 800-736-7522, 802-244-7529. Box 1266, Blush Hill Rd., Waterbury, VT 05676. This is a 1790s Cape-style house situated atop a hill with breathtaking views of Worcester Mountain Range. There are four fireplaces and large common areas for guests. Open year-round. Five rooms. $59-$130, including breakfast and afternoon/evening refreshments. (www.blushhill.com)

Grunberg Haus Bed & Breakfast, 800-800-7760, 802-244-7726. Rte. 100 South, Waterbury, VT 05676. This Austrian chalet on 45 acres, with beautiful Green Mountain views, was hand built of Vermont timber and fieldstone and boasts hand-carved balconies. The inn is hosted by Chris Sellers (a pianist and singer, who often plays at breakfast) and Mark Frohman. Open year-round. Ten rooms, including two cabins and a carriage-house suite. $59-$145, including breakfast. (www.waterbury.org/grunberg)

Lareau Farm Country Inn, 800-833-0766, 802-496-4949. Rte. 100, Waitsfield, VT 05673. Hosted by Dan (a woodworker who drives his horses for hay/sleigh rides) and Susan Easley, this 1832 Greek Revival house sits on 67 acres. Enjoy antiques, quilts, Oriental carpets, and wraparound porches with views of meadows and the Mad River. Open year-round. 13 rooms. $80-$135, including breakfast.

Millbrook Inn & Restaurant, 800-477-2809, 802-496-2405. Rte. 17, Fayston (near Waitsfield), VT 05673. This inn is run by the Gormans, who have 20 years of innkeeping experience. Their 1850s Cape farmhouse on four acres offers Green Mountain views, a quiet backyard, three sitting rooms, and a fireplaced dining room. Open December-March, June-October. Seven rooms. $78, including breakfast; $100-$140, including breakfast and dinner.

Christmas Tree Inn, 800-535-5622, 802-583-2211. Sugarbush Access Rd., Warren, VT 05674. For those who want Christmas all year long, this 1960s lodge on three acres is decked out in holiday fashion. A stay here includes access to a cozy living room, fireplaces, two pools, two tennis courts, birdwatching from the dining room, and winter views of the slopes. Open year-round. 12 rooms. $60-$115, with optional breakfast.

culture — and why, perhaps, she should be clutching a sheaf of autumn leaves.

At this point in the tour, you've already had a couple of full days, but autumn in Vermont is still calling to us. If you have the time, visit the Vermont Statehouse and the Vermont Historical Society Museum in Montpelier. The statehouse offers guided tours from July through mid-October. The atmosphere is relaxed here, and no place is off-limits to visitors. The state historical society has permanent and rotating exhibits. It is a great little museum where you can see many Vermont artifacts. In the larger back gallery, highlights from a show entitled *Generation of Change 1820-1850* are a tall case clock made by Martin Cheney from Windsor circa 1820, the handwritten minutes of the first meeting of the Vermont Anti-Slavery Society (in 1834), and a portrait of Mr. and Mrs. Daniel Thompson; he is the author of *The Green Mountain Boys* and founder of the Vermont Historical Society. Both the statehouse and the museum have nice gift shops.

Vermont Historical Society

Portrait of Daniel Thompson, author of The Green Mountain Boys, *with his wife.*

If time is limited, you can hop on Interstate 89 south and pick up I-91 south to Brattleboro, Vermont, to continue our grand New England foliage tour.

In Massachusetts we'll take you through the western hilltowns for apples, antiques, and good eating on beautiful back roads. If you can't quite leave Vermont yet, here is a (longer) scenic way to hook up with the Massachusetts itinerary.

DAY THREE OPTION From Montpelier, head northwest on Route 2. Pick up Route 100 in Duxbury and follow this south along the eastern edge of the Green Mountain National Forest. This north-south corridor, once used only by hill-town villagers, has become the way to Vermont's most popular ski resorts. It is as scenic a highway as you'll find anywhere in New England.

Near the major downhill ski areas there are great accommodations and fine food.

Just a short drive from Route 100 is Woodstock — a showcase of a town anytime, but in autumn it is stellar. For a spectacular scenic road from Stockbridge to Woodstock, take Route 107 east to 12 south. Woodstock highlights include historic architecture, impeccably maintained; a classic town green lined with sugar maples; Billings Farm & Museum, a circa-1890s farmhouse and modern farm; a raptor center at the Vermont Institute of Natural Science; and Vermont's first National Park, the Marsh-Billings National Historic Park. Leaf peepers caught without lodging should know that the Woodstock Chamber of Commerce maintains a list of private homes at which stranded travelers are graciously taken in.

To continue our tour, take Route 4 east to Interstate 91 south. Enjoy your drive through the Connecticut River Valley and pick up the beginning of the Massachusetts hill towns drive in Jacksonville, Vermont (Route 100 south off Route 9 west from Brattleboro).

ROUTE 100 IS AS SCENIC A HIGHWAY AS YOU'LL FIND ANYWHERE IN NEW ENGLAND.

– *William G. Scheller*

ESSENTIALS

Lake Champlain Regional Chamber of Commerce, 802-863-3489. Box 453, 60 Main St., Suite 100, Burlington, VT 05401. (www.vermont.org/chamber)

Smugglers' Notch Area Chamber of Commerce, 802-644-2239. Jeffersonville, VT 05464. (www.smugnotch.com)

Lamoille Valley Chamber of Commerce, 802-888-7607. P.O. Box 45, Morrisville, VT 05661.

Stowe Area Association, 800-247-8693, 802-253-7321. Box 1320, Stowe, VT 05672. (www.stoweinfo.com)

St. Albans Chamber of Commerce, 802-524-2444. 132 N. Main St., St. Albans, VT 05478. (www.stalbanschamber.com)

Woodstock Area Chamber of Commerce, 888-496-6378, 802-457-3555. 18 Central St., Woodstock, VT 05091. Information booth on town green open June-October. (www.woodstockvt.com)

P&H Truck Stop, 802-429-2141. Exit 17 off I-91, Wells River. Open 24 hours, seven days a week.

Rock of Ages Visitor Center, 802-476-3119. 773 Main St., Graniteville. Open May-October (except July 4) Monday-Saturday 8:30-5, Sunday noon-5; active quarry tours available June to mid-October Monday-Friday, departing about every 45 minutes, 9:15-3. (www.rockofages.com)

Cheese Traders and Wine Sellers, 802-863-0143. 1186

Williston Rd., South Burlington. Open Monday-Saturday 10-7, Sunday 11-5.

Cheese Outlet, 802-863-3968. 400 Pine St., Burlington. Open Monday-Friday 8-7, Sunday 10-5.

Round Church, 802-434-2556. Bridge St., Richmond. Open Memorial Day to Columbus Day daily 10-4.

Long Trail Guide from Green Mountain Club, 802-244-7037. RR 1 Box 650, Waterbury Center, VT 05677. Members $11.95, nonmembers $14.95; plus $3.75 S&H. (www.greenmountain club.org)

Historic Smugglers Notch Inn, 800-845-3101, 802-644-2412. Church St., P.O. Box 280, Jeffersonville, VT 05464. (www.smugglers-notch-inn.com)

Edson Hill Manor, 802-253-7371. 1500 Edson Hill Rd., Stowe. ($$$) Open for dinner in season daily; off-season only Friday-Saturday 6-10 P.M. Reservations required.

Ten Acres Lodge, 802-253-7638. 14 Barrows Rd., Stowe. ($$$) Open for dinner in season daily; off-season only Friday-Saturday 6-10 P.M. Reservations required.

Cliff House, 802-253-3665. Stowe Mountain Resort,

Stowe. Open for dinner Thursday-Saturday. $39 (prix fixe).

Trapp Family Lodge, 800-826-7000, 802-253-8511. Trapp Hill Rd., Stowe, VT 05672. Open year-round. 73 rooms. $180-$280 (packages vary seasonally). (www.trappfamily.com)

Smugglers' Notch Resort, 800-451-8752, 802-644-8851. Rte. 108, Jeffersonville, VT 05464. Open year-round. 460 condominium homes. Starting at $119 (double-occupancy rooms). (www.smuggs.com)

President Chester A. Arthur State Historic Site, 802-828-3051. East Fairfield. Open May 20-October 15, Wednesday-Sunday 11-5. Admission by donation.

Chester's in the Square, 802-827-3974. Sheldon Rd., Fairfield. Open Monday-Thursday 7-4, Friday 7 A.M.-8 P.M., Saturday 8-2.

St. Albans Historical Museum, 802-527-7933. Church St., St. Albans. Open Monday-Friday 1-4. $3, children under 14 free.

Jeff's Maine Seafood, 802-524-6135. 65 N. Main St., St. Albans. Open for lunch Monday-Saturday 11:30-3, dinner Tuesday-Saturday 5-9 P.M.

Black Lantern Inn, 800-255-8661, 802-326-4507. Rte. 118, Montgomery, VT 05470. Open year-round. 16 rooms. $80-$145, including breakfast. (www.blacklantern.com)

Canoeists enjoy foliage by water.

courtesy Smugglers' Notch Resort

A little girl milks a cow at Shelburne Farms.

Vermont Historical Society Museum, 802-828-2291. Pavilion Bldg., 109 State St., Montpelier. Open year-round Tuesday-Friday 9-4:30; also weekends mid-July to October 10-5. $2, seniors and students $1.

Billings Farm & Museum, 802-457-2355. Rte. 12 and River Rd., Woodstock. Open May-October daily 10-5. $7, children 13-17 $5.50, 5-12 $3.50, 3-4 $1. (www.billingsfarm.org)

Vermont Institute of Natural Science, 802-457-2779. Church Hill Rd., Woodstock. Open summer daily 10-5, winter Monday-Saturday 10-4. $6, children 12-18 $3, 5-11 $2. (www.vinsweb.org)

Marsh-Billings National Historic Park, Rte. 12, Woodstock. Open early June to mid-October daily 10-5.

Inn on Trout River, 800-338-7049, 802-326-4391. Rte. 118, Montgomery Center, VT 05471. Open year-round. Ten rooms. $86-$103, including breakfast. (www.troutinn.com)

Lemoine's at the Inn on Trout River, 800-338-7049, 802-326-4391. Rte. 118, Montgomery Center. ($$-$$$) Open for dinner nightly. Reservations required. (www.troutinn.com/restaurant2.htm)

Zack's on the Rocks, 802-326-4500. Rte. 58, Montgomery Center. ($$$) Open Tuesday-Sunday for dinner. Reservations required.

Jay Peak Resort & Aerial Tramway, 802-988-2611. Rte. 242, Jay. Open August 18-September 5 only weekends 10-4; September 18-October 11 daily 10-4. $8, seniors and juniors $5, family $25. (www.jaypeakresort.com)

Cabot Creamery, 802-563-2231. Main St., Cabot. Open June-October 31 daily 9-5; November-May Monday-Saturday 9-4; closed in January. $1. (www.cabotcheese.com)

Vermont Statehouse, 802-828-2228. State St., Montpelier. Open year-round weekdays 8-4; tours July to mid-October Monday-Friday 10-3:30, Saturday 11-2:30.

A FOLIAGE *Ramble*
IN THE
Hill Towns of Western Massachusetts

JUST EAST OF the traditional pleasures of the Berkshires lies a region known as "the hill towns." Though often overshadowed by its showier, better-publicized neighbors, this region of New England offers the best of both city and country. These hill towns are thick with creative arts, rural beauty, cultural diversity, and great music and restaurants fueled by the area's dense cluster of colleges and universities. This two-day fall-foliage ramble takes you from the Vermont border through breathtaking countryside for a night's stay in the Shelburne Falls area and then down to Northampton for a night in the "city."

In Conway, the Festival of the Hills is an autumn favorite.

courtesy Conway Festival of the Hills

DAY ONE OK, we're not yet in Massachusetts, but we couldn't pass up starting this tour in the hamlet of Jacksonville, Vermont. From Brattleboro, take 9 west (the Molly Stark Trail) to Route 100 south. Antiquers will enjoy a stop at Marillas Antiques & Country Goods, a charming multidealer shop located in an old house overlooking a lively stream in the center of town. The shop carries a variety of small and large antiques at prices that should make it easy for you to justify taking home a treasure. Up the hill, on Gates Pond Road, is the well-regarded Stone Soldier Pottery, featuring a large variety of hand-thrown stoneware pieces and other crafts. The business, run by the Burnell family (Robert is the potter and his wife, Connie, runs the shop) just celebrated its 30-year anniversary.

Heading south on Route 112, you will find the North River Winery located along the popular trout-fishing stream that runs through the foothills of Windham County. Taste and buy fruit wines, hard ciders, and Vermont-made cheeses.

Ready your cameras for the next stretch of 112 as it winds through the bucolic North River Valley toward Colrain, Massachusetts. After about five miles, the river flows for a spell between the steep granite walls of Halifax Gorge. Look for several turnouts on your right. Trails from these parking areas lead down to the gorge.

About nine miles out of Jacksonville is a farm (on the right) with the quintessential weathered gray barn and a resident gray horse to match — a classic New England photo op.

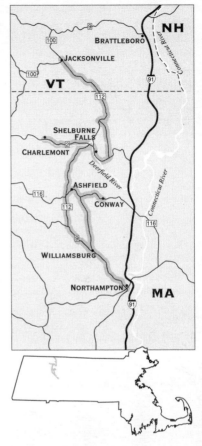

The village of Colrain boasts an interesting restaurant, Green Emporium. It is located in a circa-1850s renovated brick church, surrounded by perennial gardens and playfully decorated with neon art. Gourmet dinners, served on Fridays and Saturdays, are accompanied by a local jazz pianist. (Be sure to call ahead, as its hours are sometimes irregular.)

Now head up the hill on Greenfield Road, which becomes the Colrain-Shelburne Road toward Route 2. Any children in tow would appreciate a stop at Pine Hill Orchards on the left, a petting farm boasting well-fed sheep, goats, and ducks (adults can taste the offerings of the nearby West County Winery). Locals like to have breakfast and lunch here at Sue's

Sunrise Café. Several miles farther along the road is Orchard Hill Antiques, owned by Jeffrey Bishop, occupying an 1811 house and a barn annex full of period country furniture, lighting fixtures, clocks, and tools.

A Bridge on the Move

The **Arthur A. Smith Covered Bridge,** in the Lyonsville section of Colrain, no longer spans the North River. In 1990, teams of oxen pulled the bridge from its foundation, and it now sits on Lyonsville Road (just off Route 112) awaiting restoration. Judith Sullivan, a Colrain native who serves as town clerk, treasurer, and tax collector, is one of many locals dedicated to getting their bridge back in working order. She says, "This is one of only four 19th-century covered bridges left in the state, and it has unique arch construction that was added after its original building to withstand heavy loads from a local cider mill. We are determined to see the bridge fully restored to carry cars, but between meeting Massachusetts Historic Commission regulations and state procurement laws, we have encountered some obstacles." In order to meet new flood regulations, the bridge will have to be raised. Visitors will likely be able to watch this fascinating engineering and construction feat during the summer of 2000.

You'll come out onto Route 2 facing Shelburne Falls Coffee Roasters (with another shop in the village), perfectly placed for an infusion of coffee, cookies, and pastry.

Stretch your legs amid some lovely scenery on the trails at High Ledges, a 586-acre Audubon sanctuary in Shelburne. Turn right on Route 2 (west), take a right onto Little Mohawk Road, and bear left at the junction onto Patten Road. Continuing on Patten, go left at the next junction and then bear right. The sanctuary entrance is approximately a half mile on the left. At the cabin there, trails are posted, one of which winds up to the 1,350-foot-high ledge, affording a sweeping view of the Deerfield River valley, Mount Greylock (the highest mountain peak in the state), and the village of Shelburne Falls. The story goes that the last pair of wolves in western Massachusetts made their den somewhere among the ledges, ravines, and forest. The wolves are gone, but keep your eyes peeled for the many varieties of orchids (over 20 species line the sanctuary's extensive trail system) and ferns, as well as yellow-bellied sapsuckers, as you make your way through the lush forest.

Another excellent walk may be found right outside the Davenport Maple Farm: Go back down Patten Road, turn right onto Tower Road, and make a left onto Cooper Lane. This partially dirt road passes a lovely sheep farm with steep pastures and foliage views to die for.

For a more adventurous way to experience West County's outdoors, raft class II and III rapids along the Deerfield River through the mossy, boulder-strewn reaches of Zoar Gap. Head west down Route 2 to Charlemont. Zoar Outdoor and Crab Apple Rafting run rafting trips ranging in intensity from mild to wild.

Off Route 2 is the charming village of Shelburne Falls, a weekend destination in itself. Shelburne's generous offerings include the natural beauty of the Deerfield River, glacial potholes, several good antiques shops, tasty food, a number of local arts and crafts galleries, and the famous Bridge of Flowers. Located near the junction of routes 2 and 112, the village of Shelburne Falls straddles the Deerfield River, standing partly in the town of Shelburne and partly on the other side of the river in Buckland. Find parking on Bridge Street in the center of town, and allow at least half a day to appreciate the town. Be sure to stop at the well-staffed Shelburne Falls Village Information Center for more information about the area.

courtesy Shelburne Falls Area Business Association

Starting on the Shelburne side, you'll find several antiques shops. Shea Antiques is full of wonderful old goodies, including a collection of antique Christmas ornaments. Three doors down, Seasons Past has quality furniture and sports memorabilia. We chatted with owner Mike Charbonneau, who showed us an 8x10 signed photo of Joe DiMaggio and a couple of Hoosier kitchen cabinets starting at $600 (he sells one every few weeks). Both shops are right on Bridge Street. Look also for two offbeat stores: the Wandering Moon, with a medieval influence, and the Whistling Crow, devoted to birds and wildlife (a portion of its profits supports wildlife rehabilitation). The Art Bank has interesting exhibits as well as some evening presentations, and every fall, Pothole Pictures presents classic movies at the renovated Memorial Hall on week-

Shelburne Falls is home to the popular Bridge of Flowers.

end nights. Another Bridge Street attraction well worth a stop is the Shelburne Falls Artisans Cooperative. Here 75 artists and craftspeople feature their work.

Margo's Bistro, highly recommended for dinner, offers casual and creative gourmet fare. Ten Bridge Street Cafe serves lunch and dinner with inventive twists on traditional New England cuisine. At Mother's you'll find a tasty breakfast and lunch in a relaxed atmosphere. The menu, which exhibits a Southwestern influence, boasts five different kinds of chilies daily, as well as a variety of sandwiches and soups.

Zoar Gap

I'll admit I am no risk taker, so when the invitation to take a Zoar Outdoor white-water rafting trip on the Deerfield River came across my desk, I figured I'd pass. But the words *beginner* and *family* caught my eye, so I read on: a one-day, ten-mile trip (during foliage), with all equipment and a hearty riverside lunch provided. I thought about my husband, David, and daughter, Sara, and knew they'd never forgive me if I forfeited this opportunity.

We arrived at 10 A.M. to get our wet suits, waterproof jackets, and booties. (David was impressed that Zoar actually had equipment to fit his six-foot-five-inch frame.) There were about 50 of us — divided approximately eight to a raft, including a guide —

who gathered across the street to have a safety briefing and get the rest of our equipment: helmet, vest, and paddle. Guide Sarah explained rescue procedures (if you fall out of the raft, don't stand up, as you might get caught in a foothold; keep your feet downriver and float until you're retrieved). In practically the same breath she explained the etiquette of water fights (if your raft is attacked and you don't want to fight, make the peace sign). I looked down at my trusting daughter and wondered what we were in for.

After a bus trip to the launch site, our guide, Matt Harper (who turned out to be the older brother of Sarah, the initial-instruction-giving guide), helped us select our places in the raft; I was relieved to see he had my own

Sara directly in front of him. In a matter of minutes, we had our paddles synchronized, putting in only when Matt ordered. Most of the time we cruised, enjoying foliage reflected in the (very calm) water, gazing at the colorful hills, admiring how remote and wild much of the riverfront remains today. Matt was relaxed and made me feel confident; he knew every rapid and rock we encountered. The only challenge (and this was over before we knew it) was Zoar Gap, a class III rapid at this time of the year. The second we were through, Sara begged Matt to do it again. He laughingly replied that if she could paddle the raft upstream, he'd give her another chance. After "surviving" the Gap, we had a good lunch of sandwiches, hot chili, and wonderful homemade cookies in a quiet

If you aren't one for shopping, stop for a casting session along the rivers of West County (known for their populations of brown and rainbow trout). At Smith and Morey Sporting Goods (also on Bridge Street), you can obtain a license and find out where they're biting.

On the Buckland side of the village, a picnic or casual sit-down lunch can be found at McCusker's Market, the local health-food store and gathering place. McCusker's is also Lamson & Goodnow's "factory outlet," selling the cutlery manufactured up the street since 1851. Outdoor tables at field Zoar uses as their private picnic spot.

About the water fights — they really escalated after lunch. Maybe it was full-belly tricks as my mom would say, but we couldn't stop ourselves. In fact, the only time I felt I might fall overboard was when we got a little too enthusiastic attacking other rafts. We stood up (Sara

Riding the rapids with Zoar Outdoor.

courtesy Zoar Outdoor

included), slicing the water with our paddles, splashing and hooting war cries. Matt showed us a great technique with the bailing bucket, and before long everyone on board was drenched (the other guides taught their rafters the bucket trick, too). At one point, we hid out in a cove, camouflaging our bright yellow helmets with ferns for a sneak attack. During one particularly aggressive assault, it was hard to believe we were beginners, the way we were hopping around the raft. And once, a rafter from an enemy boat advanced quickly, calling out in a pirate's voice, "Kidnap the little girl!" Sara was in heaven.

Back at the Zoar Pavilion, we got in dry clothes for the closing — a slide show of our rafts surging through Zoar Gap. We couldn't resist buying an 8x10 picture ($18), a little large for the family album, but we all agreed we had a time worth remembering in a big way.

– *Polly Bannister*

Zoar Outdoor, 800-532-7483, 413-339-4010. Rte. 2, Charlemont. Rafting, kayaking, canoeing, and rock climbing. Gap rafting-trip weekends $75, children under 16 $60. (www.zoaroutdoor.com)

McCusker's or on Conway Street at the picnic area give you a chance to enjoy the river scenery.

Up the hill on Ashfield Street you'll find the Salmon Falls Artisans' Showroom, carrying glassware, jewelry, furniture, and other excellent handwork of more than 180 artisans. Down State Street are Bald Mountain Pottery and the newer studio of Laurie M. Goddard, whose one-of-a-kind patinated-leaf wooden bowls are more art than craft. Antiquers will enjoy a local favorite — Apple Blossoms Antiques — on the same block, as well as the collectors'-class Merry Lion.

Heading back toward McCusker's, stroll across the Bridge of Flowers. Once a trolley bridge, it was reappropriated by Shelburne Falls Woman's Club in 1929 as a pedestrian walkway and perennial garden. Gardeners will appreciate the effort taken to keep this 400-foot perennial garden in bloom throughout the season; more than 500 plant varieties line the bridge, ensuring that something is always in bloom.

Turn right onto Water Street and cross Bridge Street to find these geologic marvels: the glacial potholes, holes of all sizes bored into the Salmon Falls rockbed by glaciers (it's a real challenge to adequately photograph these curiosities). The potholes vary in size from a few inches to nearly 40 feet in diameter, and in the summer the riverbed is dotted with swimmers and sunbathers enjoying the smooth, warm rock surfaces. Crafts practically line your path down to the water: North River Glass, a working glassblowing studio open to the curious public, and Mole Hollow Candles.

Now take 112 south, through a lovely stretch of farmland and gentle hills, and make a left on 116 south into Ashfield. Ashfield's Fall Festival occurs on Columbus Day weekend and is a delightful blend of crafts, food, games, and music in a beautiful village setting. Stop at Elmer's Grocery Store —

For walkers only

On Route 116, east of Ashfield, a covered bridge spans the South River. The **Burkville Covered Bridge** (also called the Conway Covered Bridge) is one of a handful of historic 19th-century covered bridges in Massachusetts. Built in 1869, it is no longer strong enough to carry cars. It is open to walkers who can stroll through and admire the multiple-king-rod truss construction. The bridge is right off Route 116, just before you reach the town of Conway.

built in 1835 — on Main Street for excellent bakery goods and cheddar.

You are no doubt tired enough to pull out the list of B&Bs you've picked up from the Shelburne Visitors Center. Here are a few at which we've stayed while in the area. The closest B&B to Shelburne is the Johnson Homestead, where you will enjoy a full country breakfast in the surrounds of a lovely old farmhouse, accompanied by resident dogs and hummingbirds. Or stay at Bull Frog Bed & Breakfast in Ashfield, where Lucille Thibault welcomes you to her late-1700s Cape set on 27 acres of farmland, cornfields, and rolling hills. On Route 143 in Chesterfield, Doc and Denise LeDuc open their 1891 Dutch gambrel to guests under the name of the Seven Hearths B&B. On these chilly fall nights, visitors will be happy to learn that all three of the B&B's bedrooms have working fireplaces.

More than 500 plant varieties line the bridge of flowers.

DAY TWO For more Arcadian tranquillity, continue south on 116 about 1½ miles, going straight where 116 angles to the left. Follow the old-fashioned sign pointing to Williamsburg and Route 9. Ease down 2.3 miles of bumpy road to the Chapelbrook Reservation. Don't be deterred by the spectacle of serious rock climbers struggling up the face with ropes. The rest of us can follow the

You'll find everything you need (and more) at the Williamsburg General Store.

courtesy Williamsburg General Store

Where the Chef Is a Gardener

For a decade, Green Street Café has been known throughout the Pioneer Valley for its American-influenced country French cuisine. What the locals know is that owners John Sielski and Jim Dozmati grow much of the restaurant's produce in their ¾-acre home garden, located two miles west of the café. Chef John, who is native to the area, comes from a long line of gardeners. His grandfather was an onion farmer from Whately, who said the valley farmland was the best he'd ever seen, and John's parents were founding members of the Amherst Farmer's Cooperative some 30 years ago. When John was a boy, he raised cucumbers for spending money. Jim is an experienced landscape designer who fled New York City so he could finally have more than a brownstone rooftop for his garden. At the Green Street Café all baking is done on the premises and fresh-from-the-garden specialties include handmade ravioli stuffed with fresh bitter greens, squash blossom risotto, and salads with tender baby greens.

Green Street Café, 413-586-5650. 64 Green St., Northampton. Open daily for dinner ($$), weekdays for lunch ($).

marked trail up and around a sheer rock face to the summit. After taking in the vista, walk back down and follow the trail across the road to moss-covered falls (being ever mindful of the slippery rocks).

Hankering for civilization yet? Head down the Williamsburg Road (which changes to Main Poland Road and Ashfield) until you come out onto Route 9 in Williamsburg; from here it is just a few miles to Northampton.

If, however, you're a glutton for country scenery, backtrack onto 116 through Ashfield and head south again on 112 for a pretty drive. About five miles down on the left is the D.A.R. State Forest; it was established in 1929 when the Daughters of the American Revolution donated 1,020 acres to the Commonwealth. There is a nice trail along Upper Highland Lake (as well as a wheelchair-accessible trail along the lake edge that provides access to fishing) and a scenic wetland where moose, bear, and beaver are common. At the end of 112, hang a left on Route 9 through blink-and-you-miss-it Goshen and on down the hill into Williamsburg.

Visit the Williamsburg General Store, an old-fashioned (the store is over 100 years old), stuffed-to-the-gills shop, specializing in ice cream, kitchen gadgets, handmade jewelry, Christmas ornaments, and home-baked goods. It would not be fall without sampling one of their famous Wrapples — sliced, fresh apples sprinkled with cinnamon and sugar, baked in pastry, and lightly frosted. Owner Carol Majercik tells us they sell over 100 a day on weekends. Carol and her husband, David, also run the Williams House (two doors down) in a circa-1812 building. Here you'll find good New England fare served for lunch and dinner, such as their Yankee pot roast, and their signature pork with pear-pecan sauce.

In Northampton, pick up a *Valley Advocate* on the street for listings of everything from food and entertainment to movies. Main Street has enough art and craft galleries to keep you busy for hours. The Calvin Theater and the Iron Horse Music Hall are venues for big-name music groups, and the Pleasant Street Theater and the Academy of Music show interesting films. The kiosk on Main Street is a quick way to find out what's happening. If you are in the area over Columbus Day weekend, don't miss Paradise City Arts Festival, held at the Tri-County Fairgrounds on Route 9. More than 20,000 visitors attend this juried show of contemporary crafts and art. The festival features the works of over 200 artists from across the country.

If you find yourself here on a rainy day or can't resist the cultural pull of an area that boasts 30,000 students within an 11-mile radius, try visiting any of the five colleges where you'll find museums, exhibits, recitals, dance concerts, and terrific libraries.

Good friends and good food at Spoleto Restaurant.

It's hard to go wrong choosing a restaurant on Main Street. They *have* to be good to hold their own in this town. The problem: so many restaurants . . . so little time! For a special night out try Spoleto Restaurant. We recommend the mussels Poulette appetizer, then either coriander-encrusted sea bass or a Spoleto favorite: pasta shells (served with *tasso,* andouille, shrimp, spinach, fresh tomatoes, jalapeños, and herbs). Also on the main drag is upscale Del Raye Bar & Grille. Here gourmet food with international flavors is the name of the game. Our suggestions: roasted lobster with truffle butter, grilled swordfish with mango-coconut salsa, or ginger-barbecued pork loin. Both places have excellent wine lists. Just off Main Street, the Eastside Grill serves creative American cuisine. They specialize in fresh fish and seafood

with a fine selection of steaks. Warning: You may have to put your name on a waiting list at the above establishments, but strolling around town before getting seated is a fun diversion, no matter how hungry you are.

If the evening is warm enough, you'll be treated to a wide variety of street musicians as you wander after dinner. If you still have room, Bart's on Main Street and Herrell's in Thorne's basement have yummy homemade ice cream to rival the best of the best. Most places serve excellent cappuccino and latte to sip while you pour over the *Advocate* to settle on whether it will be a movie or music for tonight's entertainment.

Lodging options are Hotel Northampton, the big red-brick building conveniently located downtown. A little west, in Florence, is the Knoll, a 1910 Tudor-style house situated on 17 acres of farm and woodland. Hostess Lee Lesko boasts guests from each of the 50 states and all continents except Antarctica. In nearby Amherst, Amherst College owns the Lord Jeffery Inn, where there are 48 rooms available, eight of which are suites. Here you can choose informal dining at Elijah Boltwood's Tavern or fine dining at the Windowed Hearth.

To continue the tour into northeastern Connecticut, where more antiques, country roads, and good food await in the Quiet Corner, get on Interstate 91 southbound.

– Jan Voorhis

T IS HARD TO GO WRONG CHOOSING A RESTAURANT ON MAIN STREET IN NORTHAMPTON.

ESSENTIALS

Shelburne Falls Village Information Center, 413-625-2544. 75 Bridge St., Shelburne Falls, MA 01370. Request a map, a must for wandering the back roads. Call for a list of local bed-and-breakfast lodgings. Open May-October Monday-Saturday 10-4. (www.shelburnefalls.com)

Hampshire Hills Bed & Breakfast Association, 888-414-7664. Worthington, MA 01098. Contact for more regional lodging options. (www.hamphillsBandB.com)

Marillas Antiques & Country Goods, 802-368-7725. Rte. 100, Jacksonville, Vermont. Open year-round daily (except Wednesday) 10-5.

Stone Soldier Pottery, 802-368-7077. 64 Gates Pond Rd., Jacksonville, Vermont. Open Monday-Saturday 10-5, Sunday noon-5.

North River Winery, 802-368-7557. River Rd., just off Rte. 100, Jacksonville, Vermont. Open year-round daily 10-5, other hours by appointment. Free tastings and tours. (www.vtnatural.com)

Green Emporium, 413-624-5122. 4 Main Rd., on the common, Colrain. ($$-$$$) Open mid-April to New Year's Eve Friday-Saturday for dinner and Sunday for brunch.

Pine Hill Orchards, 413-624-3325. 248 Greenfield Rd., Colrain; turn right off of Rte. 2 at Strawberry Fields Antiques. Open year-round weekdays 7-6, weekends 8-6. ($-$$) Sue's Sunrise Café serves breakfast and lunch.

Orchard Hill Antiques, 413-625-2433. Colrain Rd., Shelburne. Open year-round by chance or appointment.

High Ledges Wildlife Sanctuary, off Patten Rd., Shelburne. Trails open daily dawn-dusk. $2, children $1.

Crab Apple Rafting Co., 800-553-7238. Rte. 2, Charlemont. (www.crabappleinc.com)

Shea Antiques, 413-625-8353. 69 Bridge St., Shelburne Falls. Open year-round daily 10-5.

Seasons Past, 413-625-2935. 55 Bridge St., Shelburne Falls. Open Thursday-Monday 10-6, Tuesday and Wednesday by chance.

Shelburne Falls Artisans Cooperative, 413-625-9324. 26 Bridge St., Shelburne. Open during foliage daily 10:30-7; other seasons Monday and Wednesday-Friday 10:30-7, Saturday-Sunday noon-5, closed Tuesday.

Margo's Bistro, 413-625-0200. 24 Bridge St., Shelburne Falls. ($$) Open Wednesday-Saturday for dinner, Sunday for brunch 11-4.

Ten Bridge Street Cafe, 413-625-6345. 10 Bridge St., Shelburne Falls. ($-$$) Open Monday-Thursday 11-8:30, Friday-Saturday 7:30 A.M.-9:30 P.M., Sunday 7:30 A.M.-8:30 P.M.

Mother's, 413-625-6300. 65 Bridge St., Shelburne Falls. ($) Open daily 7-5:30.

McCusker's Market, 413-625-9411. 3 State St., west end of the Bridge of Flowers, Shelburne Falls. Open year-round daily 7-7.

Salmon Falls Artisans' Showroom, 413-625-9833. Ashfield St., Shelburne Falls. Open Monday-Saturday 10-5, Sunday noon-5.

The Johnson Homestead B&B, 413-625-6603. 79 East Buckland Rd., Shelburne Falls, MA 01370. Open year-round. Three rooms. $60-$75, including breakfast.

Bull Frog B&B, 413-628-4493. 1629 Conway Rd., Ashfield, MA 01330. Open year-round. Four rooms. $75-$95, including full breakfast prepared with local organic ingredients.

Seven Hearths B&B, 413-296-4312. 412 Main Rd./Rte. 143, Chesterfield, MA 01012. Open year-round. Three rooms, each with working fireplaces. $65-$110, including breakfast.

A bear enjoys the foliage of the D.A.R. State Forest.

courtesy D.A.R. State Forest

Chapelbrook Reservation, Williamsburg Rd., South Ashfield (where Rte. 116 makes a sharp turn east, go for a little over two miles on Williamsburg Rd. and turn left to find the falls and pool). Good views can be found across the road at Chapelbrook Ledges. Maintained by the Trustees of Reservations.

D.A.R. State Forest, off Rte. 112, Goshen. Open year-round daily dawn-dusk. 50 sites for camping, 40 of which are reservable through Reserve America (877-422-6762, 413-268-7098). Camping May-Columbus Day weekend. $12 per night per site, $2 discount per night for Massachusetts residents. (www.reserveamerica.com/usa/ma/darf/)

Williamsburg General Store, 413-268-3036. Main St. (Rte. 9), Williamsburg. Open daily 9-6.

The Williams House, 413-268-7300. Rte. 9, Village Center, Williamsburg. ($-$$$) Open Tuesday-Sunday for lunch and dinner.

Paradise City Arts Festival, 413-527-8994. Tri-County Fairgrounds, Northampton; Rte. 9, exit 19 off I-91. Open Saturday-Sunday 10-6, Monday 10-5. $8, seniors and students $5, children $2; free parking. (www.paradise-city.com)

Spoleto Restaurant, 413-586-6313. 50 Main St., Northampton. ($$-$$$) Open daily for dinner.

Del Raye Bar and Grille, 413-586-2664. 1 Bridge St. (Rte. 9), Northampton. ($$$-$$$$) Open daily for dinner. Reservations recommended.

Eastside Grill, 413-586-3347. 19 Strong Ave., Northampton. ($-$$) Open daily for dinner.

Hotel Northampton, 800-547-3529, 413-584-3100. 36 King St., Northhampton, MA 01060. Open year-round. 99 rooms, including ten deluxe rooms and suites. $130-$205. (www.hotelnorthampton.com)

The Knoll, 413-584-8164. 230 North Main St., Florence, MA 01062. Open year-round. Four rooms. $50-$65, including breakfast. (www.bbonline.com/ma/theknoll)

Lord Jeffery Inn, 800-742-0358, 413-253-2576. 30 Boltwood Ave., Amherst, MA 01002. Open year-round. 48 rooms. $79-$178. ($-$$) Elijah Boltwood's Tavern open daily for breakfast, lunch, and dinner; Sunday brunch. ($$-$$$) Windowed Hearth open Wednesday-Sunday dinner; reservations required.

Autumn SPLENDOR IN
NORTHEASTERN *Connecticut's*
Quiet Corner

HERE'S A PERFECTLY good reason why Nathan ("I only regret that I have but one life to lose for my country") Hale came from northeastern Connecticut. Settled a generation after the rest of New England's colonizing along the coastline and the Connecticut River Valley, this area became home to many ex-Massachusetts families looking for more elbow room. Distanced from their Puritan comrades, the settlers began thinking and acting for themselves. That independent spirit eventually bred not only discontent with British rule but Nathan Hale as well.

courtesy Northeast Connecticut Visitors District

*Nathan Hale's father,
Deacon Richard Hale,
built this house
in Coventry.*

It's an independence that has never died. In the 1830s Prudence Crandall took on the establishment by opening her Canterbury boarding school to a black student. In the 1990s Austin Tanner has expanded his bucolic Brooklyn dairy farm to include a herd of American buffalo. Downtown Putnam could have become another empty crossroads when the shopping malls started going up; instead, it has transformed itself into a thriving antiques center.

DAY ONE As you travel southbound on I-91 into Hartford, be ready to make a left-lane exit onto Interstate 84 east to I-384 (toward Providence). As the freeway ends, follow signs to Coventry; a good place to start

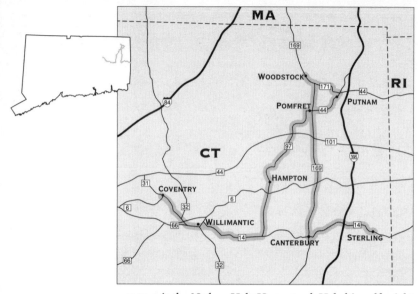

our tour is the Nathan Hale Homestead. Hale himself might not recognize the house in which he grew up. It was substantially rebuilt in the fashionable Georgian style in the year of his death, 1776. The Connecticut hero might feel familiar with the surroundings, though. The house sits in the middle of the 1,219-acre Nathan Hale State Forest, off Highway 6, a wooded setting not too dissimilar from the surrounds of Hale's boyhood 300-acre farm.

Farming persists in the region, especially in nurseries, gardens, and vineyards. Meander the area roads to find one of the best known: Caprilands Herb Farm, also in Coventry. This 50-acre herb garden started by Adelma Grenier Simmons is famous among gardeners and herbalists throughout the country. Nutmeg Vineyard is arguably the smallest of the eight northeastern Connecticut vineyards, and perhaps the least pretentious. About 1,000 cases of wine are squeezed annually from these 4½ acres of grapes. Their calling card is a delicate raspberry wine. You can visit them by backtracking on South Street, making a left turn to rejoin Highway 6, and following the signs.

To get to Coventry center, follow South Street east from the Hale Homestead, bearing right at the stop sign and soon thereafter turning left onto Cross Street/Lake Street, which intersects with Route 31. Here you can find two good places for a meal before getting back in the car: Bidwell Tavern and Bea's Country Kitchen. Bidwell's is known for chicken wings; it sells 3,000 pounds a week in 25 different varieties. It has the same number of beers on tap. Or hold out until you get to Willimantic Brewing Co./Main Street Café, a microbrewery housed in an old post office building, keeping up with national trends in Willimantic. To get there, take Route 31 south from Coventry, which merges with Route 32 and then with Route 66, into Willimantic.

Willimantic is one of many former mill towns in the Quiet Corner that helped bring prosperity to this region in the 19th century. The brick mill architecture, mansions and Victorian houses, and commercial fronts reflect the days of cotton thread and cloth production. Willimantic was nick-named "Thread City" for its production of silk and cotton thread. In the 1890s these mills were the state's largest employer. For more in-depth exposure to the milling industry visit the Windham Textile & History Museum.

Following Route 14 east (which joins Route 203 south for a while) into the town of Scotland, you might be lucky

Bidwell Tavern sells 3,000 pounds a week of its famous chicken wings.

courtesy Northeast Connecticut Visitors District

enough to come upon the annual Highland Fest held in October (always the Sunday of Columbus Day weekend). The festival features bagpipes and folk music, Highland dancing, sheepdogs, and Scottish food, all in honor of the motherland. If you've thought ahead, you can round out the international experience with a stop at the Olde English Tea Room, where afternoon tea is served (by reservation only) in Wedgwood china on lace-covered tables in a circa-1759 Colonial that sits perfectly on the village green. Hostess Pearl Dexter should know a thing or two about tea; she is the publisher of *Tea A Magazine*.

Next take Route 97 north, with Pomfret as the evening's destination. A good place to stop for a stretch along the way is Trail Wood, maintained by the Connecticut Audubon Society and formerly the property of naturalist, birder, and author

POSTCARD From

A Genius and His Puppets

While the color outside is changing, I found another burst of color at the Ballard Institute and Museum of Puppetry. In this little-known gem, about 200 puppets — dressed in bright scraps of fabric, feathers, and paper — are on display in the current show. I gazed at the walls replete with artist sketches of puppets from conception through design plans to photographs of puppets in action — all the genius of puppeteer Frank Ballard, whose collection of more than 2,000 puppets is housed in this small cottage.

Here at the only degree program of its kind in the country, University of Connecticut puppetry students act as tour guides. They answered all my questions, from how best to operate a puppet to what material is used to make Pinocchio's head. I was amazed at the range in size — I saw puppets from about three inches to more than ten feet high in all different styles, including hand, slider, rod, and marionette.

In the hands-on room, a 30-something man and his wife immersed themselves in acting out a scene between a giraffe hand puppet and a purple-haired girl rod puppet.

In the last gallery, the magic grabbed me. I envisioned *Kismet*'s wedding procession with 41 puppets, including a lumbering elephant, parading across the stage. I could almost hear the music. One visit and I know the passion and genius of puppeteer Frank Ballard is as alive as the puppets he created during his tenure in this university's theater department.

— *Katrina Yeager*

Ballard Institute and Museum of Puppetry, 860-486-4605. Weaver Rd. (off Rte. 44), Mansfield. Open late April to late November Friday-Sunday noon-5. Suggested donation $2, seniors and children $1.

Edwin Way Teale. The 156 acres feature three miles of walking trails.

Pomfret is home to the ivied and preppy-filled buildings of the Pomfret School. In the hills outside town, stop for a sandwich at the yellow barn that is Vanilla Bean Café. Pick up one of the local tourism association's excellent brochures from the rack by the door to plan your own side trips for antiquing, bicycling, or hiking.

If you are a gardener, don't miss Martha's Herbary. Martha Gummersall-Paul has lived in the Quiet Corner for 13 years and all this time has impressed neighbors with her gardens. Her shop offers unusual garden accessories, books, wreaths, herbs, and specialty plants. Martha conducts cooking classes where you can learn about medicinal herbs and make herb-flavored mustards, vinegars, and other wonderful kitchen gifts.

Sharpe Hill Vineyard has won the Taster's Guild International gold and silver medals, and you can sample their wine or tour the vineyard Fridays and Saturdays. They also serve lunch in the wine garden in good weather or fireside in the cozy tavern, where you can smell cassoulet simmering on the hearth. Or for a delicious dinner, try the Harvest. Located in a renovated 1785 homestead, it offers an eclectic and international fare that will wow you every time — from filet mignon to seared salmon with Thai lemon sauce.

A good night's rest is yours at one of these local B&Bs. Chickadee Cottage is a quiet, circa-1900 Cape decorated with antiques. Guests have a choice of a charming room in the house or their own separate cottage complete with kitchen, private deck, and sitting/dining area. Walkers can enjoy a morning stroll at the adjacent 500-acre Audubon preserve. Cobbscroft is a B&B with gift shop, gallery, and furniture

Walking Weekend

This year marks the tenth anniversary of "Walking Weekend," organized by Northeast Connecticut Visitors District. Every Columbus Day weekend the Quinebaug-Shetucket Heritage Corridor sponsors this autumn celebration of the area's rich cultural heritage and natural beauty with more than 50 free guided tours. There is something for every age and fitness level — arts, birds, vineyards, woods, rivers, mills, and more treasures from the 25-town area from Woodstock and Thompson to the north, along the Connecticut border south to Voluntown and Norwich, then west to Coventry.

Northeast Connecticut Visitors District, 860-928-1228. P.O. Box 598, Putnam, CT 06260. Request a free brochure that includes information on tours and lodging.

store. Here you can enjoy (and/or buy) watercolor, acrylic, and oil paintings by Thomas McCobb and a wide selection of pine furniture colorfully painted and stenciled. (Wooden Christmas decorations range in price from $18 for a hand-painted angel to $95 for a sled; a single pantry with three shelves runs about $300.) Celebrations Inn is enjoying a new incarnation after a long and varied history. This circa-1885 Queen Anne Victorian was once home to Miss Vinton's School for Girls; some years later the property was the site of the Pomfret Inn, and still later it was converted to apartments. A year ago, Jean and Bill Barton opened its doors again, this time as Celebrations Inn, with five rooms, each decorated according to a different theme.

DAY TWO The spine of the Quiet Corner also happens to be one of the prettiest roads in all New England. Route 169, officially sanctioned as a State Scenic Highway, weaves south from Woodstock through Pomfret and onto Brooklyn and Canterbury. Travel its curves and hills to dig deeper into this green region's past. Start your day by leaving Pomfret via Route 44 for a detour through Putnam.

*T*HE SPINE OF THE QUIET CORNER IS ONE OF THE PRETTIEST ROADS IN ALL NEW ENGLAND.

Putnam, part of Pomfret until it broke away in 1855, has been the site of textile mills since 1807. Until just five years ago, it was a place you drove through quickly on the way somewhere — anywhere — else. But then Putnam began to attract antiques dealers into the large empty spaces of its brick downtown. Today it's a changed place. The Antiques Market-place, progenitor of the shops, is a multidealer store with some fine mission-style furniture, ticking wall clocks, fine china, jewelry, and hundreds of other collectibles. Well over 200 individual dealers are represented on four floors of 350 booths and cases. Across the street, Interiors is a design ser-vice, but its storefront is packed with all that is beautifully off-beat. If the Fiestaware and the jelly cabinets wear you down, retreat to the Vine Bistro, a Soho-ish restaurant where you can sit down for lunch or dinner. Do not miss one of its frozen fruit sorbets, surely the world's quickest pick-me-up before tackling more antiques.

courtesy Northeast Connecticut Visitors District

To get to Woodstock, take Route 171 west. The town was settled in 1686 by émigrés from Roxbury, Massachusetts, and presents a tidy face of clapboard houses and trim lawns. By the mid-1800s, northeastern Connecticut was crisscrossed with railroad lines; some brought Manhattanites looking for summer retreats, one being local-boy-made-good Henry C. Bowen, who built his Roseland Cottage here in 1846. The dramatically pink Gothic Revival house retains its custom-made furniture, and it presents a taste of the good life of a Victorian summertime, from its stained-glass windows and private bowling alley to a series of tea parties and evening concerts.

The food is as great as the view at the Golden Lamb Buttery.

Tourist attractions are minimal: There are no strips of T-shirt shops and gift shoppes in the Corner. When farming declined and manufacturing ascended in the early 1800s, perhaps those who had once dubbed Woodstock and Pomfret "inland Newports" found the area too industrialized. The region boasts no big old hotels. Overnight choices tend toward small B&Bs with only a handful of rooms.

Dining is limited, too, along this corridor. Other than the Vanilla Bean and the Vine, there is the Inn at Woodstock Hill, former estate of a gentleman farmer, which serves ambitious lunch and dinner menus on its deck and inside its formal dining room. Or you'll find the venerable and very fun Golden

Lamb Buttery, full of loyal customers, farther down the road in Brooklyn. (Be sure to reserve ahead.)

Agriculture is still important to the town of Brooklyn; its fairgrounds have been in use since 1852. So it's no surprise to see cows grazing behind the old stone walls of a farm off Creamery Brook Road. What is surprising is the small shaggy herd of American buffalo, or more correctly bison, their tails and long ears twitching at flies on a Connecticut ridge. At Austin and Deborah Tanner's Creamery Brook Bison farm, you can buy various cuts of bison meat and hear about its healthy virtues. Start with the hamburgers, they suggest, if you've never tried this lean red meat before. Another example of individuality in this area can be found in Henry Riseman's eclectic collection at the New England Center for Contemporary Art, a little-known gem. Acclaimed artist and illustrator Normand Chartier offers for sale his paintings, prints, and originals of children's-book and magazine art at prices ranging from $40 to $2,500. His gallery is housed in a 100-year-old barn also on Route 169.

Just a little east, take a detour to Logee's Greenhouses in Danielson: From Brooklyn, take Route 6 east to Route 12/Main Street (in Danielson) to North Street; bear right at the split. Logee's is four-tenths of a mile on the left. Eight greenhouses nurture more than 2,000 plants. Their specialties include flowering plants, begonias, passion flowers, gesneriads, scented geraniums, and herbs. Since 1892, the Logee-

THOSE WHO CARE WANT TO KEEP THIS CORNER QUIET, FREE FROM SUBURBAN SPRAWL.

Shaggy buffalo graze at Creamery Brook Bison farm.

courtesy Creamery Brook Bison

Martin family has been growing and selling over a thousand varieties of tropical and subtropical plants. The fragrance from a walk here is guaranteed to make your heart soar.

In Canterbury, at the intersection with Route 14, the outer appearance of a handsome beige Federal suggests little more than Yankee austerity. But a tour of this, the Prudence Crandall Museum, reveals a tumultuous past. When the parents of white students pulled their daughters out of Crandall's academy over the admission of one black student in 1832, Crandall retaliated by turning over the entire school to the education of black women. Rage and lawsuits ensued, and although Crandall eventually won in court on a technicality, she closed the school when a furious mob attacked the house. Today there are few original furnishings; curators aren't even sure which rooms were used for what purposes. But there's a palpable spirit in the house, perhaps that of Prudence herself.

courtesy the Prudence Crandall Museum

Abolitionist Prudence Crandall was imprisoned and tried for educating black students.

The last leg follows Route 14, which veers hard to the left just outside of Canterbury center, through Moosup. The road also leads through charming little Sterling — named for a doctor who reneged on his promise to build the hamlet a library if it took his name.

They don't call it the Quiet Corner for nothing. But lately they've been calling this region something else, too: Heritage Corridor. If you fly from Washington, D.C., to Portland, Maine, Connecticut's northeast corner is one of the very few green spaces left that you can see from the air. Preservation of the farmland and open space has become paramount. Those who care want to keep this corner quiet, free from the rest of the Northeast's suburban sprawl. Self-dubbed the "Quiet Corner," the region offers attractions that are subtle in nature: The most rewarding discoveries come after a little digging. And the digging continues with the Rhode Island tour as you drive eastward on Route 14.

– *Janice Brand*

ESSENTIALS

Northeast Connecticut Visitors District, 888-628-1228, 860-928-1228. P.O. Box 598, Putnam, CT 06260. Request the *Getaway Guide*. (www.webtravesl.com/quietcorner)

Nathan Hale Homestead, 860-742-6917, 860-247-8996. 2299 South St. (off Rte. 6), Coventry. Open mid-May to mid-October daily 1-4. P.M. $4, children $1.

Caprilands Herb Farm, 860-742-7244. 534 Silver St. (off Rte. 44), Coventry. Open year-round daily 10-5. (www.caprilands.com)

Nutmeg Vineyard, 860-742-8402. 800 Bunker Hill Rd. (off Rte. 6), Coventry. Open year-round Saturday-Sunday 11-5.

Bidwell Tavern, 860-742-6978. 1260 Main St. (Rte. 31), Coventry. Open daily for lunch ($) and dinner ($$).

Bea's Country Kitchen, 860-742-7255. Main St. (Rte. 31), Coventry. ($) Open daily for breakfast and lunch.

Willimantic Brewing Co./Main Street Café, 860-423-6777. 967 Main St., Willimantic. ($-$$) Open Tuesday-Saturday 11:30 A.M.-midnight, Sunday-Monday 4 P.M.-midnight.

Windham Textile & History Museum, 860-456-2178. Main St./Union St., Willimantic. Open Friday-Sunday 1-5 P.M. (extended hours in summer); tours also by appointment. $4, seniors and children $2.

Olde English Tea Room, 860-456-8651. 3 Devotion Rd., Scotland. Tea served by reservation only.

Trail Wood, 860-455-0759. 93 Kenyon Rd. (off Rte. 97), Hampton. Open year-round daily dawn-dusk. Free admission.

Vanilla Bean Café, 860-928-1562. 450 Deerfield Rd. (junction of rtes. 169, 44, and 97), Pomfret. ($) Open Monday-Tuesday 7-3, Wednesday-Friday 7 A.M.-8 P.M., and Saturday-Sunday 8-8.

Martha's Herbary, 860-928-0009. 589 Pomfret St., Pomfret. Open year-round Tuesday-Sunday 10-5. (www.marthasherbary.com)

Sharpe Hill Vineyard, 860-974-3549. 108 Wade Rd. (off Rte. 97), Pomfret. Open year-round for tastings and Friday-Sunday 11-5 for lunch ($$). Reservations required. ($$$$) Dinner by prior arrangement only.

The Harvest, 860-928-0008. 37 Putnam Rd. (Rte. 44),

Pomfret. ($$$) Open Tuesday-Friday for lunch, Tuesday-Sunday for dinner, and Sunday for brunch. Reservations required. (www.harvest restaurant.com)

Chickadee Cottage Bed & Breakfast, 860-963-0587. 70 Averill Rd., Pomfret, CT 06259. Open year-round. Two rooms. $95-$125, including continental breakfast. (www.chickadeecottage.com)

Cobbscroft Bed & Breakfast, 800-928-5560, 860-928-5560. 349 Pomfret St. (junction of rtes. 169 and 44), Pomfret, CT 06259. Open year-round. Four rooms. $65-$95, including breakfast. (www.cobbscroft.com)

Celebrations Inn, 860-928-5492. 330 Pomfret St. (Rte. 169), Pomfret, CT 06259. Open year-round. Five rooms (including two suites). $85-$125, including breakfast.

The Felshaw Tavern, 860-928-3467. Five Mile River Rd., Putnam, CT 02620. Open year-round. Two rooms. $80, including breakfast.

Antiques Marketplace, 860-928-0442. 109 Main St., Putnam. Open year-round daily 10-5. (www.antiquesmarketplace)

The Vine Bistro, 860-928-1660. 85 Main St., Putnam.

courtesy Logee's Greenhouses

A plant lover visits one of eight greenhouses at Logee's.

Open Tuesday-Sunday for lunch ($) and dinner ($$).

Roseland Cottage, 860-928-4074. Rte. 169, on the Common, Woodstock. Open June 1 to October 15 Wednesday-Sunday 11-5, with tours on the hour. $4, seniors $3.50, children under 12 $2, under 5 free.

Inn at Woodstock Hill, 860-928-0528. 94 Plaine Hill Rd., Woodstock, CT 06267. Open year-round. 22 rooms and suites. $90-$155, including continental breakfast. ($$-$$$) Dining room open Monday-Saturday for dinner, Tuesday-Saturday for lunch, Sunday for brunch 11-2 and dinner 3:30-7:30 P.M. (www.webtravels.com/woodstockhill)

Golden Lamb Buttery, 860-774-4423. 499 Bush Hill Rd. (off rte. 169), Brooklyn. ($$$$) Open May-December Tuesday-Saturday for lunch and Friday-Saturday for 7 o'clock dinner. Reservations required.

Creamery Brook Bison, 860-779-0837. 19 Purvis Rd., Brooklyn. Open Monday-Friday 2-6 P.M., Saturday 9-2; wagon tours only weekends July-September at 1:30 P.M. $6, children 3-11 $4.50.

New England Center for Contemporary Art, 860-774-8899. Rte. 169, Brooklyn. Open May-November Tuesday-Friday 10-5, Saturday-Sunday 1-5 P.M. Free.

Chartier Gallery, 860-779-1104. Rte. 169, Brooklyn. Open April-Christmas Thursday-Sunday noon-5 or by appointment.

Logee's Greenhouses, 860-774-8038. 141 North St., Danielson. Open year-round Monday-Friday 9-5, Saturday 9:30-6, Sunday 11-6; off-season, store closes daily at 5.

Prudence Crandall Museum, 860-546-9916. Rtes. 169 and 14, Canterbury. Open February to mid-December Wednesday-Sunday 10-4:30. $2, seniors and children $1.

The Fairest OF THEM ALL:
Leaves, Views,
AND OTHER SURPRISES IN
Little Rhodie

I REALIZE THAT SOME travelers think of Rhode Island as a tangle of highway blocking easy access to somewhere else. I say give them a map and bid them Godspeed. I know this small and unruly state, and I can tell you for a fact that it affords more opportunities for easy enjoyment than any in New England, and there is greater variety, too.

The only thing you can't find in Rhode Island is a mountain; I suppose something had to go. After all, the entire state is only 37 miles wide and 48 miles long, and much of that is given

Venetian-style gondolas provide water taxis along the waterfront in Providence.

Richard Benjamin

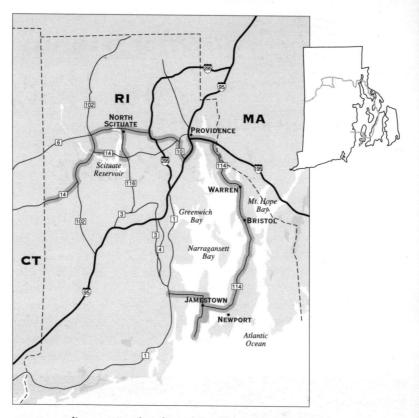

over to coastline — 460 miles of it, with literally dozens of public beaches. I know coastline doesn't spell trees, and therefore the foliage might not be what you'd see in the North Country, but believe me: We have autumn in Rhode Island. I know this, and that is why I've set out to find the best views that Rhode Island has to offer. Of course, one traveler's "best view" may be entirely humdrum to another, but to me the term implies a sense of beauty, uniqueness, joy, and inspiration.

If you're inclined to agree, come along. We will see some of the finest Colonial architecture in the Northeast, visit a classy zoo and a gem of a museum, see trees (with colored leaves) so magnificent and stately that you'd think you were in Yorkshire, gaze at mansions so elegant as to make you question the century you're in, and take in seacoast that is as picturesque as any in New England.

DAY ONE For those of you who have been with us from the Connecticut tour and are heading to Providence from the Quiet Corner, we suggest that you take Route 14 east from Sterling, Connecticut. When Route 14 merges with Route 102 North, continue on 102 to the towns along Highway 6. The area around Foster and Scituate, Rhode Island, is gentle, rural, and not at all touristy. Colorful forests, windy roads, and acres of beautifully crafted fieldstone walls dot a landscape that begs autumn rambling. A nice detour: Follow Route 14 east where it splits off from Route 102; turn right at Crazy Corners, where you'll cross the Scituate Reservoir for splendid foliage reflected in water. (Return to Route 6 via Route 116.)

Next on the tour is a visit to Roger Williams Park Zoo. Take Route 6 from North Scituate to Interstate 295; head south. Take exit 5, the very next exit, to continue east on Route 6 until the junction with Route 10. Take Route 10 southbound. Just after passing I-95, Route 10 intersects with Highway 1, also known as Elmwood Avenue; from there follow the signs. The park covers 435 acres and includes nine miles of twisting roads. It harbors a chain of ten small lakes, specimen trees, small rolling meadows, beautiful flower gardens, a replica of a Victorian carousel, and a large Japanese garden, where about a third of Rhode Island's young women pose for wedding pictures. It would be easy to spend a couple of hours here, and the polar bears and penguins alone make the zoo well worth the visit.

Retrace your steps back to Interstate 95 north, and get off again at exit 22 in Providence. In about three blocks you'll discover Waterplace Park, four reclaimed acres on Cove Basin at the confluence of

COVERED BRIDGE ALERT

Rhode Island's Only Covered Bridge

Rhode Island's only covered bridge is in Foster. Though it is the nation's newest and smallest (36 feet) covered bridge, it has a dramatic history. In the late fall of 1992, **Swamp Meadow Covered Bridge,** a latticed-truss, one-lane bridge, was built over Hemlock Brook, much to the delight of locals who took seriously the fact that Rhode Island was the only New England state without a covered bridge. On a September night one year later, teenage vandals doused the bridge with gasoline and, with the flick of a lighter, destroyed it. The townspeople were so distraught that they weren't sure they wanted to rebuild, but calls, money, and offers of support came from all over Rhode Island. A few months later, volunteers began the process that ultimately led to rebuilding. Dedicated in November of 1994, the new bridge resembles an authentic 19th-century covered bridge. To visit: From Route 6, go south on Route 94; turn right on Central Pike.

Apples Galore

On many back roads of North Scituate, you'll find handwritten signs tacked to trees and telephone poles; they read "Apples — Pick Your Own." Apples abound here. Barden Orchards offers a great selection of apples — Macs, Macoun, Empire, Cortland, Delicious, Crispin, and Jonagold — and sweet fresh peaches, too. Gilbert Barden now runs his grandfather's orchard, which was started in 1931, and also has a new location in Chepachet. His neighbor, N. H. Phillips, sells apples from White Oak Farm. Myra and Newell Phillips, who have been in the business for over 50 years, grow Paula Red (early season), Ida Red, Macs, Cortland, Macoun, Red and Yellow Delicious, Crispin, Spencer, Empire, and others. A few miles to the west, Sunset Orchards has a large operation that appears to be *the* destination for annual fall field trips for Rhode Island's schoolchildren. They offer a wide selection of fancy and baking apples, apple butter, fudge, and baked goods. There are tables inside for taking a rest while contemplating (over a cup of fresh cider) which apples to buy.

Barden Orchards, 401-934-1413. 56 Elmdale Rd., North Scituate. The address pinpoints the farmhouse, where you'll find squash, Indian corn, and pumpkins, in addition to apples and peaches. Open daily 9-5; on weekends the Bardens also open a stand on Pole Bridge Road (take 116 north from Route 6, and turn left on Pole Bridge); a second orchard on Route 44 west of Chepachet Village is open weekends and holidays 10-6.

White Oak Farm, 401-934-0749. 74 White Oak Ln. (located on the corner of Pole Bridge and Elmdale), North Scituate. Open daily 9-5.

Sunset Orchards, 401-934-1900. 244 Gleaner Chapel Rd. (follow signs north off routes 101 or 6), North Scituate. Bakery open daily 6-5 (closed in deep winter); seasonal apple picking 9-5.

the Woonasquatucket and Moshassuck rivers. If you would like, you can come back here at night and enjoy "Waterfire," unique performance art that features more than 80 bonfires set to music all along the waterway (call ahead to check the dates). Good lunch spots are easy to find. Just a short walk from Waterplace Park you can enjoy hearty sandwiches on homemade focaccia bread served at Caffe Pazzo on Steeple Street (just off South Main).

That huge, white marble landmark perched atop the rolling green lawn and looming over all else is the Rhode Island State House. Historians in this, the most heavily Roman Catholic state in the nation, say that the building's unsupported dome — the first of its kind in the nation — is second in size only to St. Peter's Basilica in Rome.

Cross the river on Waterman Street to the foot of College Hill, home to Brown University and the Rhode Island School of Design, and you're in history's lap. Straight ahead at the junction of North Main Street is the First Baptist Church in America, beautiful in its clapboard simplicity, majestic for its situation at the foot of one of the finest, most beautifully restored neighborhoods of 18th- and 19th-century homes in the Northeast. This is the capital city's historic East Side, and the next intersection is Benefit Street, its heart. Parking is dear, but don't be daunted; any side street will do.

At the Rhode Island School of Design, don't miss the Museum of Art (which houses more than 75,000 diverse works), the Providence Athenaeum, and the historic John Brown House, all of which are within easy walking distance of one another.

If you have not had lunch, try the Providence Bookstore Café (near Wayland Square), where you can browse books over everything from pizza to filet mignon. For the next leg of our trip, drive to Waterman Street and take Gano Street. At the end of Gano, hop onto Interstate 195 east. It's two miles to exit 7, for Route 114 south, the Wampanoag Trail. Reset the odometer.

courtesy RISD Museum of Art

Lady's silver writing table on display at the Rhode Island School of Design's Museum of Art.

Within four scant miles, as you pass from East Providence into Barrington, the landscape will start to change. It flattens out. The autumn light turns gold and the trees give way to riverfront and saltwater marshes, where egrets and great blue heron poke about in the tawny eelgrass. One can imagine how peacefully the Wampanoag tribe who inhabited this area (now the towns of Barrington, Warren, and Bristol) must have lived, hunting and fishing this lush land.

We hope that you will rest as peacefully tonight. Comfortable lodging and good food await in the quiet of East Bay (see box at right for editors' picks).

Where to Stay and Eat in East Bay

Nathaniel Porter Inn, 401-245-6622. 125 Water St., Warren, RI 02885. Considered one of the state's best-preserved Colonial homes, this inn has three rooms — each with private bath — and a very good restaurant ($$-$$$). Open year-round (closed some holidays). $89, including breakfast; $99 special package for two (includes continental breakfast and two dinner entrées).

Candlewick Inn, 401-247-2425. 775 Main St., Warren, RI 02885. A charming turn-of-the-century Sears-kit home. Open year-round. Three rooms, one private bath. $85-$125, including full gourmet breakfast.

The Parker Borden House, 401-253-2084. 736 Hope St., Bristol, RI 02809. A recently restored circa-1798 Federal with a water view; located across from East Bay Bike Path. Open year-round. Three rooms — one with private bath, another shared. $70-$85 shared bath, $95 private bath; including breakfast.

The Rockwell House Inn, 800-815-0040, 401-253-0040. 610 Hope St., Bristol, RI 02809. This circa-1809 Federal Victorian is located in the heart of Bristol. The innkeepers provide bathrobes and hair dryers, serve sherry, and offer a gourmet breakfast. You'll find the largest and oldest tulip poplar tree in the state right in the backyard here. Open year-round. Four rooms (two with fireplaces, all with private baths). $85-$150, including breakfast. (www.rockwellhouseinn.com)

Bradford-Dimond-Norris House, 888-329-6338, 401-253-6338. 474 Hope St., Bristol, RI 02809. This circa-1792 building is one of Bristol's best-known landmarks, called the "Wedding Cake House." Open year-round. Four guest rooms, all with private baths and central air-conditioning. $80-$110, including breakfast. (www.edgenet.net/bdnhouse)

HotPoint Restaurant, 401-254-7474. 31 State St., Bristol. ($$-$$$) This is the newest restaurant in town and growing in popularity by the day. Only 12 tables, so the dining is intimate and the food is superb. Open Tuesday-Sunday for dinner, also Sunday 11:30-3 for brunch. (www.hotpointrestaurant.com)

Redlefsen's Rotisserie and Grill, 401-254-1188. 444 Thames St., Bristol. ($$-$$$) This restaurant is highly recommended by locals and visitors alike, who enjoy the European bistro atmosphere. Its Wiener schnitzel has been called the best in New England. Open Tuesday-Saturday for lunch, Tuesday-Sunday 5-9:30 P.M. for dinner.

Quito's Restaurant, 401-253-4500. 411 Thames St., Bristol. ($-$$) Don't be misled by plastic chairs and paper plates. The seafood is so fresh that you can watch it being unloaded from Quito's boat right on Bristol Harbor; it is also a wholesale fish market. Open May-September Sunday, Monday, Wednesday-Saturday for lunch and dinner; October-April Thursday-Sunday for lunch and dinner.

DAY TWO Three towns, all located on Route 114 between Providence and Newport, make up East Bay. Barrington is largely a bedroom community for Providence; Warren is authentic New England at its best; and Bristol is a historic seaport with all the amenities of a tourist town. These Bristol County towns share Narragansett Bay, miles of salt marshes dotted with shorebirds, a 14-mile scenic bike path, stunning architecture, and a preponderance of excellent antiques shops.

In the town of Bristol, you'll notice the center line turns red, white, and blue as a reminder that this is the annual site of one of the nation's oldest and biggest Fourth of July parades. Exactly 11.3 miles from the start of the Wampanoag Trail, turn right into Colt State Park.

This is the former property of industrialist Colonel Samuel Pomeroy Colt, and it sprawls over 443 well-tended acres on Narragansett Bay. It's a great place to walk, bike, fly a kite, play boccie, have a picnic or a barbecue, or just while away a quiet hour sitting on the seawall watching terns and gulls play across the water. The pavement is usually sprinkled

Awesome Antiquing

Of East Bay's three towns, I've found that Warren and Bristol offer the best destinations for antiquing. I can park the car (once) and wander in and out of shops. The Square Peg, on the corner of Water and Miller streets in Warren is one of my favorites. Owner Gil Warren started the antiques craze here 35 years ago, and his shop is jam-packed with evidence of a lifetime's collecting. When asked what his most desired objects are, he laughs, "The last 20 things I bought." There are artifacts from the Fall River steamboat line, thousands of antique buttons ranging in price from five cents to $30, fountain pens, watches, lead soldiers, Gorham silver, and literally hundreds of other wonderful things. Another fun shop, the Lady Next Door, is right around the corner on Water Street. Here female inventory reigns — vintage clothes of sumptuous velvet, satin, and silk; shoes, handbags, stacks of textiles and linens; glassware, toys, dolls, and jewelry. I could divide a whole day between these shops, but more treasures await in the dozen-plus antiques stores in town. And then there's Bristol....

– Polly Bannister

The Square Peg, (no phone). 51 Miller St., Warren. Open most days noon-5.

The Lady Next Door, 401-831-7338. 196 Water St., Warren. Open Thursday-Saturday 1-5 P.M.

with bits of broken quahog shells; the gulls take them up high and drop them until they break open and yield their clams. In the middle of the site is a long, low stone barn. It's now home to park management, but the picturesque building once housed Colt's prized cattle. In fact, verdigris-coated bronze statues of two of Colt's favorite bulls flank the entrance and exit to the grounds.

Blithewold Mansion is planted with more than 2,000 species of flowers, shrubs, and trees.

For a clearer taste of what it was like to actually live in such comfort, take a right turn out of the park and continue for a couple of miles on Route 114 south through downtown Bristol; follow the signs to Blithewold Mansion & Gardens. This is a simple but comfortable 45-room manor, a summer residence in the tradition of those that dot England's countryside.

The manor is set on 33 acres, lavishly planted with more than 2,000 species of flowers, shrubs, and trees, many of them Asian, for that was the fashion in 1908, when Pennsylvania coal magnate Augustus Van Wickle established Blithewold. The manor's "Great Lawn," a broad expanse stretching down to Narragansett Bay, was used for the drying of the massive canvas sails. These powered the grand 12-meter yachts that first sailed from Narragansett Bay in the 1930s to capture one America's Cup after another.

In the distance is Poppasquash Point and beyond that Prudence Island, but don't let the panorama lull you into missing Blithewold's gardens and especially its trees. Three are particularly striking: a small Chinese weeping pagoda tree that dates back to 1876 (the oldest tree in the collection), a giant sequoia so tall at 94 feet that for preservation it needs its own lightning rod, and an 80-foot European weeping beech,

my favorite. Within the sanctum of its dense, shading boughs, the temperature is easily four or five degrees cooler, and you can look straight up its majestic trunk and know why the rich are different. To plant a slow-growing tree such as this, you would have to believe that your money and position and power and cultural tradition would long outlive you, that it would all pass down through the generations with your house and property intact, and that one day your distant scion, and perhaps the entire state, would think well of you for it.

Neither is it an accident that many more magnificent beeches line the best streets in Newport, which is only about 30 minutes away. To get there, hop back on Route 114 south, cross the Mount Hope Bridge, and just follow the signs. The road takes you right into Queen Anne's Square, where a stop at Trinity Church is well worth the trouble of finding a place to park. The church dates to 1726, and it has been in continuous use ever since. George Washington, Queen Elizabeth II, and Archbishop Desmond Tutu all prayed here. Trinity's pulpit rises in three tiers. Some of its pews are flanked by magnificent stained-glass windows crafted by Louis Tiffany, and its organ, imported from London in 1733, is said by some historians to have been tested by George Frideric Handel.

Follow the "Mansions" signs down Thames Street's cobblestones, and they'll take you to Bellevue and Ochre Point avenues, where you can visit and tour the awesome trappings of great wealth till your heart turns green. The majestic homes all have names, and not quaint ones like "Art and

A mannequin models vintage tennis dress at the Newport Casino & International Tennis Hall of Fame.

courtesy Newport Casino & International Tennis Hall of Fame

Betty's Bungalow" or "Dunrovin." Here are the Breakers, Beechwood, Chateau-Sur-Mer, the Elms, Kingscote, Belcourt Castle, Marble House, and Rosecliff.

The Newport Casino & International Tennis Hall of Fame and Museum are down at the end of Bellevue. Take a right turn onto Memorial Boulevard and you can park on the street to take the Cliff Walk; the entrance is right by the big Cliff Walk Manor overlooking Easton's Beach.

The first third of the walk is easy, but the rest is work. It is not suited for all of its length to small children, strollers, bicycles, or anyone who is disabled. If you go far enough — and how can you not, in the presence of lively surf and grand mansions — you'll be clambering over big rocks and along seawall, and depending on the tide and wind, you may get a bit of saltwater spray in your face, too. The view is breathtaking: There's Rhode Island Sound stretching out for miles off Newport. Sunlight shimmers across the water like hammered silver. The surf slaps the rocky base of the walkway, sending fountains of salt spray into the air to be caught briefly on the wind and gently sprinkled on the thickening hedgerows of beach plums that gird parts of the meandering path. Just beyond and to my right are the manicured lawns and sprawling, stately backyards of some of the most magnificent mansions in the country.

Halfway down the walk, behind Marble House, is an exquisite replica of a Chinese teahouse. A concrete tunnel passes discreetly beneath it, and on my way back I notice that some fool has spray-painted "Share your wealth" on the foundation. Is this not a unique kind of wealth, this no-fee walk of more than three miles through the backyards of the rich and famous who lived and loved and played on Bellevue Avenue? They are the historic "haves" of New England's smallest and unruliest of states, and I suppose the kid with the spray paint was one of the "have-nots" who always yearn for somebody else's wealth.

But they don't have to. There's enough here in this smallest of states to go around; we've been enjoying it for days — and we won't even get to Second Beach in Middletown, East Beach in Charlestown, Watch Hill in Westerly, or Mohegan Bluffs on Block Island.

Sunlight shimmers across the water like hammered silver.

I cross the Newport Bridge, pay my $2, and drive onto Conanicut Island and Jamestown, which was burned by those zany Brits in 1775, and head south on the island's thoroughfare, North Main Road (which becomes Southwest Avenue, merges with Hamilton Avenue, and becomes Beavertail Road), to Beavertail State Park and Lighthouse Museum, which is a fitting place to let the day wind down. In fact, Beavertail offers one of the finest ocean views in the ocean state.

The wind is up. The fall air is still warm and redolent of distant marsh and ageless salt. The setting sun is bright red, and it paints the sky a rich and darkening vermilion, like an ember. "Share your wealth." Indeed.

Speaking of embers, Providence and the 80-fire display along the river is only a 40-minute ride from here. Just return to Route 138 and follow it across the Jamestown Bridge to return to the mainland. Route 4 north will get you back to 95. Route 4 south will take you to Route 1.

Naaw, you go ahead. I think I'll stay a while. If you second this, a great place to stay in Jamestown is the Bay Voyage Inn. This inn with 32 rooms is known statewide for its Sunday brunch (reservations are a must). It is open year-round with a dining room that overlooks the harbor and serves classic American cuisine — filet mignon, rack of lamb, and an extensive seafood menu, including baked-split lobster paella.

– *Wayne Worcester*

ESSENTIALS
....

Rhode Island Tourism Division, 800-556-2484, 401-277-2601. Rhode Island Economic Development Corporation, 1 West Exchange St., Providence, RI 02903. (www.visitrhodeisland.com)

Providence/Warwick Convention & Visitors Bureau, 800-233-1636, 401-274-1636.

1 West Exchange St., Providence, RI 02903. (www.providencecvb.com)

East Bay Chamber of Commerce, 888-278-9948, 401-245-0750. 654 Metacom Ave., Suite 2, Warren, RI 02885. (www.eastbaychamber.org)

Newport County Convention & Visitors Bureau, 800-976-5122, 401-849-8048. 23 America's Cup Ave.,

Newport, RI 02840. (www.gonewport.com)

Roger Williams Park Zoo, 401-785-3510. 1000 Elmwood Ave., Providence. Open daily April-October, weekdays 9-5, weekends 9-6; off-season daily 9-4; $6, seniors and children $3.50. (www.users.ids.net/~rwpz/)

Waterplace Park, 401-272-3111. Francis St., between

Elephants snuggle at Roger Williams Park Zoo.

courtesy Roger Williams Park Zoo

College Hill and downtown Providence. Call or check the Web site for a schedule of bonfires. (www.waterfire.org).

Caffe Pazzo, 401-421-1667. 9 Steeple St., Providence. ($-$$) Open Monday-Friday 7-7 , Saturday 8-5.

Rhode Island State House, 401-222-2357. Providence. Call ahead to reserve a guide. Self-guided tours Monday-Friday 8:30-4:30. Free.

First Baptist Church in America, 401-454-3418. 75 N. Main St., Providence. Tours Monday-Saturday 10-3, Sunday after morning services. Donation.

Benefit Street. Skirting College Hill, the city's "Mile of History" is lined with one of the finest collections of 18th- and 19th-century buildings in the country. Includes the 1774 Baptist church, east and uphill from Waterplace Park along the river.

The Providence Preservation Society, 401-831-7440. 21 Meeting St., Providence. Offers self-guided tour and other visitor information.

Museum of Art at the Rhode Island School of Design, 401-454-6500. 224 Benefit St., Providence. Open Wednesday-Sunday 10-5, Friday until 8 P.M. $5, seniors and college students $4, children 5-18 $2. (www.risd.edu/museum.html)

Providence Athenaeum, 401-421-6970. 251 Benefit St., Providence. Open Monday-Thursday 10-8:30, Friday-Saturday 10-5, Sunday 1-5 P.M.; closed weekends in summer. Free. Here in the fourth-oldest library in the country, designed by William Strickland, you will see one of the few remaining complete sets of Audubon's *Birds of America,* Napoleon's commissioned book *Description de L'Egypte,* and unique 19th-century col-

lections in natural history and travel.

John Brown House, 401-331-8575. Corner Benefit and Power sts., Providence. Look for the two-acre lawn at this 1786 brick Georgian-style mansion owned by a wealthy Providence merchant. John Quincy Adams described the house as "the most magnificent and elegant private mansion that I have ever seen on this continent." Open Tuesday-Saturday 10-5, Sunday noon-4. $6, college students and seniors $4.50, children 7-17 $3, family $15. Walking tour brochures available here.

Providence Bookstore Café, 401-521-5536. 500 Angell St., Providence. ($$) Open daily for lunch and dinner.

Colt State Park, 401-253-7482. Rte. 114, Bristol. Open sunrise to sunset. Free.

Blithewold Mansion & Gardens, 401-253-2707. 101 Ferry Rd. (Rte. 114), Bristol. Grounds open daily 10-5; guided tours of mansion and grounds April-Columbus Day Tuesday-Sunday and most Monday holidays 10-4. In the following prices the lower fare is for grounds only, and the higher is for a guided tour of mansion and grounds: $5/$8, students and seniors $4/$6, children 6-17 $3/$4.

Trinity Church, 401-846-0660. Queen Anne Sq., Newport. Open July-early September daily 10-4, spring and fall 10-1; the 1733 organ is played at the 10 A.M. Sunday service in the summer, 10:30 A.M. in the fall. Donation.

The Newport Casino & International Tennis Hall of Fame and Museum, 800-457-1144, 401-849-3990. 194 Bellevue Ave., Newport. Open in summer daily 9:30-5. $8, seniors and students $6, children $4. (www.tennisfame.org)

Cliff Walk, Newport. Start at Memorial Blvd. at Easton's Beach, and if you go all the way, you'll end up at Coggeshall Ledge near the end of Bellevue Ave. Open daily 9-9.

Beavertail State Park and Lighthouse Museum, 401-423-3270. Beavertail Rd., Jamestown. In the museum you can see more than 30 models of Rhode Island lighthouses and other artifacts. Open in summer daily 10-4; park open year-round daily dawn-dusk.

Bay Voyage Inn, 401-423-2100. 150 Conanicus Ave., Jamestown, RI 02835. Open year-round. 32 rooms. $60-$200. Open daily for dinner ($$-$$$); Sunday brunch two seatings — 10 A.M. and 2 P.M., reservations required.

The Loveliest AND WILDEST LAND: The Kancamagus

ANCHORED IN THE EAST by Conway Village and to the west by Lincoln, this scenic highway is driven by more than 750,000 vehicles every year and is some of the loveliest and wildest land in the White Mountain National Forest. The Kancamagus Highway is a groove cut through a wall of trees and lies mostly in the town of Albany, New Hampshire. It bisects the Pemigewasset Wilderness, which is roughly square. The highway is known chiefly for three things: scenery, difficulties with the name, and moose.

The scenery is identified by eye and sign along the 34.5 miles of highway. Of the four pronunciations of the name in wide use, one is correct: "Kanca-MAW-gus."

Loggers worked for White Mountain timber barons.

courtesy the Lumbermen's Museum, Patten, Maine

NEW HAMPSHIRE

LINCOLN
CONWAY
112

Moose are gentle and somewhat improbable creatures, combining as they do the best features of the cow, the giraffe, and the chandelier. This gives them an endearing quality. They are dedicated vegetarians and they require large amounts of greenery, so they're most often seen along the swampy low-lying sections of the highway. Motorists should keep a sharp lookout at night; moose are black on top and gray lower down, which makes them extremely difficult to see against car-lit pavement and the dark forest beyond.

The most interesting part of the Kancamagus Highway is less obvious than its scenic and recreational treasures because it is hidden in the early years of our century.

It is important, however, because without it there might be no Kancamagus Highway.

Except for the occasional hunter or fisherman, this land did not feel a human footstep from the time the planet cooled until shortly after our Civil War. That would change with dizzying speed. In 1866, a group of hardy souls named themselves the Pemigewasset Perambulators and essayed a modest exploration of the north rim.

In 1882, a gentleman and three ladies set out to traverse the wilderness. The women were turned out in leg-of-mutton sleeves and skirts that swept the ground, and they often required the aid of two sturdy woodsmen who had been engaged to find a way through the untracked forest. The crossing took a week.

Most of the White Mountains land was state-owned until the middle of the 19th century; then it was more or less given away to private owners. Timber barons headed the list of recipients: Three operators divided up the Pemigewasset Wilderness, and the Kancamagus Highway runs for its entire length on the skid ways and railroad beds they built. This was the heroic age of American history and the approach of these three men defined the choices of American enterprise then and even to this day.

One tract of 75,000 acres went to Daniel Saunders, an unlikely woodsman who had a law degree from Harvard and the look of a rector in an English cathedral town. Indeed, he was a highly placed authority on legal matters in the Episco-

*E*XCEPT
FOR THE
OCCASIONAL
HUNTER OR
FISHERMAN,
THIS LAND
DID NOT FEEL
A HUMAN
FOOTSTEP
UNTIL SHORTLY
AFTER OUR
CIVIL WAR.

Conway Lumber Co., Conway, N. H.

pal church, and in 1876 he started a mill town at the northern edge of the wilderness that would eventually include 150 residents and up to 200 choppers in the woods.

At one time, the sawmill at the Conway Lumber Company produced 125,000 feet daily.

Selective cutting is the practice of taking only mature trees and leaving the rest to grow while the choppers move on to the next mature stand. This term was not in the timber baron's vocabulary or even widely understood when Mr. Saunders went to work. He was the only operator who used this method. The Saunders family was so careful that they cut over most of their land three times and still had virgin trees standing after 41 years of work.

Fire was the great enemy. The timber barons were interested in only the long trunks of the trees and thus often left behind immense piles of limbs and the slender upper sections of the trees — what the British call "lops and tops." These vast tinder boxes could be ignited by lightning, by a careless match, or even more easily, by sparks from the wood-burning locomotives of the timber railways. It's a measure of the Saunders family's devoted stewardship that no fire ever burned in their domain.

The largest of the operators was J. E. Henry, who advanced into the wilderness from the Zealand Valley in the north and then from Lincoln in the west, a company town

*Employees at
A. C. Kennett's
Spool Manufactory.*

built and personally owned by Mr. Henry. He was in business from 1881 to his death in 1912, and he was relentless. His men worked 11-hour days, which were regulated by 47 posted rules, 28 of which concerned the proper care of horses. Mr. Henry paid each of his men in person while carrying a gun on his hip, and he brooked no arguments. When one of his choppers settled up his account at the end of the winter, he saw a substantial deduction for tobacco at Mr. Henry's store. "I don't use tobacco," said the chopper, "you can ask any of the men." "That's all right," snapped Mr. Henry. "It was there if you'd wanted it."

The property lines of the timber barons' vast holdings were often disputed, and these were not trivial matters. The first serious disagreement involved the Saunders operation, and it went all the way to the U.S. Supreme Court. Local ingenuity settled other arguments. There was, for instance, the line along the height of land between mounts Carrigain and Kancamagus. It divided the Saunders and Henry holdings, and the two men did not agree on the exact location, so Mr. Henry sent the sheriff to arrest the Saunders choppers near the height of land, and he jailed them in Lincoln. Independent investigation found that the Henry choppers were at fault. Then Mr. Henry returned to thought and came up with a more subtle plan: It was said that he counted noses and then sent so many of his men to live in Livermore that they could form a voting majority and redefine the property lines.

Unlike the judicious Saunders family, the Henry ideal was to mow the wilderness, to clear off the land so completely that logs could be rolled down the mountainsides to the skid ways and then hauled to his mills by train. These were not narrow-gauge railroad lines; they were full commercial width, and their location as well as the labyrinth of skid ways made for complicated undertakings.

This was the work of Levi "Pork Barrel" Dumas, an unlettered French Canadian, whose instinct for location and gradient would be the envy of today's best civil engineers. While most loggers had a single-track operation, Mr. Henry built an empire with more than 20 deep-woods camps and more than 50 miles of railroad for six engines and extras he leased as needed; the trains would make two or three runs a day — a top haul was 28 laden cars — and telephone lines connected the camps and regulated traffic in "Henry's Woods."

Mr. Henry's profligate ways led to three major fires: 12,000 acres burned in 1886, 10,000 in 1903, and 35,000 in 1907. Writers told of the "devastating efficiency" and "abomination of desolation" of the Henry operations. In the summer of 1907, the sky was darkened by smoke as if from a volcanic eruption. When the land had cooled, scientists declared that the ground was profoundly destroyed, that it was sterilized into the upper layers of bedrock, and that no green thing might ever grow there again. When the Henrys sold out in 1917, they transferred 100,000 acres largely given to stumps and ashes.

Sabbaday Falls and Bear Notch Road

At approximately the midpoint, about 20 miles east of Lincoln, look for a barely visible National Forest sign — on the south side of the Kancamagus Highway — marking the trailhead to Sabbaday Falls. A ten-minute hike on a gentle, wide trail leads to a striking flume and waterfall. Walls of stone rise about 40 feet skyward, while below, water has carved a four-foot pothole at the base of the falls. There's a bridge crossing the falls that lets you watch the cascades gush down a granite chute. From the Sabbaday Falls trailhead, it's about 15 miles to Conway, the eastern terminus of the highway. During peak foliage weekends, both Lincoln and Conway can be snarled with traffic; an escape route is Bear Notch Road (paved, but closed in winter), 21 miles west of Lincoln and 13 miles east of Conway. The nine-mile road hooks up with Route 302 in Bartlett, passing through young forest, affording mountain views to the east, and bypassing some of the heaviest tourist traffic.

– Carol Connare

*T*HE WOODS AGAIN BELONG TO HIKERS AND HUNTERS AND FISHERMEN.

The third member of this epochal trio was Oakleigh Thorne, who started into the wilderness from Conway on the east side. He was as different from the other two giants of the Pemigewasset as they were from each other; he was a cultured New York financier and a member of the Tennis and Racquet Club and the Westminster Kennel Club. He used to arrive in the North Country riding in a seat attached to the running board of his chauffeur-driven Packard roadster.

Mr. Thorne began work in 1906 and would eventually build 20 miles of track. However patrician and picturesque Oakleigh Thorne might have been, he was an absentee owner: He let work out to subcontractors, and his operations were so anonymous that local residents and imported workers alike spoke only of "the Company," the very model of a modern corporate life. This did not indicate a lack of character, however, and work habits were strictly enforced: One morning the foreman lit a stick of dynamite under his choppers' shanty to hasten their way out to the cuttings.

"The Company" ceased operations in 1916, the last of the rapacious Henrys was gone in 1917, and the saintly Saunders left their woods in 1927. Nature sees things in a longer span than we do. The railroad beds and skid ways laid out by Pork Barrel Dumas are still engraved on the land, and hikers still find iron artifacts remaining from those wilderness empires, but it is impossible to find any differences in the woods once claimed by such completely different men. Now it again belongs to hikers and hunters and fishermen, the same as before any of the timber barons began their immense work.

– *Nicholas Howe*

ESSENTIALS

Lincoln-Woodstock Chamber of Commerce, 800-227-4191, 603-745-6621. The information center at the Depot Mall on Main St. is also a reservation service for area lodging.

Lincoln Woods, at Lincoln Woods Trail parking off Rte. 112, just east of the Loon Mountain main entrance. This comfy log cabin serves as a warming hut in winter and information center all year long. National forest rangers give personal advice about trails and campgrounds on the Kanc.

White Mountain Visitors Center, 800-346-3687, 603-745-8720. P.O. Box 10, North Woodstock, NH 03262; at base of exit 32 off I-93. Open daily 8:30-5; in summer until 6 P.M.

White Mountain National Forest Saco Ranger Station, 603-447-5448. Kancamagus Highway (Rte. 112), just off Rte. 16, Conway. Pick up campground information and a free map to eight terrific hiking trails that range from a half mile to five miles long. Open seven days a week 8-4:30. Saco Ranger Station is also the place to find out about historic Russell-Colbath House, an 1830 homestead located midway on the Kancamagus Highway, just west of Jigger Johnson Campground. Exhibits and costumed interpreters tell the story of the family who lived here. Open in June Saturday-Sunday, July to mid-October Wednesday-Monday; 9:30-4:30.

Loon Mountain, 800-229-5666, 603-745-8111. Rte. 112, Lincoln. Not just for skiing: Ask about bike rentals and tours, horseback riding, in-line skating, and other activities in summer and fall. (www.loonmtn.com)

The Common Man, 603-745-3463. Pollard Rd., Lincoln. ($$) Simple country cooking and decor with a cozy fire-placed lounge. Open daily 5-9 P.M. for dinner (pub menu

from 4 P.M.); open Friday-Saturday until 9:30.

Café Lafayette Dinner Train, 800-699-3501, 603-745-3500. Rte. 112, North Woodstock. Enjoy a five-course movable feast in a 1924 Pullman car or a 1952 Pullman Dome car. The train and its passengers embark on a two-hour journey along the Pemigewasset River. Open Memorial Day-October, and also the month of December; Saturday, Sunday, Tuesday, Wednesday, Thursday; 6 P.M. departure time. Price includes five-course meal, tax, and train fare; $41.95, children 6-11 $24.95. (www.cafelafayette.com)

Gordi's Fish & Steak House, 603-745-6635. Rte. 112, Lincoln. ($$) House favorites are lobster, beef, and seafood. Open Memorial Day-Columbus Day daily for lunch and dinner; off-season daily for dinner.

Peg's, 603-745-2740. 97 Main St., North Woodstock. ($) Breakfast where the locals do (served all day). July 4-November 1, 5:30-4; off-season 5-2:30.

Kancamagus Motor Lodge, 800-346-4205, 603-745-3365. Rte. 112 and Pollard Rd., Lincoln, NH 03251. Open year-

round. 34 rooms. $68-$89. Brittany's Café open daily for breakfast and dinner ($$). (www.kancmotorlodge.com)

The Mountain Club on Loon, 800-229-7829, 603-745-2244. Rte. 112, Lincoln, NH 03251. Slopeside accom-modations right on Loon Mountain. Open year-round. 234 rooms, 116 of which are suites with kitchens and mountain views. $89-$429. (www.mtncluboonloon.com)

The Mill House Inn, 800-654-6183, 603-745-6261. Rte. 112, Lincoln, NH 03251. Open year-round. 95 rooms. $79-$169, including resort ameni-ties. (www.millatloon.com)

Woodstock Inn, 800-321-3985, 603-745-3951. 135 Main St., North Woodstock, NH 03262. Open year-round. 21 rooms. $67-$150, including breakfast. Clement Grille ($$-$$$) for bistro dining, the more casual Woodstock Sta-tion ($-$$), and a brewpub ($-$$); all open daily for din-ner, except Christmas Eve and Christmas. (www.woodstockinnnh.com)

"YONDER ARE THE *Redcoats*": THE *Molly Stark* TRAIL

G REAT ROADS, like great stories, take shape around a turning point. That is my opinion, at any rate, having grown up in New England. Midwesterners might say otherwise — that roads and stories get straight to the point — but I like the challenge, the switchbacks over tall mountains that make the end seem earned. So the story of the Molly Stark Trail is, for me, a good one. It is a road that marks the first serviceable route through Vermont's Green Mountains, bending for 46 miles along streambeds, from Bennington in the west to Brattleboro in the east. And it carries with it

Bennington Battle Monument commemorates our defeat of invading British forces in 1777.

BIRD'S-EYE VIEW, BATTLE MONUMENT, BENNINGTON, VT.   62-B

FAIRCHILD AERIAL SURVEYS, INC.

Yankee archives

a story that marked a turning point in the Revolutionary War.

It was an August day in 1777 when General John Stark stood on a rail fence near Bennington, Vermont, and spoke the words that have not been forgotten since: "Boys, yonder are the redcoats, and they are ours or this night Molly Stark sleeps a widow." When the Battle of Bennington was won, John Stark turned his horse toward home. The road he took was an old military trail studded with stumps. It rose steeply from Bennington and was, in the opinion of Stark's companion, the worst road he'd ever seen. In Brattleboro, Stark and his companion had to swim their horses across the Connecticut River, but Stark arrived at last in what is now Londonderry, New Hampshire, where Molly was waiting.

The Molly Stark Trail has everything I like in a road — the twists and turns that follow the rock-strewn streams, the wooded roadside that never reveals what is next until you are upon it, the dips and dives, the drama of the emergency brake ramps for trucks — clues that you are indeed passing through the Green Mountains. I like the "100-mile view" from the Skyline Restaurant on Hogback Mountain; the mounted-animal museum in the basement of the Hogback Mountain Gift Shop in Marlboro; the symmetry of the road, which runs from New York's border to New Hampshire's with the lovely village of Wilmington smack in the middle. I like intersecting the Long Trail with my car, even if I don't get out and hike it. And I'm glad, too, that on a fresh fall day I can stop at the Molly Stark State Park, climb a mile and a half, and be high on Mount Olga, looking out from the tower toward Hogback Mountain.

Molly's name is everywhere: the Molly Stark Motel, Molly Stark Antiques, Molly Stark Inn, the Molly Stark Cannon. She is our heroine within reach — our mother, our spouse, our home fire. In the Old Bennington cemetery, a common gravestone marks the casualties of the Battle of Bennington. About four miles northwest of here, on Harrington Road, lies the battle-eve campsite of General Stark, engraved with the

GREAT ROADS, LIKE GREAT STORIES, TAKE SHAPE AROUND A TURNING POINT.

famous words he said for Molly. More places bear Molly's name than that of her heroic husband.

There is a painting of Molly that shows up almost as often as her name. She is round of face and kind of eye. The portrait was done by John Singleton Copley when he was an itinerant painter. I like her look and so was disappointed to learn

Don't Drive — Paddle Instead

The Molly Stark Trail, Route 9, is a lovely road, but on weekends, especially during peak foliage, it can be bumper-to-bumper with leaf-peeping traffic. The moving water, easy enough for beginner paddlers. Bring your own boat or rent one at Vermont Canoe Touring Center. Owner John Knickerbocker rents canoes and

BRIDGE OVER CONNECTICUT RIVER   ROUTE 9
Brattleboro, Vermont

courtesy Brattleboro Historical Society

best time to drive its length is midweek, but if you find yourself in the area on a busy autumn weekend, consider parking your car and paddling instead.

The Connecticut River, from Bellows Falls to the Vernon Dam below Brattleboro, is a 32-mile stretch of slow-

Drivers today still enjoy this view of the Connecticut River.

kayaks, guides trips (including overnight camping excursions), and offers a shuttle service. (If even *floating* downriver seems too strenuous, consider a leisurely cruise on the *Belle of Brattle-*

boro, a stately 49-passenger riverboat.)

The views from the water are not as vast as from the overlooks on Route 9, but they are just as colorful. You'll pass cornfields, railroad bridges, riverfront homes, and marinas at a pace that gives you time to look around; no white knuckles on the steering wheel here. Remember to look skyward for hawks, geese, and other southbound birds; the Connecticut River is a major flyway for migrating fowl.

– Carol Connare

Vermont Canoe Touring Center, 802-257-5008. At the cove at Veterans Memorial Bridge, Rte. 5, just north of the junction with Rte. 30, Brattleboro. Open Memorial Day-Labor Day daily 9-7; spring and fall only weekends.

Belle of Brattleboro, 802-254-1263. Connecticut River Tours, Putney Rd., Brattleboro. Cruises Memorial Day-Columbus Day Tuesday-Sunday plus holidays.

recently from Joseph Parks, the former Bennington Museum librarian, that her portrait came from the artist's imagination. No one knows what she really looked like or what she thought. She left no diaries. "The Molly Stark story," says the current museum librarian, Tyler Resch, "is one that has been subject to many variations and imaginative interpretations over the years."

Haystack Mountain, one of many sites along the Molly Stark Trail.

But it is not so much the imaginative interpretations that historians take issue with as the actual route taken on John Stark's historic journey home. "The present route of the Molly Stark Trail didn't exist until the 1840s," says Joseph Parks. "It climbs straight up the face of that mountain, about 1,200 vertical feet in a series of switchbacks, along the City Stream. It was horrendously steep, and a completely different road had to be built as part of the Windham Turnpike to even get a stagecoach up there."

Windham Turnpike eventually became Route 9, and in 1967 the highway department petitioned the state board of libraries to have it named the Molly Stark Trail. People have since made the story part of their own lives and commerce. "The commercialism doesn't offend me historically — you make out of it what you can," says Parks. "And maybe it isn't so bad since, as you get over to Brattleboro, past Wilmington, you are on the same road that Stark went on, and the name is probably correct."

When I ask the man at the Bennington Bookshop what he knows of Molly Stark, he says, "Besides the quote and the trail, there's nothing to know. She was basically a stay-at-home sort of person."

One quote, one road. That's all that is left. But that is more than most of us will have 200 years from now. The Molly Stark Trail is the road home, with all the turns and hardships endured to get there. We should be glad that much remains.

– *Christine Schultz*

ESSENTIALS

The Marina Restaurant, 802-257-7563. On the Connecticut River, Putney Rd., Brattleboro. ($-$$) Pasta, burgers, fish — and great sunsets. Open year-round for Sunday brunch; spring-fall Monday-Saturday for lunch and dinner; winter Wednesday-Saturday for lunch.

The Latchis Hotel, 802-254-6300. 50 Main St., Brattleboro, VT 05301. Listed on the National Register of Historic Places, the Latchis is one of only two truly art deco buildings in Vermont. Greek Revival theater, three cinemas, and live performances on the premises. 30 rooms. $55-$155, including full breakfast.

Latchis Grille and Windham Brewery, 802-254-4747. ($-$$$) This dining facility, residing in the basement of the Latchis Hotel, is a cozy, friendly place to enjoy a full gourmet dinner or café fare. Open nightly, except Tuesday, for dinner; Friday-Sunday noon-3 for lunch. (www.brattleboro.com/latchis)

Molly Stark State Park, 802-464-5460. Rte. 9, Wilmington, VT 05363. From the campground, a short hiking trail ascends Mount Olga (2,145 feet) where a summit fire tower affords excellent views

Cozy cabins once dotted the Molly Stark Trail.

courtesy Brattleboro Historical Society

of the region. Open early May to mid-October. 34 campsites, including 11 lean-tos. $11-$15.

Alonzo's Pasta & Grille at Crafts Inn, 802-464-2355. W. Main St., Wilmington. ($-$$) Fresh pasta, extensive grill menu. Open daily 4-10 P.M. for dinner.

The Nutmeg Inn, 800-277-5402, 802-464-7400. 153 Rte. 9W, Wilmington, VT 05363. This romantic circa-1777 Vermont farmhouse features 11 wood-burning fireplaces, in some of the rooms and in all of the suites. Ten rooms and four suites. $89-$299, including full breakfast. (www.nutmeginn.com)

White House of Wilmington, 800-541-2135, 802-464-2135. 178 Rte. 9E, Wilmington, VT 05363. The *New York Times* calls this "one of the ten most romantic places in the world." From the sunset-view patio to the Continental cuisine in three dining rooms ($$-$$$), we think so, too. 23 rooms. $138-$208, including full breakfast. (www.whitehouseinn.com)

Molly Stark Inn, 800-356-3076, 802-442-9631. 1067 E. Main St., Bennington, VT 05201. Country-style inn one mile east of village center. Six guest rooms. $90-$125, including full breakfast. (www.mollystarkinn.com)

Four Chimneys Inn, 802-447-3500. 21 West Rd., Rte. 9, Bennington, VT 05201. Pamper yourself with a good night's sleep in one of these deluxe rooms. 11 rooms. $125-$185, including breakfast. ($$$) Better yet, treat yourself to a gourmet meal in the inn's posh dining room. Open daily for lunch and dinner. (www.fourchimneys.com)

Bennington Station, 802-447-1080. Depot St., Bennington. ($-$$) The railroad-themed menu is tasteful, and you'll enjoy the fare even more in this beautifully restored train station built in 1897. Open daily for lunch and dinner.

Motion
WITHOUT EFFORT:
THE *Mohawk Trail*

I F THIS WERE A WORLD of perfect fit and just proportions, only automobiles built during the teens and twenties would be allowed on the Mohawk Trail. Running from Greenfield to Williamstown, Massachusetts, and marked on maps as Route 2, the Mohawk Trail officially opened on October 22, 1914. And this two-lane road has not changed much since then. It is the only motor road of the pre-World War I era still in use in the United States.

The trail is fitted to the speed of the era — 30 miles per hour — and to the gee-whiz wonder of automobiling: Look! We're scaling mountains! Take a picture: me and Ma and the kids and the motor car enjoying the view. Another picture: a roadside picnic, the car gathered into the family circle. In that adventurous era of motor touring, one had closer contact with the countryside. Today's cars are sleek metal capsules with tinted glass and interiors padded with music, phones, and enough cup holders to hold drinks for a horse. The countryside goes by like a silent video.

When the Mohawk Trail opened, it was marked by "red bands on telegraph poles at all points of doubt," as one 1916 travel handbook said. The points of doubt were many in the early days of motoring. The guide advised that there were long hills on the trail "and water tanks should be filled before starting."

LONG VIEW, MOHAWK TRAIL MASS.
The Tower With A 3 State View

To get to know the Mohawk Trail, we chose a car to match the road: Ed Gienty's 1916 Cadillac touring car. Behind the wheel, smiling all the time, Ed is a calm captain. When he gathers a long line of cars following behind him, he pulls over and waves them on. When I see milky-white water and steam spitting out the right side of the car — looking much like a biplane that's been shot in a dogfight — he explains that it's water-pump fluid and chuckles. He says there is a chance of overheating. I see us in another tableau of the era: sitting under a tree as the car cools off.

So what if we don't have front brakes, turn signals, bumpers, windshield wipers, side windows, seat belts, or cup holders. The Cadillac, with its large wooden-spoked wheels and black-formal-wear look, is reassuringly solid — all 2½ tons of it. The large headlights give it an expressive face that inspires trust. The canvas top fits the car like a man's cap of the era, dressing it like a proper gentleman. When they see us drive by, many people along the route smile, flash their lights, or wave. When the Cadillac is parked, people come out as if pulled by a steady magnetic charge. They often pose for pictures. (Ed occasionally takes the car to the retirement home where his wife works as a nurse and gives everyone a ride.)

We have a 77-horsepower V-8 engine, three-gear manual transmission, electric starter, and room for seven. The Model T

Three-state view from the Mohawk Trail.

*T*HE TRAIL IS FITTED TO THE SPEED OF THE ERA — 30 MILES PER HOUR.

This postcard depicts a frighteningly steep-sided slope on the Mohawk Trail.

of the era had one-third the horsepower, had to be started with a hand crank, and could be purchased for one-fourth the cost of a Cadillac.

Starting the car is a ritual that bonds driver to machine: Ed pushes a lever in the center of the steering wheel to the left to retard the spark. Then he reaches toward the dash and pumps up the pressure for the fuel system; next he adjusts the choke, flips the starter switch (no key), and finally engages the starter motor with a foot pedal. The 80-year-old engine is surprisingly smooth — the 80-year-old gears are sometimes like people at that age, a little stiff.

"We should be back in one piece," I had joked to Ed's wife, Beverly, as we were getting in the car earlier to leave.

"Well, he's packed some work clothes," she'd responded.

"And tools," Ed had added.

I look now under the jump seats. There are a lot of tools. And a gallon jug of water. I, too, have packed my breakdown kit — the Sunday *New York Times*. Now I wish I had packed a book — maybe Dickens, anything over 500 pages.

Ed looks up the road carefully. Old brakes are inferior to modern brakes. "If someone pulls out in front, you don't stand a chance," he says.

The Mohawk Trail is an old-fashioned story — with a beginning, a middle, and an end — about an old-fashioned landscape: village, farm, and forest. Interstates are endless. The trail is almost perfectly punctuated with interesting villages, places to stop to swim or hike, mountain views, and little shops selling antiques and souvenirs.

We begin in Greenfield, stop for lunch in Shelburne Falls, a vibrant village, and travel on to take the highest point, Whitcomb Summit; we then head down around the famous

WHAT THE LOCALS KNOW

West County Winery

Nothing tastes better on a crisp, autumn day than a glass of cider. Or so we thought until we tried the delicious fruit wines crafted at West County Winery. The winery's tasting room is in a cottage behind the farmhouse and bakery at Pine Hill Orchards. (This orchard supplies some of the apples used in the cider and wine making.) The scenery here is pure country: Ducks preen in a pond set beside a barnyard with hens and goats.

We began by tasting the ciders: Baldwin Dry (which is effervescent and full of apple flavor, and which packs a kick — 6.4 percent alcohol); Extra Dry (lighter and more bubbly); and Cidre Doux (Normandy style, with 3.7 percent alcohol). These were all delicious — like taking a bite of an October morning.

But the fruit wines won us over, too. The Orchard's Edge blended the fragrance of raspberry with the tang of apple. It was light and semi-dry. The Blueberry-Apple wine was pleasing, too — dry enough to have with food and sweet enough for sipping on its own.

Owners Terry and Judith Maloney produced their first commercial hard cider in 1984. They moved from northern California to Franklin County in 1972 and couldn't find grapes to make their year's supply of wine. Instead, they found their neighbors were making a tasty hard cider using their own apples.

With abundant orchards in the area, they followed suit and were seduced by the variety and complexity of cider. They fermented their first vintage for sale, thus becom-

ing the first U.S. winery to specialize in hard cider.

The Maloneys have an orchard of about 1,000 trees of English, French, and American varieties of cider apples. Cider varieties are grown especially for pressing: Their concentrated flavors make them unpleasant to eat. After the apples are harvested and selected, they are pressed at Pine Hill Orchards.

In the end, we couldn't decide if cider or wine better complemented our perfect fall day, so we took home several bottles of each, as well as homemade jam and some of the Maloneys' own cider vinegar.

– *Carol Connare*
West County Winery, 413-624-3481. At Pine Hill Orchards, 248 Greenfield Rd., Colrain; turn right off Rte. 2 at Strawberry Fields Antiques. Open June-December Thursday-Sunday 11-5; during foliage season daily; January-May call ahead.

hairpin turn and on into a valley through the "odd couple" of the road, the mill city of North Adams and well-bred Williamstown, where the Mohawk Trail ends.

Mornings are the best time to be rolling along. The mist is rising off the fields and by the river. The trees overhead glisten. The countryside is waking up. At 30 miles per hour, with engine working away, sitting high up, you are at a nearly ideal fulcrum between the machine world — motion without effort — and the pleasures of rocking on a front porch. The day is opening up, and you feel as if you could go on forever. We would have missed that in an ordinary car.

"Purring along like a kitten," says Ed. "That shifted beautifully. Nice and smooth. If you double-clutch, it works fine." He drives his car by feel, using an acutely developed machine sense. Ed is 67 years old. He taught wood and metal shop for 20 years at a high school in Peterborough, New Hampshire. He has owned about ten old cars in his life, including several Model Ts. He bought one Model T in college that was just a running chassis — you sat on the gas tank. He never did buy a body for it.

When he bought this Cadillac, it had been sitting in barns for 42 years and looked like the forlorn jalopy of John Steinbeck's Okies. He took the car apart down to the chassis. For five years, the car was in his cellar in pieces, "all in little cat-food cans. Nuts and bolts — all labeled. My wife said I'd never get that back together, but I did."

"Let's make a run for this hill," he says as we approach Whitcomb Summit, at 2,240 feet, in the oddly named town of Florida. The Cadillac's most impressive gauge sits right at the top of the radiator, dead center, a red-thermometer hood ornament. At a glance you are warned if the car is going to overheat. As we climb the long hill, the red thermometer begins to climb as if it were registering altitude. It becomes a question of which will reach the top first — the red line or the car.

A long line of cars is strung out behind us. It turns out that the one side mirror — a "recent" 1925 accessory — is quite limited. I become the second rearview mirror, twisting around to count cars and to let Ed know when they are pass-

OTHER GIFT SHOPS SOON OPENED, EACH WITH A LOOKOUT TOWER AND AN AMAZING VIEW.

ing, lost in a blind spot large enough to hide several circus elephants. A Model T would have faded to half our speed, grunting up the hill at just about 15 miles per hour.

Short of the top, at a gift shop and overlook, we stop. Ed pours in a couple of quarts of water. Early cars still shared the thirst of animals. They stopped at the same side-hill springs as horses. The car cools off. We push on to the top and are rewarded with a view of four states and free ice cream.

The trail's first tourist shop opened on the summit. A Mr. Canedy realized that by the time a car got to the summit, both the car and the driver needed a drink, and he would be the one to sell it to them at a handsome profit. Other gift shops soon opened, each with a lookout tower and an amazing view. The shops are still there — the Wigwam and the Longview among them, but only a couple of towers remain.

The opening ceremonies for the Mohawk Trail were held up on the summit. Two thousand people attended. Most walked. There were few cars on this rare paved road. Dignitaries came out from Boston to mark the first route from Boston to Albany that didn't require a railroad or an oxcart.

We reach Williamstown by late afternoon. The day's heat has gathered, and I am ready to step down from the machine. Traveling at 30 miles per hour has lost some of its charm; I want a shower and a hot meal. And I feel toward the car *Taking a breather before hitting the road.*

Yankee archives

THE FAMOUS HAIRPIN TURN, MOHAWK TRAIL, MASS.

almost as you would toward a horse — it's time it rested. I have been aware of its working all day long.

The next day we reverse the trip, skirting a serious thunderstorm. Some rain spills into the car, blowing in crosswise and under the windshield. But before the storm arrives, we make it home. Ed pulls into his garage. I drive away in my vintage car, a 13-year-old Subaru, and the muffler pipe snaps. Using the cover of the thunderstorm, I boom along and turn up the radio, another metal-and-glass capsule trying to make time, all the while losing the present.

– Howard Mansfield

ESSENTIALS

For more suggestions, see the driving tour for the hill towns of western Massachusetts, p. 58

Main Street Café, 413-458-3210. 16 Water St., Williamstown. Great food here, where all the summer stars eat during the theater festival. Choose between fine-dining and bistro menus. The bistro offers salads, seafood, and oven-baked pizza, while the fine-dining menu has impeccable pasta and seafood specialties, such as wok-seared shrimp sautéed in garlic sauce, with fresh herbs and plum tomatoes over linguine. Open Tuesday-Saturday for lunch ($-$$) and daily for dinner ($$$). Reservations recommended.

Hobson's Choice, 413-458-9101. 159 Water St., Williamstown. ($$$) One of Williamstown's most popular eateries, with turn-away crowds most weekends. As you make your way through the salad bar, you'll see chef-owner Dan Campbell grilling the steaks, prime ribs, and seafood. Open daily for dinner.

Wild Amber Grill, 413-458-4000. 101 North St. (Rte. 7), Williamstown. ($$$) Eclectic American cuisine served in a warm, sophisticated atmosphere. Choose from standards like filet mignon and osso bucco, as well as sesame-seared tuna with a soy-ginger vinaigrette, seared scallops with red-pepper sauce, and smoked mozzarella served over black-ink squid pasta. Good wine list. Lighter fare on the bar side. Open daily for dinner. Reservations recommended.

1896 House, 413-458-1896. Rte. 7, Williamstown. ($$$) Extensive menu ranging from "Yankee" comfort foods (pot roast, turkey dinner, apple crisp) to contemporary fusion cuisine (pesto salmon filet, encrusted with hazelnuts; sautéed pork medallions with foie gras, caramelized apples, Normandy Calvados, and Brie). Dine in wing chairs and note the Oriental carpets covering the wide floorboards of this circa-1896 barn. Recent winner of *Wine Spectator*'s award of excellence. Open year-round daily for dinner; Sunday for brunch, lunch, and dinner.

1896 House Brookside & Pondside, 413-458-8125. Rte. 7, Williamstown, MA 01267. Two motels flanking the 1896 House restaurant. Open year-round. 30 rooms total. $60-$160. (www.1896house.com)

The Orchards, 800-225-1517, 413-458-9611. 222 Adams Rd. (Rte. 2), Williamstown, MA 01267. Don't let the modern exterior fool you; this hotel is stylishly decorated with English antiques and Oriental accent pieces. 47 rooms. $165-$230. The four-star (rated by AAA) restaurant in this hotel serves gourmet food (two popular dishes: seared veal loin with herbed wasabi butter, paired with lemon risotto and pickled ginger salad; oven-roasted squash glazed with maple syrup on green tagliatelle, with a white balsamic sauce). Open year-round daily for breakfast, lunch ($$), and dinner ($$$-$$$$); Sunday for brunch ($-$$). (www.orchardshotel.com)

The Williams Inn, 413-458-9371. Main St. (junction of routes 2 and 7), Williamstown, MA 01267. Located right in the heart of Williamstown, this good-size hotel is a favorite among Williams College parents. Open year-round. 100 rooms. $95-$185. Restaurant open year-round for breakfast, lunch ($-$$), and dinner ($$-$$$) and is a local favorite for Sunday brunch ($-$$).

Field Farm Guest House, 413-458-3135. 554 Sloan Rd., Williamstown, MA 01267. This intimate house, surrounded by 296 acres of protected farmland, is filled with modern art and 1950s-style Danish modern furnishings. Each of its guest rooms has a private bath, and guests have access to tennis courts, a swimming pool, and miles of hiking trails. Open-year round. Five rooms. $125, including breakfast.

Steep Acres Farm B&B, 413-458-3774. 520 White Oaks Rd., Williamstown, MA 01267. An antiques-decorated 1900 country cottage on 50 acres, perched high on a knoll with spectacular views of the Berkshire Hills and Green Mountains. There is a pond for swimming, fishing, and canoeing. Open year-round. Four rooms. $85, including breakfast.

The Williamstown B&B, 413-458-9202. 30 Cold Spring Rd., Williamstown, MA 01267. This restored 1881 Victorian, with a large front porch and comfortable dining and living rooms, is located within walking distance to town. Open year-round. Four rooms. $90-$105, including breakfast. (www.williamstownbandb. com)

River Bend Farm, 413-458-3121. 643 Simonds Rd. (Rte. 7N), Williamstown, MA 01267. This authentic circa-1770 tavern (a Georgian Colonial) is listed on the National Register of Historic Places. Local history tells us that the original tap room was where the Battle of Bennington was planned. Its guest rooms are filled with antiques. Open April-October. Four rooms. $90, including breakfast.

A *Highway* WHERE THE EYE IS FILLED WITH *Beauty*: THE *Merritt Parkway*

One can build a concrete highway anywhere.... But the Merritt Parkway is different. More than any "futurama" at the World's Fair, more than any dream of the futuristic designers, it shows what the highway of the future should really look like — a highway where the eye is filled with beauty and the mind with peace, as the car purrs safely along.

– Bridgeport Post, January 7, 1938

DRIVING WITH ME along the Merritt Parkway recently, my mother recalled the time, years ago, when her uncle arrived in a tizzy at the family homestead outside Boston. The excitement, he said, was the "new road" he had taken from New York through Connecticut. Not only did it cut down traveling time (the 67-mile stretch from the Holland Tunnel to Bridgeport) to just two hours, but it was beautiful besides. He launched into an enthusiastic description of the trees, flowering bushes, and highway bridges along the way. "Such a road," he said in awe.

Such a road indeed. Today, 60 years after the Merritt Parkway, formally Route 15, opened — the New York-to-Bridgeport stretch in June 1938, the Bridgeport-to-Stratford length in September 1940 — it is still a thing of beauty. It is a trendsetter that has paved the way, literally and figuratively, for roads nationwide.

The building of the road came about in response to a call during the 1920s from Robert

Moses, then director of public works in New York, to build an extension of the proposed Hutchinson River Parkway in Westchester County. Connecticut residents frustrated with the slowness of Route 1 (which presented a daunting 108 stoplights between New York and Bridgeport alone), as well as New Yorkers who had started to weekend in Fairfield County, jumped on the bandwagon.

For Connecticut, just climbing out of the Depression, the project was a godsend. While politicians wrangled over the proposed route, what land to take and how much to pay for it (in the end the road cost $20 million to build — but then again, gas was 12¢ a gallon), the state began hiring, bringing together a team of talented young engineers, architects, and landscape designers to answer the call.

Chief among them were Earl Wood, the engineer who envisioned a highway that would blend seamlessly with the natural environment; Weld Thayer Chase, the landscape architect who implemented Wood's vision with mountain laurels (the state flower), dogwoods, and other native plants; and George Dunkelberger, the architect who created the parkway's most conspicuous feature, 68 different bridges in

Each bridge on the Merritt Parkway is distinctive.

courtesy Connecticut Department of Transportation

37.5 miles — from Italian to art deco, from exuberant to whimsical, with embellishments from Nike wings to hollyhocks — that soared beyond their utilitarian function to become pieces of sculpture. For these gentlemen, the parkway became a cause. As Wood said at the time, "I never knew a man who worked on that parkway who did not have a sense of what we were trying to do. They felt they were really making a contribution to Fairfield County and the nation. . . . It was a tremendous, cooperative venture fired with the enthusiasm of youth."

Today, the volume of traffic on the Merritt Parkway has grown far beyond the imaginings of its creators, who in fact

Weir Farm National Historic Site

Bring a sketch pad to the former summer country retreat of Impressionist painter J. Alden Weir (1852-1919). The rustic landscape of Weir's home, studio, barns, and outbuildings is sure to get your creative energies flowing as it did for the artist for 40 summers.

Weir came here to this area of Ridgefield and Wilton, Connecticut, known as "Branchville," to escape the swelter of New York City. The bucolic scenery often served as subject matter for many of his paintings. His contemporaries came here to visit and paint, too, so the farm has been captured by the likes of Childe Hassam, Albert Pinkham Ryder, and John Twachtman.

The landscape and the Federal-style farmhouse remain much as they did when Weir worked and lived here. The Historic Painting Sites Trail leads visitors to certain points on the property where the artists worked, and you can compare the scene before you with the painting it inspired.

Sculptor Mahonri Young (1877-1957) married Weir's daughter, Dorothy, in 1931 and subsequently built his own studio on the property. The Youngs eventually made the farm their year-round residence, and while living here, the sculptor worked on some of his most famous and demanding projects (among them the statue of Brigham Young in the Capitol building in Washington, D.C.; Mahonri was the grandson of Brigham Young).

Weir Farm National Historic Site, 203-834-1896. 735 Nod Hill Rd., Wilton. The state's only national park service site — and the country's only one dedicated to a painter (J. Alden Weir) — represents a unique fusion of nature and art. Wander the garden, meadows, and woods, and hearken back to a time when most of the state — not just this farm — was the stuff of which Impressionist landscapes were made. Grounds open year-round daily dawn-dusk; visitor center open Wednesday-Sunday 8:30-5; studio tours at 11 A.M. 1 P.M., and 3 P.M. Free. (www.nps.gov/wefa).

– *Carol Connare*

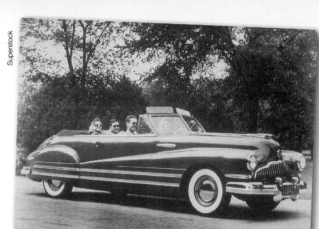

Travelers have been enjoying the Merritt for over 60 years.

never saw it as a commuting road at all. While it has remained free of commercial vehicles, bicyclists, pedestrians, billboards, and U-turns across the landscaped median divider, it has suffered with the passage of time. Most of the mountain laurel and dogwood have died off, bridges have deteriorated, and graceless interchanges with Route 7 in Norwalk and routes 25 and 8 in Stratford have disrupted the integration of road and countryside.

And it has its limitations. The parkway has a minimum of service stations, offers no restaurants, and is far enough inland (4½ miles from Route 1 through mainly residential areas) to require backtracking to reach most commercial destinations. Motorists must put up with long stretches between some exits; foremost among these is the 7.5-mile "No Man's Land" in Fairfield, a concession to Greenfield Hill residents, who together with backcountry Greenwich residents seem to have feared a New York onslaught the most. And with just two lanes, construction and accidents can wreak havoc.

Then there's the problem of night travel. The Merritt is not equipped with lights. This can pose a hazard at night, particularly in bad weather and along the more winding stretches. Those of us who have had near-death experiences with deer appearing out of nowhere can attest to that.

Why, then, do so many drivers opt for the Merritt? Simply because, as Bruce Radde, author of *The Merritt Parkway* (Yale University Press, 1993), points out, it is the "saner, more

*T*HE MERRITT IS A TRENDSETTER THAT HAS PAVED THE WAY FOR ROADS NATIONWIDE.

humane alternative to the bleakness and aggressiveness of I-95." The quirky charm of the bridges, the arching canopies of trees, and the uninterrupted vistas make for a drive that is almost therapeutic. At the same time, as Radde says, "the architecture, sculpture, and landscaping combine to make not just a great highway but also a great work of art."

And like a great work of art, the Merritt produces a high in the mind of the driver. This high is best experienced in autumn. If business or pleasure brings you to Connecticut this season, try the Merritt. Doubtless you will find more than one spot — say, as you round a bend — where the dramatic burst of crimson and gold from the oaks and maples framing a bridge will leave you in awe. Thank you, Messrs. Wood, Chase, and Dunkelberger, for ourselves, and for posterity.

– Dale B. Salm

ESSENTIALS

Long Ridge Tavern, 203-329-7818. Exit 34, 2635 Long Ridge Rd., Stamford. ($$) This historic tavern, which has seen restaurants come and go, has hit its stride with new owners and creative country fare. Open Tuesday-Saturday for lunch and dinner, Sunday for brunch 11:30-2:30. (www.longridgetavern.com)

Tuscan Oven, 203-846-4600. Exit 40B, 544 Main Ave., Norwalk. Don't be put off by its location on busy Rte. 7, right next to the Motor Vehicle Department. This upscale trattoria offers sophisticated Northern Italian dishes in a setting that makes you think you are, well, in Tuscany. (Pizza and salads; too.)

Winner of *Wine Spectator*'s award of excellence. Open daily for lunch ($-$$) and dinner ($-$$$).

The Three Bears, 203-227-7219. Exit 41, Rte. 33, Westport. This pretty Colonial building houses a restaurant that is a perennial local favorite in the New American category. Ask for a garden-view table. Open Tuesday-Saturday for lunch ($-$$) and dinner ($$$-$$$$); also open Sunday for brunch ($$) noon-3 and dinner until 8 P.M.

Trumbull Marriott, 203-378-1400. Exit 51N/51S, 180 Hawley Ln., Trumbull, CT 06611. This large full-service hotel is one of a few such located right off the Merritt. 323 rooms. $109-$179,

based on availability, most including breakfast.

Silvermine Tavern, 203-847-4558. Exit 40A, 194 Perry Ave., Norwalk, CT 06830. With an updated American menu, a barn's worth of Early American tools, and an idyllic waterside/waterfall setting, this picture-book, circa-1785 inn is quintessential Connecticut country. Open year-round. 11 rooms. $99-$120, including continental breakfast. Open Wednesday-Monday for lunch ($-$$) and dinner ($$$).

SECTION II:

The Leaves

WHEN THE
Red Gods Call

WE DID NOT ALWAYS know fall as the time when we chased the color, as if it were an elusive animal that we could somehow corral. Our grandparents knew a time when the leaves turned color without fanfare, a process as natural as the wind, the southward flight of birds, and the gathering cold. The beauty of our autumn filled the towns and villages then no less than today, but we stayed put, tending to the life in front of us.

Arthur Tauck Sr. was the first person we know of who envisioned the commercial possibilities in chasing the fall colors. He had invented the aluminum coin tray for use in banks. He crisscrossed the region selling the trays. He had an eye for beauty and an entrepreneurial spirit. On a fall day in 1925, he loaded his seven-passenger Studebaker with customers who paid $69 and embarked on a journey along the Mohawk Trail; he had made arrangements for overnight lodging and meals. He carried on lively conversation with his passengers, telling them the history of (as well as legends about) the places they were seeing. Word of mouth brought new passengers, new trips. The guided-tour industry was born.

A decade later, Kodak introduced color film, and every year, improvements brought color photography into the hands of the masses. By 1970, over 50 million Americans had

> *October is the month for painted leaves. Their rich glow now flashes round the world. As fruits and leaves and the day itself acquire a bright tint just before they fall, so the year near its setting. October is its sunset sky; November the later twilight.*
>
> – Henry David Thoreau

purchased Instamatic cameras. Nothing brought out the hunger to capture beauty on film like a New England autumn — the time when "the red gods call," as *Yankee* writer Ben Rice wrote more than 50 years ago.

Now fall arrives full of hype and hope, a singular New England sport, an intricate guessing game filled with leaf "scouts," charts, schedules, and statistics from past seasons. Our New England states compete for the right to claim "best viewing." We argue about the glories of past years. "You should have been here in 1997" is a common refrain. "That was the best color I've ever seen." The fall of 1999, once expected to be the runt of the litter due to a lengthy summer drought, surprised everyone with its comeback.

New England is an understated region. We have no special festive weeks, no Mardi Gras, no Kentucky Derby. What we do have to set us apart has always been with us — fall. The color marching up the hillsides, the morning snap of cold that gives way to warm afternoon sun, the startling sight of leaves blowing across our path, giving us bounce to our step. Feeling so alive, we enjoy spending money — hundreds of millions of dollars flow into our states in a few short autumn weeks. Our towns and villages have long prepared for the tourists. The inns are fully staffed. We hold harvest suppers and crafts fairs, pumpkin festivals and classic-car shows. Apple orchards, where we once came to simply pick fruit, have become family entertainment centers, a carnival of mazes, hayrides, and hot doughnuts, fresh from the deep fryer. If summer days are carefree, autumn is when we feel most alive.

I was born in New England. I have lived in New England for most of my middle-aged life. I would like to see peak color. Just once. Every year I miss the grand moment. I am not exactly sure how. Sometimes I am too early and see swatches of green, healthy leaves still in the middle of the scene. Other times I am too late. Bare branches are skeletons dancing in the background. I never am there in the moment when the picture is snapped for the postcard.

– Leigh Montville

Many visitors are lured here because there is genius behind the marketing of our fall colors. To not be here, say the tourism campaigns, is to miss out on something rare and special. Every Columbus Day weekend, typically the season's final hurrah of peak color, over half a million visitors squeeze into New Hampshire. Locals call them "stall-and-crawl" leaf peepers. But we feel pride that so many people want to see what we live with every day.

Yes, fall foliage is hyped. But know this: All of the hype is valid. There are hundreds of white-sand tropical beaches in the world, hundreds of ski mountains, many great cities. But nowhere on earth can you duplicate the duration and the intensity of color we see in New England. We know the season is fleeting, we sense that urgency, our hearts race a bit faster driving northward into the color. Be there, our hearts say, or it will be gone. It is our most intimate love affair with nature, a few weeks each year when we can do nothing but admire what the sun and soil and cold offer to us. All of our technology cannot alter nature's way with our leaves, and we love it all the more because of that. You never know exactly what you will see. Each tree, each bend in the road, each pond, each meadow — each brings the possibility of something new.

It is the time when we really notice what's around us. When people ask me the secret to enjoying these weeks, my reply is simply *notice*. Pay attention. If one tree lacks fire-engine red — the prima donna of our colors — notice the variations of color, the russets, the pale purples, the soft yellows, the tinges of green. The magic of a New England fall lies in the shadings, all the colors in between the exuberant scarlets.

I write this in late October. The full foliage season in the North Country is gone. The vacancy signs have returned

*A*re there not dull days enough in the year for you to write and read in that you should waste this glittering season when Florida & Cuba seem to have left their seats & come to visit us with all their shining Hours.

– Ralph Waldo Emerson

···

*T*HE SCARLET OF
THE MAPLES

CAN SHAKE ME LIKE A CRY

OF BUGLES GOING BY.

– William Bliss Carman

···

I SAW OLD AUTUMN IN THE MISTY MORN

STAND SHADOWLESS LIKE SILENCE, LISTENING

TO SILENCE.

— Thomas Hood

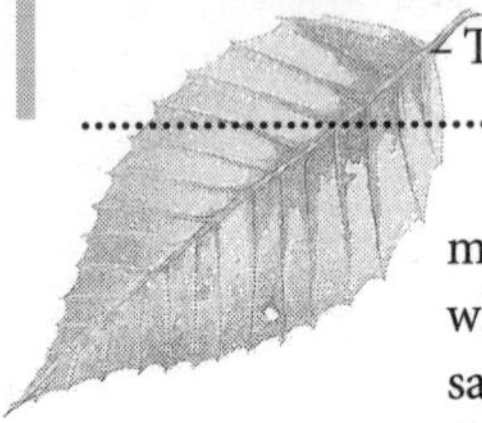

outside the inns. When I drive my sons to school in the early morning, I see more bare branches than I do trees with color. But there, in the heart of town, stands a sugar maple on the lawn of a bank — with barely a leaf missing. It may be the most beautiful tree I have seen this year. Tomorrow it may be different, and I know soon the leaves will lie in thick mats around its trunk; the gray threat of winter cannot be stopped by this single sugar maple in town. But as long as that single tree holds on, then I will, too. If Leigh Montville is still chasing after peak color, I say, come, today. It's all here, on this one tree by the bank in the center of our town.

– Mel Allen

Capturing the Color: HOW TO Make THE FINEST FOLIAGE Photographs

Ｈow is the foliage going to be this year? It's more than a passing interest for us at *Yankee* Magazine. It's an obsession. During the long, rainless summer of 1999, I hoped the leaves were loving the drought and would reward us with rich reds and yellows come September. During the heavy rains and strong winds of Hurricane Floyd, I gave only a fleeting thought to losing power or having trees crash down around me. As the storm raged outside my New Hampshire home, I worried that the leaves would be stripped off before our photographers got out on the road to shoot this year's foliage stories.

I've worked in *Yankee's* art department for 15 autumns, and I know New England's color is always beautiful. Some years it's a little redder or the leaves turn a little earlier or later than the year before. But it is always beautiful. Always. Even in the years leaf peepers are greeted by gray skies and a steady drizzle, the leaves are magnificent. Actually, they look more brilliant in the rain, as if given a shiny new coat of paint.

I have looked at more than 500,000 foliage photographs as picture editor for *Yankee.* Not all of them were beautiful, but some were so spectacular I wanted to climb right into them — perch in the strong arms of a sugar maple ablaze against a brilliant blue sky, or walk that deer path through muted colors of birches and ash in the early morning mist.

I asked Kindra Clineff and Alison Shaw, two of *Yankee's* finest foliage photographers, how they capture on film, season after season, the breathtaking images that preserve the essence

SOME PICTURES WERE SO SPECTACULAR I WANTED TO CLIMB RIGHT INTO THEM.

of autumn. Here are some of their tips to help you bring better photographs back from your New England foliage safari. Some of these suggestions are for those who have cameras with interchangeable lenses, but most of these words of wisdom can be used by anyone, whether you are using a disposable box camera or a sophisticated 35mm camera.

Words of Wisdom

Film: If you want handy prints to pass around or put in an album, use print film. ASA 100- or 200-speed film will give you better color than faster films (such as ASA 400) and will allow you to make crisper enlargements. If you want the absolute best images, shoot slide film. Most *Yankee* photographers choose Velvia (ASA 50), a transparency film favored for its rich color saturation. This is very slow film, so in low-light situations, you will need a tripod.

Kindra urges anyone serious about their photographs to pay the extra money for professional film from a proper camera shop, not the local drug store, because the color density is better. It has been perfectly aged and properly stored. She says, "Film is like fruit. The professional film is ripe."

Processing: If your prints come back looking grainy or gray, do not automatically assume it is your technique or your camera. It could be the processing. Old chemicals result in washed-out prints. Spend a little extra for better-quality processing. Ask to see samples before you trust anyone to process your film.

Composition: Keep it simple. Look for a dominant element, like one tree in a field or a single branch of leaves against the sky. Alison suggests that "the photographer should isolate elements by using a shallow depth of field. This allows you to have one tree or part of a tree in focus while everything else is out of focus." The sharp part of the photo is then your dominant subject.

"Change your point of view," advises Kindra. "Get down on your belly and shoot through things, letting objects in the foreground go out of focus. This will give you a nice wash of color in the foreground and lead you into the background that you've kept in focus. Or you can keep the foreground sharp and let the background go soft."

Filters: In sunny conditions, try a polarizing filter to cut glare and capture brighter color in the leaves and sky. This will offer better overall definition. Look through the filter and see what it does, turning it for more or less polarizing effect.

When to photograph: Early morning and late afternoon provide the most interesting light. But don't grumble on an overcast or rainy day. Alison insists that she loves to shoot foliage in these conditions: "Overcast days will show color better than sunny ones."

Kindra's favorite time to shoot is during the 30 minutes before and after sunrise and sunset. But she adds, "Don't put your camera away in the middle of the day. And forget all that advice about keeping the sun behind you when you photograph." She prefers shooting into the sun,

Alison Shaw

so her subjects are backlit. If you've ever seen a sugar maple with the sun punching through the leaves, you'll agree. Be sure to protect your lens from sun flares. A lens hood, a piece of cardboard, or the shadow of a friend can shade your lens from the sun.

Lenses: "Avoid wide-angle lenses," says Alison. If you want the big, long view, "buy the postcard." Alison suggests that a photographer should "come in closer, focusing on a single tree — or just part of it." A single red leaf on a stone in a brook can be beautiful, more artistic, and pack a lot more punch than a huge view that has no definition or sense of scale.

But I want the view: Well, then do what Kindra does: "Be sure to have something interesting in the foreground to frame the view." This can be a porch railing, a tree, or whatever you like. Remember backlighting when applicable.

Motion: Alison reminds us that "everything doesn't have to be in focus. If you're near running water, put your cam-

Simple graphic compositions make perfect photographs.

Alison Shaw

era on a tripod and focus on some bright leaves on a rock just above the water. Set your shutter speed for one second or longer. This will give you a sense of movement in the brook, while capturing the still part of the frame as you see it."

On a windy day, use a tripod and focus on a beautiful tree or row of trees. Be sure the trunk is in focus, and expose your film at one-half second or slower. The trunks

A child's fall fun captured in motion (right). *Foliage against a steeple beckons us to look heavenward in Newfane, Vermont* (below).

Alison Shaw

Kindra Clineff

Kindra Clineff

will be sharp, and the moving leaves will create a lovely, fiery look. Experiment with slower and slower shutter speeds.

Reflections: Early morning is the best time to capture perfect reflections in a lake or pond. The water is more likely to be still, and you may get the added bonus of a nice mist rising off the water.

When asked how she keeps photographing foliage in fresh ways, Kindra answers, "It is such a short season every year — fleeting really. I don't have time to get bored with it. So at the end of each autumn, I look forward to the next one, when I can go to new places or return to some of the old favorites and try something different."

– Ann Card

Kindra Clineff

Sunrise on Franconia Ridge from the Sunset Hill House, Sugar Hill, New Hampshire (above). *Golden leaves and white fence in Old Bennington, Vermont.*

THE *Most Leaves*
IN THE
Shortest Time:
DRIVE-TO-THE-TOP
Mountains

"CLIMB EVERY MOUNTAIN," sings the Mother Superior in *The Sound of Music*... but she doesn't say you have to do it on foot. Even in New England, where there is a long tradition of associating hard work with just rewards, there are times when *being there* beats *getting there* by a long shot. We want our foliage vistas, and we want them now — so, onward and upward, in our cars. Herewith, a rundown of nine New England mountain summits attainable by auto road. Some are among the region's loftiest and most majestic mountains; others are mere bumps on the landscape — but bumps with a view.

The blue water of Camden Harbor is a perfect backdrop to fall colors as seen from Mount Battie.

William H. Johnson

Mount Greylock: Rockwell Road, the eight-mile route to the highest point in the Berkshires — and in Massachusetts — begins at the Mount Greylock Reservation Visitor Center in Lanesboro. Views from the 3,491-foot summit stretch across the Taconic Range and southern Green Mountains, and far to the east beyond the Hoosic River. This is mostly hardwood forest, and the colors are intense in early October. If you've made reservations, the Appalachian Mountain Club will put you up at its Bascom Lodge on the summit (private and bunkroom accommodations); the

AMC also serves meals. At the tippy-top of Greylock is a 1932 war memorial tower that looks like an upside-down Art Deco golf tee.

Mount Greylock Reservation, 413-443-0011 (ext. 10 for Bascom Lodge reservations). Rte. 7, Lanesboro, MA 01237. Road open mid-May to mid-October dawn-dusk; Bascom Lodge keeps the same schedule.

Pack Monadnock Mountain: The road to the top of New Hampshire's "other" Monadnock is only 1.2 miles long, but the 2,290-foot summit offers uninterrupted 360-degree views, carpeted with

Fog and ridgelines, looking north from Mount Greylock.

color in autumn. Climb to an observation platform on a radio tower to see Mount Monadnock, Vermont's Green Mountains, and Mount Wachusett in Massachusetts. On a clear day, you can make out the Boston skyline, 55 miles distant. (Ask for a map of the view at the entry station.)

Miller State Park, 603-924-3672, or West Region State Park supervisor 603-547-3373. Rte. 101, Peterborough,

(continued on page 137)

Bagging the Peaks

LET'S START by noticing that one person's peak is another person's near miss. Temperature and moisture are different every year. That's why we've given you a range of dates to look for peak foliage all over New England. If you miss it in one place, you can always look somewhere else later — at least until the end of October.

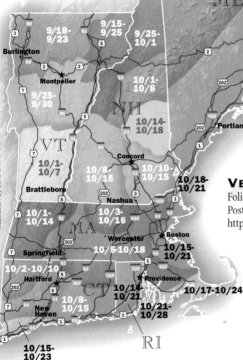

9/27-10/9

10/2-10/16

9/18-9/23

9/15-9/25

9/25-10/1

Burlington

Montpelier

10/1-10/8

9/25-9/30

NH

10/14-10/18

Augusta

Portland

VT

10/1-10/7

10/8-10/15

10/10-10/15

Concord

10/18-10/21

Brattleboro

Nashua

10/1-10/14

10/3-10/16

MA

Worcester

Boston

10/15-10/21

Springfield

10/5-10/18

Hartford

10/2-10/10

Providence

10/14-10/21

10/17-10/24

CT

10/8-10/15

New Haven

10/21-10/28

RI

10/15-10/23

ME

MAINE
Foliage hot line: 800-533-9595
Public information: 207-287-4909
Foliage views with routes, towns, and exact locations can be picked up at http://www.state.me.us/doc/foliage/foliage.htm.

VERMONT
Foliage hot line: 800-837-6668
Posted reports are at http://www.travel-vermont.com.

NEW HAMPSHIRE
Foliage hot lines:
800-258-3608; 800-262-6660
For foliage updates on the Web, visit http://www.visitnh.gov.

MASSACHUSETTS
Foliage hot line: 800-227-6277
Web site address is http://www.mass-vacation.com.

RHODE ISLAND
Foliage hot line: 800-886-9463
A foliage map with suggested routes is on the state tourism's Web site: http://www.visitri.com.

CONNECTICUT
Foliage hot line: 800-282-6863
Web site: http://www.ctbound.org

How Leaves Change Color

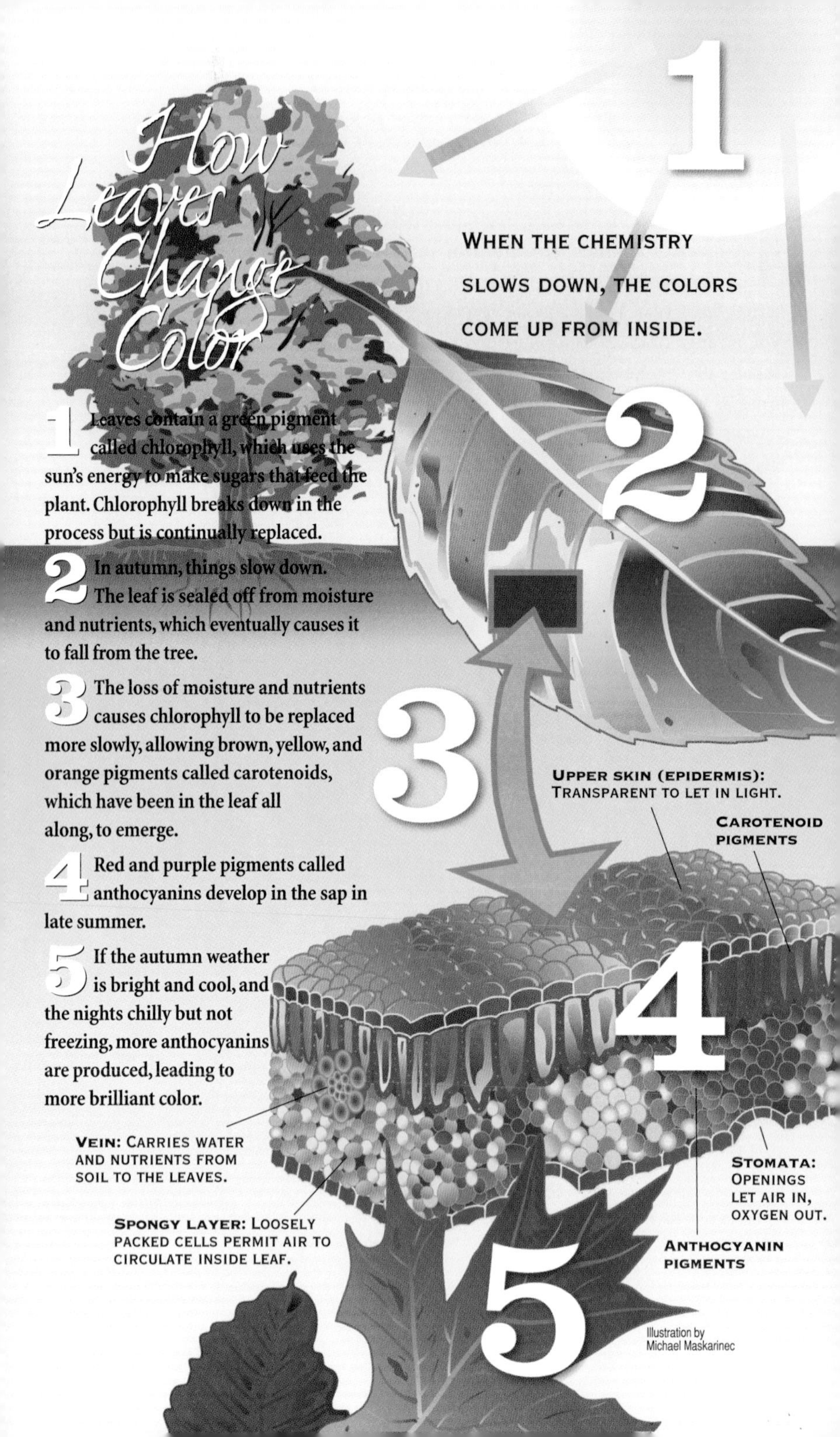

WHEN THE CHEMISTRY SLOWS DOWN, THE COLORS COME UP FROM INSIDE.

1 Leaves contain a green pigment called chlorophyll, which uses the sun's energy to make sugars that feed the plant. Chlorophyll breaks down in the process but is continually replaced.

2 In autumn, things slow down. The leaf is sealed off from moisture and nutrients, which eventually causes it to fall from the tree.

3 The loss of moisture and nutrients causes chlorophyll to be replaced more slowly, allowing brown, yellow, and orange pigments called carotenoids, which have been in the leaf all along, to emerge.

4 Red and purple pigments called anthocyanins develop in the sap in late summer.

5 If the autumn weather is bright and cool, and the nights chilly but not freezing, more anthocyanins are produced, leading to more brilliant color.

UPPER SKIN (EPIDERMIS): TRANSPARENT TO LET IN LIGHT.

CAROTENOID PIGMENTS

VEIN: CARRIES WATER AND NUTRIENTS FROM SOIL TO THE LEAVES.

STOMATA: OPENINGS LET AIR IN, OXYGEN OUT.

SPONGY LAYER: LOOSELY PACKED CELLS PERMIT AIR TO CIRCULATE INSIDE LEAF.

ANTHOCYANIN PIGMENTS

Illustration by Michael Maskarinec

**DRIVE-TO-THE-TOP
MOUNTAINS**

(continued from page 134)

NH. Open year-round for hiking; May-Veterans Day road access (conditions permitting). $2.50 per person, N.H. residents over 65 and children under 12 free.

Mount Washington Auto Road: Superlatives reign on the Northeast's highest peak. At 6,288 feet you'll find the strongest wind speeds on earth, the worst weather in New England, and the oldest man-made attraction in the United States. That's the eight-mile auto road, which has been open since 1861 (horses took four hours; you'll take about a half hour each way by car) and which can tug at the nerves of the squeamish with its narrow, guardrail-free route to the clouds. On roughly one day out of three, vistas from the summit range 30 to 40 miles; when it's really clear, you'll see beyond the Green Mountains to New York's Adirondacks and all the way to the Atlantic Ocean in Portland, Maine. At the summit is the renowned Mount Washington Observatory and its interesting little museum. Foliage isn't much of an issue up here, as you're way above treeline, but the *views* of it

from here rank among the best.

Mount Washington Auto Road, 603-466-3988. Rte. 16, Gorham, NH (Pinkham Notch). Open mid-May to mid-October; 8-4 in fall, extended hours in summer. Car and driver $16, each additional adult $6, each child $4; motorcycle and driver $8; guided tours in vans are $20 per person.

Mount Agamenticus: Located near the southern tip of Maine's long coastline, 691-foot Agamenticus looms over the town of York and its beaches, offering views of the ocean and of the dappled forests of the Maine and New Hampshire hinterlands. The road is only a little more than half a mile long and ends at an odd stone cairn that is said to mark the grave of St. Aspinquid, a 17th-century Native American medicine man. If you're not venturing farther north to our next two Maine coastal mountains, this is a great place to watch the sunrise.

Mount Agamenticus, 207-363-1040. Mountain Rd., York, ME (a left turn off Rte. 1, just north of York Beach, if you're heading north). Open year-round dawn-dusk. No charge.

Mount Battie: This is one of the finest vantage points on Maine's midcoast — an easy, 1.6-mile drive through a state park to an 800-foot summit that looks out over all creation — or at least that part of it blessed with a Penobscot Bay address. Beyond the white spires of Camden, set against fall colors, you can look out across Vinalhaven, Deer Island, and Isle au Haut, with Blue Hill in the distance. For an even better vantage point, climb the squat stone tower that has stood on the summit for nearly 80 years.

Camden Hills State Park, 207-236-3109 (entrance booth); 207-236-0849 (off-season). Rte. 1 (just north of Camden, ME). Open May 1-October 31 9A.M.-sunset. $2, over 65 free, children under 12 50¢.

Cadillac Mountain: Good morning, sunshine — this is the place to go when you want to be first in the United States to greet the first rays of dawn. The Cadillac summit road winds for just over two miles to the windblown, pink granite, 1,530-foot crest that stands as the East Coast's loftiest spot. Along with that first glimpse of the sunrise (you'll share it with a small throng; after all, this *is* popu-

Hikers ramble the peaks of Mount Mansfield.

Alden Pellett

lar Acadia National Park) are sweeping vistas of Bar Harbor, the islands of Frenchman's Bay, the Schoodic Peninsula, and the vast Maine blueberry bushes, which in autumn turn fire-red. Mount Katahdin stands over 110 miles to the north-northwest, just in case conditions are optimal, but there's nothing wrong with being content with that salt-sprayed realm directly below.

Acadia National Park, 207-288-3338. Rte. 3, Bar Harbor, ME. Open year-round, though the Cadillac summit road is not plowed in winter; road closed from midnight to one hour before sunrise (sunrise times posted at main visitor center). Park loop road pass (good for seven days) $10.

Mount Mansfield: The rooftop of Vermont doesn't belong only to Stowe skiers and Long Trail hikers; the 4.5-mile Toll Road, an intermediate ski trail in winter, snakes to a 3,850-foot elevation just under the "nose" of Mansfield, a mountain said to resemble the profile of a reclining human (the high point is the 4,395-foot chin). At the lower elevations, the surrounding autumn hardwoods are spectacular; higher up, they give way to distant panoramas with a muted, heathery palette. The nearer views include the forbidding rock walls of Smugglers' Notch, with the adjacent ski trails of Spruce Peak and Madonna Mountain; beyond, north to south, are distant Jay Peak, Mount Washington, and Camel's Hump. To the west, the Champlain Valley unfolds: The great lake sprawls north to south, framed by the high peaks of the Adirondacks.

Mount Mansfield Toll Road, 802-253-3000. Rte. 108 (the Mountain Road), Stowe, VT; Stowe Mountain Resort. Open mid-May to mid-October daily 9-5. Cars $12, motorcycles $7.

Mount Equinox: Southwestern Vermont's most prominent peak is in the Taconics, not the Green Mountains —

and it's the property of a Carthusian monastery. The 5.2-mile Sky Line Drive traverses the monks' mountain fastness, climbing to a 3,835-foot elevation that commands views of the Battenkill valley, the Massachusetts Berkshires, the Green Mountains, and — under superlative conditions — the White Mountains in New Hampshire and the Adirondacks to the west. (We're a little skeptical, however, about the claim regarding Mount Royal at Montreal.) Up top, there's a skein of hiking trails and — unusual for Vermont summits — a small inn (Equinox Mountain Inn, 802-362-1113), making lodging available (from mid-May to mid-October) and offering meals to the public.

Sky Line Drive, 802-362-1114. Rte. 7A, just south of Manchester Village, VT. Road open May 1-November 1 8 A.M.-10 P.M. Car and driver $6, each passenger over 12 $2.

Burke Mountain Toll Road: Tucked away in Vermont's Northeast Kingdom is the most remote — and one of the most rewarding — of our summit drives. Burke Mountain, at 3,267 feet, is the training ground for many American Olympic skiers. It also offers a route to the top, replete with hair-raising switchbacks, knockout foliage (the yellows of birches dominate in these parts), and views that take in virtually the entire northern portion of the Green Mountain State. That's Lake Willoughby over there to the west, nestled between mounts Pisgah and Hor; farther south is the profile of Mount Mansfield. Over to the east is Mount Washington; up north, it actually looks as if winter is about to come lumbering over that nameless jumble of Canadian hills.

Burke Mountain Ski Area, 802-626-3305. Off Rte. 114 in East Burke, VT; follow signs, and use the second (mid-Burke) entrance to the resort — the summit road is the first left. Open mid-May to mid-October daily until a half hour before sunset. Free.

– *William G. Scheller*

Secrets OF THE MAINE *Leaf Spotters*

ORE THAN ANY OTHERS, Maine's forest rangers watch the trees. Their job is to protect the Maine woods, and they peer from fire towers and airplanes, and from the windows of their trucks, looking for fires or illegal cutting.

And for a few weeks in September and October, the forest rangers tell the rest of us where and when to see the leaves turn color in Maine. They've done this since 1959, writing down the percentage of color change in the hundreds of square miles they patrol each week. Once a week, they phone a forest-service dispatcher in Augusta, who then compiles the data into a neat foliage report for each of Maine's seven foliage zones, to be used by newspapers, foliage hot-line callers, and, of course, Internet browsers.

They begin in mid-September, when the nights in northern Maine snap with cold and the tops of the hardwood ridges tease the eye with the first hints of red and yellow and orange. Within days, the color sweeps down the hills and mountains, heading southward toward the sea, until October arrives and the entire state seems engulfed in the autumn flames.

Each year the rangers note when peak arrives in their region and when the leaves tumble off. They are the scorekeepers in the real fall classic.

ZONE 6
Wildlands
From the Allagash and St. John rivers area, north of Baxter State Park. Earliest peak September 26; latest October 9.

ZONE 7
Aroostook County
North of Houlton and east of Route 11. Earliest peak September 24; latest October 9.

ZONE 5
Western Mountains
From Fryeburg north to Dole Brook Township and northeasterly to Patten, including Rangeley and Moosehead lakes. Earliest peak September 27; latest October 8.

ZONE 4
Eastern Central
From Bangor to the Canadian border, between Calais and Houlton. Earliest peak September 28; latest October 16.

M A I N E

ZONE 3
Western Central
From the New Hampshire border east to Bangor; south of Moosehead Lake, including the Sebago Lake area. Earliest peak October 1; latest October 16.

ZONE 1
Southwestern Coastal
Within 20 miles of the ocean, from Kittery to Penobscot Bay. Earliest peak October 2; latest October 16.

ZONE 2
Eastern Coastal
Within 20 miles of the ocean, from Penobscot Bay to Calais; includes Acadia National Park. Earliest peak October 4; latest October 16.

ZONE 1

Southwestern Coastal

Within 20 miles of the ocean, from Kittery to Penobscot Bay. Earliest peak October 2; latest October 16.

BRUCE SMALL is the head forest ranger for the Saco River District, with headquarters in Gray. He oversees rangers from York, Cumberland, Androscoggin, Oxford, and Sagadahoc counties. He has been a forest ranger for 24 years.

What makes his area special: "You don't need to climb a tall mountain to get 50-mile views."

His secret spot: "It's less than a half-mile hike to the summit of Bradbury Mountain, but you'll see great color in the forests and views of the Casco Bay islands. Bradbury Mountain State Park is a favorite place for hawk watching in September."

To get there: Drive west from I-95, take exit 20 to Route 136 in Freeport, and immediately turn left on Pownal Road. Drive four miles to Pownal center and turn right on Route 9. The park is less than a mile; the climb to the summit is three-tenths of a mile. 207-688-0712.

ZONE 2

Eastern Coastal

Within 20 miles of the ocean, from Penobscot Bay to Calais; includes Acadia National Park. Earliest peak October 4; latest October 16.

DOUG GETCHELL is the head forest ranger for the Down East District, with headquarters in Jonesboro. He supervises southern Hancock and Washington counties. He has been a Maine forest ranger for 27 years, with most of his time spent in the Ellsworth-Bar Harbor area.

What makes his area special: "The views here are unique: the coastal plain, with really beautiful lakes."

His secret spot: "It seems like a cop-out, but I never get tired of the view from Cadillac Mountain in Acadia National Park. You can drive or hike to the summit. At the top, you're at 1,500 feet, the highest point along the eastern seacoast. The whole panorama, looking out on the islands of Frenchman Bay and the other mountains of Acadia, is truly special."

To get there: There are several driving routes to Acadia National Park (207-288-3338). The fastest is usually I-95 to Bangor; 395 east to Route 1A to Ellsworth; then Route 3 south. Bar Harbor Chamber of Commerce: 800-288-5103. Mount Desert Chamber of Commerce: 207-288-3411.

LESLIE THORNTON is the district ranger for the Damariscotta District, based in Jefferson. He has been a ranger for more than 20 years.

What makes his area special: "The woods and the lakes."

His secret spot: "I don't know a finer spot than the Blueberry Hill overlook in the town of Rome. You're on the west side of Long Pond *[where Ernest Thompson, author of* On Golden Pond, *summered – Ed.]*, and you look across the string of lakes. That's awfully nice color in there. That's where you see lots of people stopping for photos."

To get there: From Route 27, just south of Belgrade village, take Castle Island Road west about three miles to Watson Pond Road. Turn right and continue about 1.5 miles.

MAYNARD THORNTON is the district ranger for the St. Croix District, with headquarters in Lee. He has been a ranger for 29 years.

What makes his area special: "We have so many rivers and lakes — and lots of hardwoods."

His secret spot: "I always go to Almanac Mountain in Lakeville. We have a fire tower up there that you can drive to; you're about 1,000 feet high there. Then you walk behind it on a trail and you come to a ledge. You look across to Junior Lake and all the lakes and streams in the Grand Lake Stream region. It's some country."

To get there: Follow Route 6 east from Lincoln to Springfield. Take a right on South Springfield Road, about four miles.

BRAD BARRETT is the assistant district ranger for the Rangeley District, with headquarters in Oquossoc. He has been a ranger for 27 years.

What makes his area special: "This is a hardwood forest with a lot of scenic overlooks across our lakes. Perfect for foliage viewing."

His secret spot: "The ride through Grafton Notch State Park is just fabulous. This is one of the premier scenic areas in the state. You have viewing places like Eyebrow and Table Rock along the road, as well as picnic spots with views of the Mahoosuc Mountains and the Presidential Range. There are

ZONE 3
Western Central
From the New Hampshire border east to Bangor; south of Moosehead Lake, including the Sebago Lake area. Earliest peak October 1; latest October 16.

ZONE 4
Eastern Central
From Bangor to the Canadian border, between Calais and Houlton. Earliest peak September 28; latest October 16.

ZONE 5
Western Mountains
From Fryeburg north to Dole Brook Township and northeasterly to Patten, including Rangeley and Moosehead lakes. Earliest peak September 27; latest October 8.

hiking trails in the park, and there's an old fire tower that's been fixed up. You get a tremendous view from the observation deck there. Just outside is Screw Auger Falls Gorge, which is just spectacular."

To get there: From Bethel take Route 2 east to Route 26 north for 7.8 miles. Turn left at the Getty station and go toward New Hampshire for 8.7 miles. Screw Auger Falls Gorge is one mile farther on Route 26. Grafton Notch State Park: 207-985-6890.

ZONES 6 & 7
Wildlands and Aroostook

From the Allagash and St. John rivers area, north of Baxter State Park. Earliest peak September 26; latest October 9.

DARCY LABBE is the district ranger for the Allagash District, with headquarters in Portage. He has been a ranger for 25 years.

What makes his area special: "This is the big woods, with two of the most famous wilderness rivers in the East."

His secret spot: "I don't believe you'll find a nicer drive than Route 11 from Fort Kent through Eagle Lake to Portage. I especially like to stop about halfway between Portage and Eagle Lake, where you come to Knoles Corner and Hedgehog Mountain. It's really colorful there."

To get there: Route 11 from Fort Kent to Portage is a Maine Scenic Highway.

ZONE 7
Aroostook County

North of Houlton and east of Route 11. Earliest peak September 24; latest October 9.

PETER UMPHREY is a field ranger in the Aroostook Waters District, with headquarters in Daaquam. He has been a ranger for 17 years.

What makes his area special: "We have the hardwoods covering the hills, but unlike other areas, we have the backdrop of all the farms. You can just drive over a rise and look out over the farms and lakes; the horizon is unlike any other in the state."

His secret spot: "Right about the first of October, everyone up here makes the same driving loop. It takes you through parts of Zones 6 and 7. You leave Presque Isle on Route 163. You go through Mapleton, then head to Ashland, where you get on Route 11 to Portage. Then you go north on Route 11 to Eagle Lake. You stay on 11 to Fort Kent, then get on Route 161 south to Caribou."

To get there: Take I-95 to Houlton, then go on Route 1 north to Presque Isle.

– Mel Allen

Trophy Trees

NOT FAR FROM Portsmouth, New Hampshire, stands a black gum tree. In autumn, its glossy green leaves turn a brilliant orange-red, but from a distance, the tree itself is rather unremarkable, standing in a wooded wetland on private property.

Josh Allen examines a black gum tree that began life when Christopher Columbus was 15 years old.

The location of the tree, however, is a jealously guarded secret, and an up-close inspection of its ancient, weathered bark reveals why. When this tree began its life, Christopher Columbus was 15 years old. Scientists say this black gum might be the oldest known deciduous tree in North America.

Foresters estimate that, give or take a few million, New England has over 26 billion trees. With so many, it is easy to miss the trees for the forest. Sometimes it is worth a detour to gaze at just one tree, to know its story, or to consider how much has happened during its life.

What follows are just some of New England's most notable trees. Like the New England forest itself, they are a mixture — some are distinctive for the role they have played in history, or their sheer jaw-dropping size, or their breathtaking loveliness. Or because of the hand that planted them.

Carole Allen

Carole Allen

Students from the April Melluzzo School of Dance play ring-around-the-sycamore.

A Family Tree

THE PINCHOT SYCAMORE is the largest tree in Connecticut: Ninety-three feet high, with an average branch spread of 138 feet, its trunk measures 25 feet 8 inches in circumference. Families often link hands to circle the tree.

Where: *Cross the steel bridge over the Farmington River on Connecticut Rte. 185, south of Simsbury Center. The tree stands in a small park.*

The Survivor

WELL-KNOWN TO Dartmouth College students, the Parkhurst elm is loved for its tenacity as well as its beauty. It's a majestic tree, 94 feet tall, whose leaves turn yellow-gold in autumn. This elm survived the Hurricane of 1938, then Dutch elm disease. Twenty years ago, some of its roots were severed during a road project, but the elm continues to thrive.

Where: *On North Main St. in Hanover, New Hampshire, in front of Parkhurst Hall.*

New England's Largest Turkey

WITH A TRUNK almost 17 feet in circumference, this is a magnificent specimen of the turkey oak (*Quercus cerris*), 64 feet high — New England's largest. Native to Europe, it has wavy-edged leaves and large acorns with bristly cups. Some say it's called a turkey oak because its leaves look like the fanned-out tail of a tom turkey.

Where: *Bushnell Park, Hartford, Connecticut.*

The Tree That Saved Connecticut's Liberty

ALTHOUGH NOT a rare species and not the largest of its kind, this is probably the most notable tree in Connecticut. It is a scion — or first-generation offspring — of Hartford's famous Charter Oak, which played a key role in how Connecticut got its nickname: the Constitution State. It is the state tree of Connecticut.

In October 1687, on the order of the English Crown, Sir Edmund Andros, governor of Massachusetts and Rhode Island, was sent to Hartford with some 60 heavily armed troops to seize Connecticut's charter, which authorized the colony to operate independently. During a long and increasingly tense meeting held at the Old State House, all of the candles were knocked over, plunging the room into darkness. Captain Joseph Wadsworth of Hartford whisked the charter out of the room, ran down Main Street, and hid it in an old hollow oak tree, where it remained for almost two years. In 1689, the people of Connecticut voted to reestablish the government according to the old charter. The significance of all this is that, among the 13 original colonies, only Connecticut maintained self-rule up to the American Revolution. The original Charter Oak grew at the corner of Charter Oak Avenue and Charter Oak Place. It blew down in 1856. A marker designates the spot. (The original Connecticut charter may be seen at the Connecticut State Library, across from the capitol.)

Where: *Bushnell Park, Hartford, Connecticut.*

WITH A TRUNK ALMOST 17 FEET AROUND, THIS IS A MAGNIFICENT SPECIMEN OF THE TURKEY OAK.

The Trees the Settlers Saw

GIFFORD WOODS, a small, under-ten-acre stand of old-growth forest in a Vermont state park, gives visitors a glimpse of how the New England forest looked to the first settlers. Some trees rise more than 100 feet from the forest floor. Most of the sugar maples date from Revolutionary times, and there is also a 400-year-old hemlock. A state park and campground allows visitors to sleep within sight of these trees.

Where: *Gifford Woods State Park, Sherburne, Vermont, one-half mile north of Rte. 4 on Rte. 100.*

The Tree of Independence

THIS VERY LARGE and beautiful horse chestnut was planted by one of the signers of the Declaration of Independence, William Whipple, upon his return from Philadelphia in 1776.

Where: *On the lawn of the Moffatt-Ladd House on Market St., Portsmouth, New Hampshire.*

"The Forest Primeval"

ALONG THE Elwell Trail at Paradise Point Nature Center is a stand of giant hemlocks that began their lives in the 17th century, well before Longfellow wrote of "the murmuring pines and the hemlocks" in "Evangeline."

Where: *Paradise Point Nature Center, 603-744-3516. North Shore Rd., East Hebron, New Hampshire.*

The Endicott Pear

THE OLDEST living fruit tree in the United States has blossomed and borne fruit for more than 300 years. In 1964, vandals cut off its branches, but the tree was saved by grafting.

Where: *On Endicott St., behind the Sylvania Plant in Danvers, Massachusetts; take exit 24 off Rte. 128.*

"Tree at My Window, Window Tree ..."

FROM 1900 TO 1909, Robert Frost lived on a farm in Derry, New Hampshire. He once wrote, "I might say the core of all my writing was probably the first five years I had there." His children may have played by this magnificent maple near the barn.

THE OLDEST LIVING FRUIT TREE IN THE UNITED STATES HAS BORNE FRUIT FOR MORE THAN 300 YEARS.

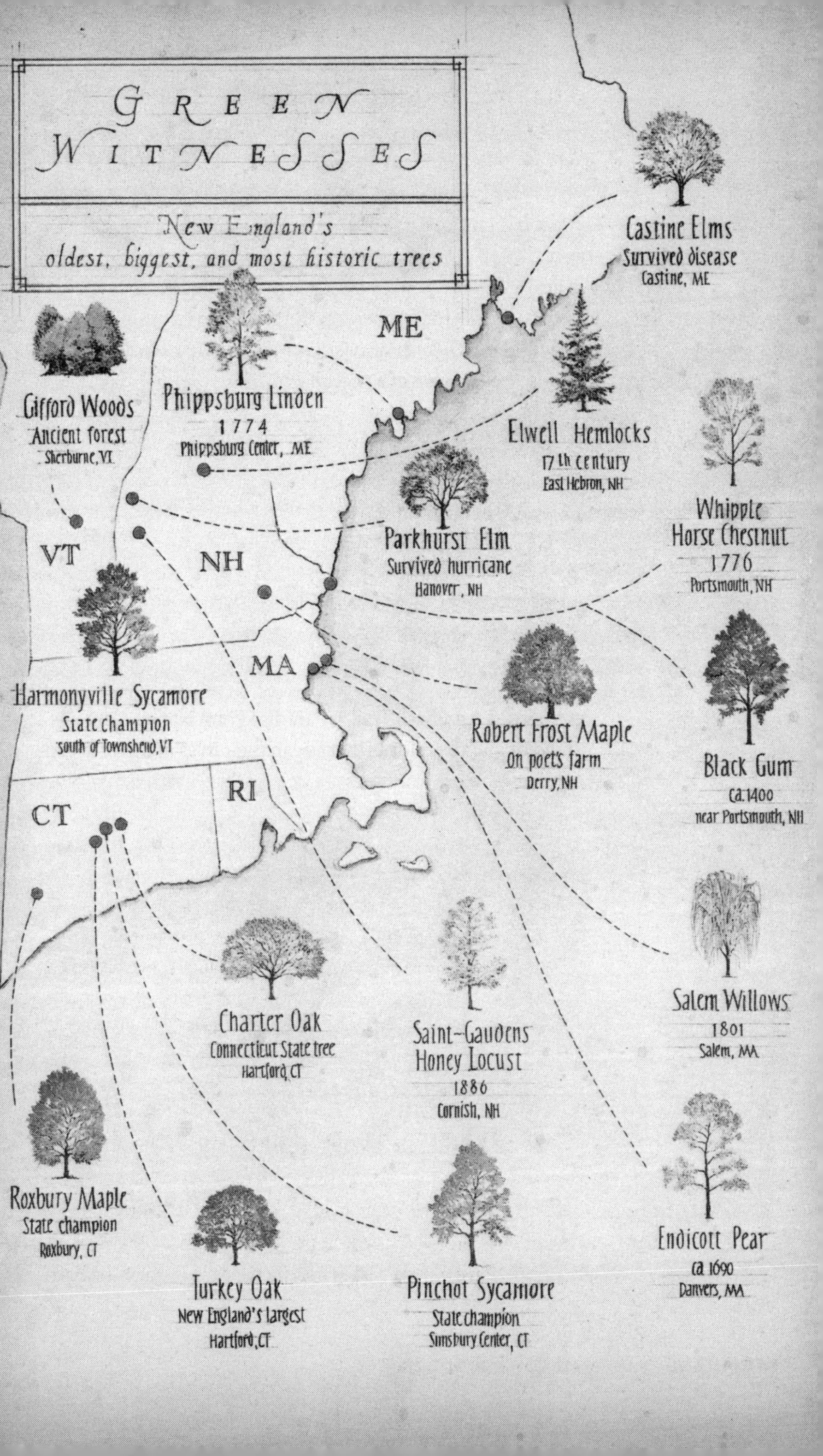

GREEN WITNESSES

New England's oldest, biggest, and most historic trees

Castine Elms
Survived disease
Castine, ME

Gifford Woods
Ancient forest
Sherburne, VT

Phippsburg Linden
1774
Phippsburg Center, ME

ME

Elwell Hemlocks
17th century
East Hebron, NH

Parkhurst Elm
Survived hurricane
Hanover, NH

Whipple Horse Chestnut
1776
Portsmouth, NH

VT

NH

Harmonyville Sycamore
State champion
south of Townshend, VT

MA

Robert Frost Maple
On poet's farm
Derry, NH

Black Gum
ca.1400
near Portsmouth, NH

CT

RI

Charter Oak
Connecticut State tree
Hartford, CT

Saint-Gaudens Honey Locust
1886
Cornish, NH

Salem Willows
1801
Salem, MA

Roxbury Maple
State champion
Roxbury, CT

Turkey Oak
New England's largest
Hartford, CT

Pinchot Sycamore
State champion
Simsbury Center, CT

Endicott Pear
ca.1690
Danvers, MA

Map/Illustration Erick Ingraham

Where: *Frost Farm, 603-432-3091. 1¾ miles south of Derry Circle on Rte. 28. Open June only weekends 10-6; July 1-Labor Day Thursday-Monday 10-6; Labor Day-Columbus Day only weekends 10-6.*

The Sculptor's Honey Locust

THIS TREE STANDS in front of the house where famed sculptor Augustus Saint-Gaudens lived. It was planted by Saint-Gaudens in 1886 and is the largest honey locust in New Hampshire.

Where: *Saint-Gaudens National Historic Site, 603-675-2175. Cornish, New Hampshire. Take I-89 to exit 20, drive south on Rte. 12A. Open Memorial Day-October 31 daily, buildings, exhibits, and grounds; November 1-late May 8 A.M.-dark, only grounds.*

The Spirit-of-America Maple

THIS MAJESTIC 375-year-old maple stands on the front lawn of the home of the late Vermont painter William Dean Fausett. He maintained that the tree, the subject of his painting "The Spirit of America," is on the site where Ethan Allen's Green Mountain Boys met.

Where: *Nichols Hill Rd., Dorset, Vermont.*

The Salem Willows

SET IN A landscaped park overlooking the Beverly, Massachusetts, waterfront on one side and Salem Sound and the coast from Marblehead to Cape Ann on the other side, the willows were planted in 1801 to form a shaded walk for patients at the smallpox hospital. The trees now form the backdrop for one of New England's old-fashioned amusement areas.

Where: *Salem Willows Park; follow signs along Derby St. to Fort Ave.*

The Castine Elms

CONSIDERED ONE of the finest stands of elms in New England, over 300 of these great trees grace the village of Castine, Maine. Townspeople helped their trees withstand Dutch elm disease, and these elms are among Castine's treasures.

Where: *Especially notable along Main St., Castine, Maine.*

Carole Allen

The Hold-Fast Sycamore

AN ESPECIALLY beautiful Vermont state champion, well worth the visit. Its yellow-green leaves hold on longer than almost any other tree around.

Where: *Just south of Townshend, Vermont, on Rte. 30, you come to the Harmonyville General Store; the tree is right next to the bridge.*

Hold-fast sycamore friends stand guard on the state champ.

The Phippsburg Linden

IN A LOVELY coastal setting in Phippsburg, Maine, this huge linden was planted in 1774.

Where: *Go south on Rte. 209 until you come to the Phippsburg General Store; turn left on Parker Head Rd. into Phippsburg center. The tree stands between the Congregational church (1802) and a small cemetery.*

A Monster Maple

IN ROXBURY, Connecticut, stands the state champion sugar maple, nearly 20 feet around, 94 feet high, with a 99-foot spread of branches.

Where: *18 Mallory Rd., Roxbury, Connecticut; from the Seth Warner monument in the center of town, take South St. south about 2.8 miles to Mallory Rd., turn left on Mallory, and the tree will be on your left.*

Living Dinosaurs

THIS STAND OF 60-foot-high firs with a lush understory of ferns is in a deep gully, so when you descend into it, according to people who've seen it, "You feel as if you're back in the age of dinosaurs."

Where: *At Katahdin Iron Works (a state historic property) in Brownville Junction, Maine; it's a short walk from the parking lot that serves the trailhead for the Gulf Hagus Trail. Be sure to get good directions from the gatekeeper.*

– Mel Allen

Leaf Everlasting:
HOW TO
Preserve the Colors
OF FALL

W HEN I WAS a little girl, I had a three-block walk
to school. On these walks in the fall I played a
game, a treasure hunt of sorts, where I would find
the tiniest perfect leaf and the largest perfect leaf. These I
would present to my mom before lunch. I walked those three
blocks with my head down, selecting candidates, comparing
them against the few carefully held in my hand by the stems,
and gently tossing the rejects on the slate sidewalk. My
mother examined the day's catch and then served me my
soup and sandwich.

Today I play the same game with my daughter, Sara. I
send her out to find the most perfect specimens, smallest and
largest. We preserve these, and when the days turn shorter
and colder, we set up the card table by the fireplace. Then we
glue the colorful leaves on note cards and bookmarks for holiday gifts.

Here are a couple of ways we preserve the leaves:

◆ Start by selecting the best specimens. Pick a sunny day and
collect only dry leaves. Avoid leaves with any damage, because
these imperfections will be accentuated when the leaves are
dry. Try to find at least four or five leaves from each species so
that you will have a good representation.
◆ Within a half hour of collecting, place each leaf between
two layers of paper towel or blotting paper (you can find this
at an art-supply store). If you wait much longer, the leaves

begin to dry out and lose color. The trick to keeping the colors sharp is to remove the moisture as quickly as possible.

+ Gently put the leaf with its blotting paper between the pages of a large book. When I was a child, we used a big telephone book, but I prefer a large coffee-table book — the pages are thicker and therefore more likely to withstand moisture, and when it comes to adding weight for pressing, a big hardback book like this is less likely to shift and damage the leaf. Keep at least ten pages between leaves, and don't put in too many — use a second book if you have a lot of leaves.

+ Stack at least five more books (aim for about five pounds of pressure) on top, and let them sit for ten days or more. Keep the books in a dry room, one with no humidifier. For the best results, change the blotting paper after the first few days of pressing.

+ If you have just a few leaves and want quicker results, try ironing them dry. Set your iron on dry medium heat, and place the leaves between single layers of absorbent paper or paper towels. Press for about ten minutes, turn the leaves over, change the paper, and press the second side for about five minutes. To prevent scorching, keep the iron moving constantly. Then sandwich the leaves between two layers of waxed paper (wax side on the leaf), and set the iron on high. To protect my iron, I cover the waxed paper with another layer of paper. Press for about a minute, or until leaves adhere and are coated with wax. While the leaf is still warm, peel off the paper. This thin coating of wax will nicely preserve your autumn color.

– Polly Bannister

The View

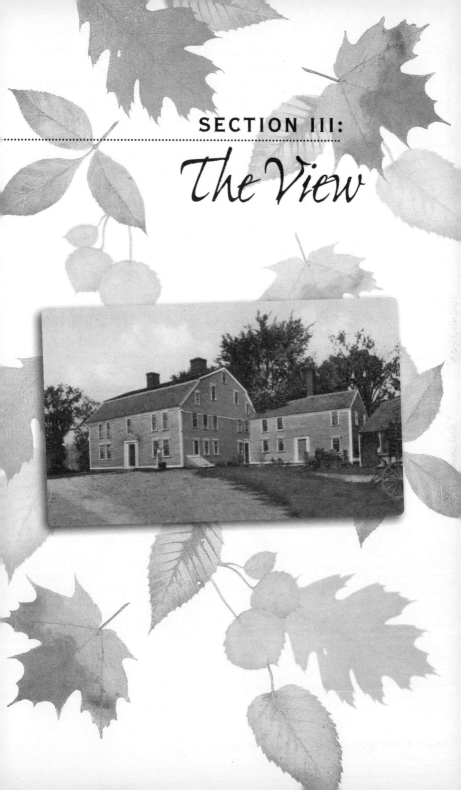

View WITH A *Room*

W E ALL KNOW WHEN some-
thing stops us in our tracks —
when we see a breath-stopping
view that makes us say, "Oh, my gosh!" I
travel all over New England in every season, and the views from the following
places in New Hampshire still have the
power to stop me in my tracks.

Heading north on I-93, I approach
Bungay Jar via Route 112W and 116N,
passing beaver ponds and shallow
riverbeds along the hidden Easton Valley. The byway is laced
with surprises just like Bungay Jar, a renovated 18th-century
barn. When I first stumbled onto this B&B, the front facade
looked ordinary enough, but when I moved to the backyard
— wow! Approaching from the wooded front yard and
closed-in valley, you get no hint of the unfolding drama: Exuberant gardens lace the foreground and slope down the ridge,
while the Kinsman Range rises beyond, providing a suitably
dramatic backdrop. It feels close enough to touch.

Most of the whimsically decorated guest rooms feature
these magnificent mountain views from private decks, but for
those that don't, the sweeping spectacle is exactly the same
from the common porch, overflowing with potted perennials
and trickling water fountains. The Kinsman Range won't let
me take my eyes off her — whether from the breakfast nook

*Perennial gardens
and water-lily pond
at Bungay Jar
Bed-and-Breakfast.*

or the porch adjacent to the sauna. Still, I cannot resist being drawn down winding pathways through natural arbors to a lily pond, actively cultivated to look wild. My world telescopes from macro to micro, from grand mountainsides to quiet secret garden. I'm alone but for the dragonflies and butterflies.

I developed great expectations for this next inn based solely on the property's name: Sunset Hill House. Luckily, this inn is true to its name. Yes, it roosts on a hill in the town of Sugar Hill, and it's well-positioned for taking in sunsets. But the true autumnal spectacle is the hill itself, lit as if on fire by a high concentration of noble sugar maple trees. From the inn's porch, pool, and fine dining room, far beyond the meadows and stone walls, my gaze roams 180 degrees north and south, across the entire Presidential Range. The Kinsman and Franconia ridges dominate the foreground, as do the "three little cannon balls" (known locally as the Three Graces) of Cannon Mountain. An antique wall map in my room helps me identify each and every mountaintop seen from this completely renovated late-19th-century hotel. All rooms are decorated with tasteful floral Victorian overtones.

The Notchland Inn sits on 100 acres surrounded by the White Mountain National Forest.

By sunset, the eastern summits blaze a spectacular but fleeting alpenglow. To the west, beyond the nine-hole hilltop

courtesy Notchland Inn

Miles of porches encircle the Mount Washington Hotel.

golf course, the sun quickly settles behind the Green Mountains. Pick your perspective: Odd-numbered guest rooms face east, while even-numbered ones face west.

The Notchland Inn is situated above the road just south of dramatic Crawford Notch, with its spectacularly sheer walls and waterfalls, putting me smack in the midst of an extensive wilderness area. Rather than keeping the mountains and forest at arm's length, at the Notchland Inn I am in and of the view. I am enveloped by the mountain and dwarfed by it, as is the sturdy granite gabled inn. Across the road, a short path leads down to the pebbly shores of a pure mountain river, or you can follow the 150-year-old Davis Path that leads to the summit of Mount Washington. Humility and respect settle in as I begin the ascent.

Set on 400 acres of undeveloped property, great for cross-country skiing as well as hiking, the romantic inn exudes warmth from the outset. The sight and scent of wood-burning chimneys (every room has a fireplace) beckons me in from the all-too-early arrival of dusk. After a lovely five-course meal, I head out into velvet darkness for a soak in the wood-stoked outdoor hot tub, adjacent to a spring-fed pond. From the tub, I can feel the overarching presence of the mountains, even if I can no longer see them holding up the glittering celestial canopy.

The dramatic siting and architecture of the Mount Washington Hotel & Resort make it such a traffic-stopper that it has its own designated highway overlook. The resort squarely faces the indomitable mountain, greatest of the Presidential Range. There is no civilized place I'd rather while away an afternoon than in a white wicker chair on the veranda, a porch so long — 900 feet — it appears to be made with mirrors. I even have a favorite chair, one that, after much pseudo-scientific testing, I have decided encompasses the best of all available views. (See if you can find it.)

On a clear day, I can see from the porch the weather observatory atop the barren peak and smoky clouds from "the little engine that could," the Cog Railway, which chugs up the near-35-degree incline. I prop my feet on the white railings, sip a drink, and engage in an internal struggle between reading and gazing. The lilting strains of piano music wafting from the glassed-in conservatory tip the scales toward gazing. Although the porch also overlooks the resort's action-packed facilities (clay tennis courts, horse trails, walking trails along a shallow riverbed, sculpted golf fairways, a swimming pool, croquet), I'm not tempted to budge. The glowing palette of changing leaves and light provides action enough.

Not only does West Side Road bypass snarled North Conway traffic, but it also deposits you, after a long, winding driveway of sorts, at the White Mountain Hotel and Resort, a modern three-story hotel that sits directly beneath dramatic Cathedral Ledge. On the approach, there's one spot where the sheer ledge meets a golf fairway. Conveniently, a flower-

AFTER A LOVELY FIVE-COURSE MEAL, I HEAD OUT INTO THE VELVET DARKNESS FOR A SOAK IN THE OUTDOOR HOT TUB.

bedecked gazebo is perfectly positioned to take advantage of the view. No doubt you'll stop here, too.

Resident English springer spaniels greet guests at the Spalding Inn.

Although the standard-issue hotel rooms are fine, with upscale reproduction furnishings, the view from the dining room is what really draws me here. The main course at every meal is Mount Cranmore, served in all its glory across the broad valley. I eat slowly to savor the visual feast. After lunch, meander down a short path to Echo Lake and appreciate the glorious vista from another perspective.

About 20 miles north of the northern edge of "the Whites," the Spalding Inn offers an exceptional value for families, in guest-house suites as well as in adjoining rooms, each with a private bath. Located in Whitefield, known as "the friendly town with a beautiful point of view" (reason alone to come), the inn is also a convenient base for launching journeys to the less explored Mount Cabot and Crescent Range.

The Spalding Inn used to boast an absolutely fabulous long view, but trees grow, and now the distant but still powerful mountains are exposed only in snippets and snatches. For me, the hide-and-seek heightens my anticipation; just a few hundred yards up the road, the vista is still magnificently panoramic. Another bonus: The drive south yields broad views that will entrance you for miles and miles on your way home.

– *Kim Grant*

ESSENTIALS

Bungay Jar, 800-421-0701, 603-823-7775. Easton Valley Rd. (Rte. 116), Franconia, NH 03580. Six rooms and one cottage. $115-$195, including full breakfast. Two-night minimum stay during foliage; rates lower before and after foliage. (www.bungayjar.com)

Sunset Hill House, 800-786-4455, 603-823-5522. Take Rte. 117 to Sunset Hill Rd., Sugar Hill, NH 03585. 27 rooms and five suites. $95-$250, including breakfast. Higher rates and two-night minimum stay during foliage. (www.sunsethill.com)

The Notchland Inn, 603-374-6131, 800-866-6131. Rte. 302, Hart's Location S.R., Bartlett, NH 03812. Seven rooms and five suites. $225-$285, including breakfast and dinner ($50 less if you choose not to have dinner). Three-night minimum stay during foliage; midweek packages are available. (www.notchland.com)

The Mount Washington Hotel & Resort, 800-258-0330, 603-278-1000. Rte. 302, Bretton Woods, NH 03575. 200 rooms and various suites in the Grand Hotel. $210-$510 ($360-$580 for a family of four in two rooms), including breakfast and dinner, plus 8 percent service gratuity; higher rates for corner rooms and suites. Wheelchair accessible. (www.mtwashington.com)

The White Mountain Hotel and Resort, 800-533-6301, 603-356-7100. West Side Rd., North Conway, NH 03860. 67 rooms and 13 suites. $129-$199. Two-night minimum on weekends; lower rates at other times. (www.white mountainhotel.com).

Spalding Inn, Mountain View Rd., Whitefield, NH 03598. 800-368-8439, 603-837-2572. 36 rooms and suites, each with private bath; $190 for a family of four, including breakfast. Six guest-house cottages; $170-$350 daily, $800-$1,400 weekly. All rates plus 15 percent gratuity. (www.nettx.com/spalding. htm).

Six INNS, Four STATES, Two Billion COLORED LEAVES

SIX OF THE REGION'S finest inns recently joined together to form "The Original Historic Inns of New England." All boast spots on local and national historic registers; all were originally built as inns (not converted residences); and all have provided good food, drink, and lodging to man and beast since the days of the stagecoach. There is no better time than autumn to set out on this inn-to-inn tour.

I started from the Boston area and looped through Massachusetts, New Hampshire, Vermont, and Connecticut. I stayed at a different inn each night. I covered more than 400 miles of the region's most beautiful back roads in a week,

The original Longfellow's Wayside Inn, Sudbury, Massachusetts.

courtesy Longfellow's Wayside Inn

everything from coastal Connecticut to the Green Mountains of Vermont.

There is no inn operating in America older than Longfellow's Wayside Inn in Sudbury, Massachusetts. It has been licensed since 1716 on the Boston Post Road, midway between Boston and Worcester. It is so old that it has its own staff of historians, six of them, and they can tell you some stories. The walls don't need to talk at the Wayside — the people do.

This is the place where Henry Wadsworth Longfellow came in 1862 to console himself after his wife's tragic death. He had not written a word since her passing, but sitting with friends beside the tavern's fire, he found inspiration enough to later compose *Tales of a Wayside Inn*. History made from heartbreak.

My parents had brought us here as children to picnic beside the mill (where the inn's cornmeal and wheat flour are ground for muffins), and I was glad on my return to find it as I remembered — a sprawling Colonial structure with cradled floorboards, paneled wood, and ladder-steep stairs to low-ceilinged rooms.

Some places lend themselves to good company; the Wayside is one. I ate dinner with three strangers. We sat by the warmth of the fireplace, with its beehive oven, and we ate blue point oysters, broiled fresh swordfish, and Indian bread pudding; we drank Longfellow Winter Ale and talked late into the night.

The history I love best is the kind you can cart home — creaky antiques. There are no better roads for discovering old stuff to buy than the old Boston Post Road and Route 119 north toward New Hampshire. There are so many antiques shops that Boston tour buses pass this way. I followed after.

I'd been told that Delaney Antique Clocks in Townsend, Massachusetts, must not be missed. When I entered the red-carpeted barn, it was like entering a living being; I tell you, the clocks ticked and pulsed. More generations of grandfathers in one raftered room than I had imagined in the world. It is, in fact, the largest selection of American antique tall clocks in the country. I lost track of time in a place that sold only time. The clocks smelled of finished wood, with sides as smooth as

*T*HERE IS NO INN OPERATING IN AMERICA OLDER THAN LONGFELLOW'S WAYSIDE INN.

flesh. Little stories were typed out and tacked beside them like introductions to a party of personalities. And then the bells began to ding, dok, and dop in every tone, and I was Alice in another land.

Farther up Route 123, in Peterborough, New Hampshire, I made a stop at Rosaly's Garden Center. Fields of seasonal art hung on the vine — vegetables by the sackful, flowers to cut and carry off. In town, at the Sharon Arts Center, I stopped again to see the world through the eyes of the area's talented artists. Then on to the Hancock Inn, New Hampshire's oldest, where I would spend the night.

Hancock was my childhood home. The people in those stately clapboard historic houses were my neighbors. We are used to hearing the steepled clock sound as often as the village gets named one of the prettiest in New England.

Historic Hancock Inn.

But it was the first time I had stayed in my hometown as a tourist, and so I saw it from a new perspective, a little smaller, a little more relaxed. Friends joined me for dinner — Shaker cranberry pot roast,

courtesy Hancock Inn

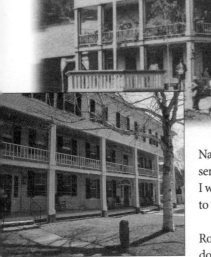

The long porch of the Old Tavern Inn beckons guests to sit a spell.

Nantucket seafood chowder, Indian pudding — served by a waitress in 18th-century dress. Since I was feeling so at home, it seemed a surprise not to do the dishes.

After breakfast the next day, I followed rural Route 123 toward the Vermont border, with a dogleg north on 12 to see the Fort at No. 4. A short ride over the Connecticut River to I-91, then south to 121, brought me through Saxtons River to Grafton, Vermont.

Grafton is a classic New England town — white-clapboard and redbrick houses, a general store, barns of horses, fields of sheep, two covered bridges, and the Old Tavern Inn. Three decades ago, Dean Mathey, a man with money, had the foresight and generous spirit to set up the Windham Foundation, which has since saved 55 of Grafton's 19th-century buildings — all part of this working village, with its galleries, gift shops, and 600 residents.

I am happy to leave my car for the long porch of the Old Tavern, a former stop on the Boston-Montreal line, and count myself in good company; presidents Grant, Wilson, and Roosevelt have creaked these boards; writers Hawthorne, Emerson, Thoreau, and Kipling (who honeymooned here), too.

In the morning, I walked the maple-lined road to the old cemetery. I visited the blacksmith shop with its wrought-iron tools and toured the Grafton Village Cheese Company down the road, with its award-winning cheese. Then continuing west on 121 to Route 100, I turned north and stopped at the Vermont Country Store. Backtracking south on 100, then west on routes 11 and 7A, brought me to the designer factory stores in Manchester Center and the regional crafts from the Southern Vermont Art Center.

Route 7 is a pretty drive south across the Massachusetts border into the Berkshire Hills, through Williamstown and Lenox, and into Stockbridge. There isn't a better place to porch-sit than the Red Lion Inn, a rambling old hostelry of more than 100 rooms, originally built in 1773 on the stagecoach route from Albany to Boston. Colonial revolutionaries used to meet there to pass resolutions protesting English taxation (despite the inn's crest, which represents the crown of King George III). A green tail painted on the inn's red lion showed sympathy with the colonists' cause.

Inside the inn, there's an old-world bustle. Porters carry your bags, guests anchor velvet

The Red Lion Inn was originally built in 1773.

The Deerfield Inn is at the center of village life.

couches beside the lobby fire, a birdcage elevator whirs between floors, and a maid turns down my feather-pillowed, canopied bed, while I dine on a traditional turkey dinner. Staffordshire china on the table, Colonial pewter, 18th-century furniture, Oriental rugs, antique sideboards in the halls ... a gift shop and the original Country Curtains flagship store on the first floor.

After a good night's rest and a hearty breakfast, I drive east on the Mass Pike (I-90), then north on I-91 to my second-to-last stop on the tour, Historic Deerfield. I am impressed, as always, with this tidy place, with the 15 historical museum houses, three working farms, three private schools, the surrounding hills, the open fields, and the winding Connecticut River. Deerfield was once a Colonial outpost, and to this day farmers still plow up bones and ax heads from the 1704 Indian raid. It is peaceful now.

At the center of village life sits the Deerfield Inn, Jane and Karl Sabo at the helm. In a town built on tradition, each afternoon they serve afternoon tea, with freshly baked cakes and cookies, in the inn's Beehive Parlor beside the fireplace. I ate more duck and drank more wine than I should have for dinner, then woke to the smell of freshly ground and brewed coffee in the hall, and again ate more than I should have for breakfast. Gladly, I took advantage of the opportunity to work it off on a lovely running loop past the farm fields, river, and 300-year-old village.

Last on my tour was the Griswold Inn in Essex, Connecticut, about two hours south on I-91 and Connecticut Route 9. The "Gris" is a seaside village inn, filled with Antonio Jacobsen maritime art and Currier & Ives steamboat prints. On Monday nights, yachtsmen, overland travelers, and townies all come to pound the walls and tabletops and belt out the words to old sea chanteys in the handsome taproom.

For fine food and lodging try the Griswold Inn.

Over clam chowder and meat pie, innkeeper Doug Paul told me that Essex was once an important shipbuilding town that the British navy laid siege to during the War of 1812. They forced a quick surrender and commandeered the Griswold Inn for headquarters. It is testimony to the inn's sense of tradition that its staff continue to serve the British-inspired Sunday Hunt Breakfast buffet. And it is tes-

courtesy Griswold Inn

timony to the townspeople's good-natured spirit that they continue to celebrate with the annual Losers Day Parade. After browsing the fine boutiques, exploring the Connecticut River Museum, and sitting on the dock watching yachts and fishermen go by, I can understand how easy it is to stay in good spirits in a showcase place like this.

I took the little ferry from Chester (another great river town) across the Connecticut River to East Haddam. I visited the Goodspeed Opera House, sampled the restaurants, and poked through the shops, all the while aware that I'd be needing to make my way back to Boston, leaving all this behind, but I would be back. Having seen these six inns in these four states, I can tell you that they represent the best mix of New England inns and towns that I've seen in a decade of traveling. New England in the fall cannot be matched. You will agree when you see it with your own eyes.

– Christine Schultz

ESSENTIALS

Longfellow's Wayside Inn, 800-339-1776, 978-443-1776. 72 Wayside Inn Rd., Sudbury, MA 01776. Open year-round. Ten rooms. $87-$145, including breakfast. (www.wayside.org/wayside.html)

Hancock Inn, 800-525-1789, 603-525-3318. 33 Main St., Hancock, NH 03449. Open year-round. 15 rooms. $106-$210, including breakfast. (www.hancockinn.com)

The Old Tavern, 800-843-1801, 802-843-2231. 92 Main St., Grafton, VT 05146. Open May-February. 63 rooms. $135-$260, including break-

fast and afternoon tea. (www.old-tavern.com)

The Red Lion Inn, 413-298-5545. 30 Main St., Stockbridge, MA 01263. Open year-round. 112 rooms. $75 (with shared bathroom) to $185 (private bath); suites $175-$400. (www.redlioninn.com)

The Deerfield Inn, 800-926-3865 (out-of-state only), 413-774-5587. 81 Old Main St., Deerfield, MA 01342. Open year-round. 23 rooms. $241, including breakfast and afternoon tea. (www.deerfieldinn.com)

The Griswold Inn, 860-767-1776. 36 Main St., Essex, CT 06426. Open year-round. 31 rooms. $90-$195, including

continental breakfast. (www.griswoldinn.com)

OTHER ATTRACTIONS

Delaney Antique Clocks, 978-597-2231. 435 Main St., Rte. 119, West Townsend, MA. Open year-round Saturday-Sunday 9-5, plus most days by chance, appointments anytime. (www.delaneyantiqueclocks.com)

Sharon Arts Fine Craft & Fine Art, 603-924-2787. 7 School St., Depot Sq., Peterborough, NH. Open year-round Monday-Saturday 10-5, Sunday noon-5. (www.sharonarts.org)

The Fort at No. 4, 888-367-8284, 603-826-5700. Springfield Rd., Rte. 11, Charlestown, NH. Open Memorial Day weekend-late October daily 10-4. $6, children 6-11 $4, under 6 free. (www.fortat4.com)

Grafton Blacksmith Shop, School St., Grafton, VT. Shop open May-October Thursday-Monday 10-3. Free public demonstrations 11 A.M. and 1 P.M.

Grafton Village Cheese Company, 800-472-3866, 802-843-2221. 533 Townshend Rd., Grafton, VT. Open year-round Monday-Friday 8-4, Saturday-Sunday 10-4. (www.graftonvillagecheese.com)

The Vermont Country Store, 802-824-3184. Rte. 101, Weston, VT. Open July 4-Columbus Day Monday-Saturday 9-6; off-season Monday-Saturday 9-5. (www.vermontcountrystore.com)

Southern Vermont Art Center, 802-362-1405. West Rd., Manchester, VT. Open May-October Tuesday 10-8, Wednesday-Saturday 10-5, Sunday noon-5; December-March Monday-Saturday 10-5. (www.svac.org)

Historic Deerfield, 413-773-7415. Rtes. 5 and 10, Deerfield, MA. Open year-round daily 9:30-4:30. $12, children 6-17 $5, under 6 free. (www.historic-deerfield.org)

Connecticut River Museum, 860-767-8269. 67 Main St., Essex, CT. Open year-round Tuesday-Sunday 10-5. $4, seniors $3, children 6-12 $2, under 6 free. (www.connix.com/~crm)

Goodspeed Opera House, 860-873-8668. Goodspeed Landing, Rte. 82, East Haddam, CT. Open April-December, performances Wednesday-Sunday. (www.goodspeed.org)

THE
Cultivated Hiker

F OR PEOPLE to whom hiking is not just about elevat-
ing your heart rate, these hikes provide a lot more than
aerobics and rocky terrain. If you are looking for great
views, colorful ridges, history, church spires, and a beautiful
harbor, all with a hearty dinner and cozy lodging at the day's
end, read on.

Crowd-free Hiking in the White Mountains

HIGH SUMMER brings the thickest knots of hikers into the
White Mountains, especially to the brawny and dramatic
Presidential Range. Throughout July and August, the challenge is finding less-trammeled pathways. Try to abandon
core hiking areas, traveling lesser-known trails instead. In the
same vein, focus on the lower peaks, which don't attract quite
as many People Who Wear Lycra.

The area around Philbrook Farm Inn (about five miles
outside of Gorham, New Hampshire) permits these strategies
for crowd-free hiking. This venerable inn is off the beaten
path on 1,000 private acres in the Androscoggin River Valley
against the base of a forested ridge. It offers a variety of nearby
trails, including several that ascend low peaks with fine, open
views of the valley and surrounding hills of the Carter Range.
As one of the inn's owners, Ann Leger, observes, the walking
opportunities can be neatly broken down to a choice of
"strolls, short walks, long walks, and hikes."

Five generations of Philbrooks (including Leger) have
owned the inn since 1854 (the original farming Philbrooks

started taking in summer boarders in 1861), and the three-story white clapboard inn with green shutters and prominent gables is one of the more handsome and formidable in the valley. The common rooms and the 19 guest rooms (ten of which have a private bath) are comfortable rather than fussy. It's not hard to imagine spending a rainy day indoors perusing both antique and contemporary volumes of local natural history in the library.

Take one of Leger's "strolls" soon after arrival to sample the flavor of the place and limber up. It's about a ten-minute walk through open fields from the inn to the Androscoggin River. (Effluents from the paper mill in Berlin, far upstream, make swimming ill-advised.) There's also the quiet Cottage Road behind the inn, which meanders by the inn's five house-keeping cottages and leads to the hiking trails. A quiet exploration of the grounds prepares you for the inn's dinner of traditional New England fare.

Day hikes are plentiful from the inn's backyard. And two relatively easy climbs reward hikers with superb views. The 1.8-mile Yellow Trail winds through relatively level forest land before crossing Austin Brook and beginning the ascent of 1,412-foot Mount Crag. Although Crag has a low summit compared with other peaks hereabouts, the sheer south face gives a grand view of a bend in the river and the mountains beyond. Allow about 1½ hours round-trip.

Choose from a number of hikes and views in the northern White Mountains.

Stephen O. Muskie

Another easily accessible peak is Crow's Nest, a 1,287-foot dome to the east of the inn. Ascend on the White Trail, which is moderately challenging until the end, when a steep spur strikes to the top. While the summit is wooded and overgrown, a vantage point slightly farther along affords good views. One-way distance is 1.3 miles, or about 1½ hours.

For a more ambitious day's outing, several waterfalls and high mountain ponds are accessible along the trail network that stems from the Austin Brook Trail. (Note: Consult the most recent edition of the Appalachian Mountain Club's *White Mountain Guide* before navigating this sometimes-tricky terrain. All the rules of backcountry travel apply: Bring plenty of food and water and backcountry basics such as rain gear, matches, knife, and compass.)

The 300-foot Dryad Falls are said to be the highest waterfalls in the White Mountains — high, yes, but not always spectacular. The falls are usually reduced to a trickle by midsummer, but in spring, or after a few days of steady rainfall, the falls become a tumultuous, dramatic sight. While just 2.4 miles from the inn, the trek is rugged and demanding. Start off on the Yellow Trail, head north on the Austin Brook Trail, then veer west on the Dryad Falls Trail. The base of the falls is a half mile beyond the last trail intersection.

Another attraction in this trail network is lovely Gentian Pond. The ascent to this quiet mountain tarn taxes most hikers. The round-trip from North Road to the pond is just seven miles, but be sure you have sturdy boots and plenty of stamina.

If a weekend's hiking isn't enough, housekeeping cottages can be rented by the week, letting you sample the nearby Evans Notch region or the rugged, remote hills of Grafton Notch to the north. If you're feeling saucy, you could stage a commando raid on one of the Presidentials, hitting a summit at dawn and returning before the Lycroids have even finished their coffee.

ESSENTIALS

Philbrook Farm Inn, 603-466-3831. 881 North Rd., Shelburne, NH 03581. Open May 1-October 31 and December 26-March 31. 19 rooms; $115-$145, including breakfast and dinner. Five cottages; $700 per week. Picnic lunch $6 extra per person. (www.innbook.com)

A Late Autumn Ramble in the Northeast Kingdom

The Inn on the Common is a perfect base for autumn hikes.

LATE FALL HIKES in northern New England tend to be chancy: The border between fall and winter is indistinct. High ridges are regularly buffeted by bitter northwest winds, and even low peaks can be unexpectedly dusted with snow. But by sticking to the lower elevations, you can enjoy the unique sense of melancholy that comes from wearing an oversized sweater and shuffling through newly fallen leaves.

Some of the best late-fall, low-elevation hiking may be found in Vermont's Northeast Kingdom. Remote at any time of year, by mid-October this area seems light years from the foliage crowds that clutter the roads to the south.

Craftsbury Common, founded in 1779, is a perfect base for late-autumn hikes. The village — an uncommonly well-preserved collection of Federal homes and churches — sits on a low, broad ridge surrounded by rolling countryside. Hilly farmlands are interspersed with dense forest, and the entire region is laced with lightly traveled but well-maintained dirt roads — perfect for rambles.

You have a choice of several accommodations in the area, including two at opposite ends of the budget spectrum. In the village itself, the Inn on the Common offers deluxe accommodations: 16 rooms in three meticulously restored Federal-era homes. The guest rooms, each with private bath, are well-appointed and comfortable, as are the gracious common areas. Meals served in the homey dining room follow the seasons and the whim of chef Gene Cote; in the fall, that might include roast quail and squash.

*T*HIS TRIP CLIMBS A GENTLE RIDGE WITH QUINTESSENTIAL VERMONT VIEWS OF PASTURES AND FARMS.

The Craftsbury Outdoor Center, about 2.5 miles north of Craftsbury Common, is easier on the budget. On the 140-acre grounds of the former Cutler Academy (a modest and ill-fated prep school), the center opened 25 years ago as a cross-country ski center and has expanded to include a variety of sports, such as canoeing, mountain biking, and walking. Guest rooms in the old dormitories and cottages on the lake are comfortable but simple and rustic. ("This wasn't St. Paul's or Choate," says Russell Spring, the center's founder.) The best deal is full board — until the kitchen closes in mid-October. Perhaps the most popular walk is the Ten-Mile Loop, also called the Creek Road Loop. Directions are relatively foolproof: Head northward from the Craftsbury Outdoor Center and make a right at every intersection.

This trip starts out along a white-cedar swamp, then climbs a gentle ridge with quintessential Vermont views of pastures and farms. To the east, the hills roll in from New Hampshire's White Mountains; to the west, you can spy Mount Mansfield and Camel's Hump, which may be white with early snow.

The road then angles southward through white pines and spruce. Eventually you reach an overlook of Mill Village, once a thriving milling center at the southern tip of Little Hosmer Pond. From here it's back down below the Craftsbury Common ridge. Two rights bring you northward (and through Mill Village, now a residential area) before you return to the center. (This trip can also originate from Craftsbury Common: Follow the paved road northward about three-quarters of a mile; look for the "Craftsbury Outdoor Center" sign instructing you to bear right on the first dirt road.)

If your trip happens to coincide with Indian summer weather, mountain hiking is available in the Lake Willoughby region, a 40-minute drive east of Craftsbury. The southern end of this handsome lake is flanked by the 7,300-acre Willoughby State Forest, which encompasses Mount Hor and Mount Pisgah. With sheer cliffs and superb overlooks, these mountains offer remarkable views along the lake of locales as far north as Lake Memphremagog, which straddles the Vermont-Quebec border.

For the Mount Pisgah hike, park on the west side of Route 5A about one-half mile south of the lake. The trailhead is across the road; the blue-blazed trail to the summit is 2.7 miles.

To find the trailhead for Mount Hor, follow a CCC-made gravel road from the right side of the Mount Pisgah parking lot, bearing right when you come to a fork; continue for 1.8 miles. The 3.5-mile trail to the summit leaves from the small parking lot at the end of this road. Allow about three hours for either of these round-trips.

Smaller cross trails and faint blazes can confuse the casual hiker. A good topographic map can be helpful: *Northern Vermont Hiking Trails* (Map Adventures, 1997) is available for purchase at the Willough Vale Inn, which also makes a great place for a meal or a bed at the end of a weary day.

ESSENTIALS

The Inn on the Common, 800-521-2233, 802-586-9619. Main St., Craftsbury Common, VT 05827. Open year-round. 16 rooms. $240-$260, including breakfast and dinner. Two-night minimum stay during foliage and Christmas seasons. (www.innonthecommon)

The Craftsbury Outdoor Center, 800-729-7751, 802-586-2514. Lost Nation Rd., Craftsbury Common, VT 05827. Open year-round. 50 rooms. $118-$188, including all meals; cottages with kitchenettes $195-$215. (www.craftsbury.com)

Willough Vale Inn, 800-594-4123, 802-525-4123. 793 Rte. 5A, Westmore, VT 05860. Open year-round except first two weeks of November and April. Nine rooms. $119-$145, including continental breakfast; lakefront cottages $1,100-$1,200 per week. ($$-$$$) Dining room and taproom open daily. (www.willoughvale.com)

Llama treks are a trademark of the Telemark Inn.

Dances with Ruminants, New England Llama Treks

DEBORAH FROCK unpacks lunch for eight hungry hikers atop Chocorua Mountain — a craggy, rock-capped summit. The buffet keeps growing: quiche, raspberry turnovers, fresh fruit salad, poppy-seed cake, frozen chocolate-covered bananas (for the kids), and vats of juice, tea, and coffee (both hot and iced).

She reserves her greatest flourish for the flatware — a heavy pile of stainless knives, forks, and spoons that she lays out on the red-and-white-checked tablecloth covering a slab of granite. "No plastic here," she says triumphantly.

For hikers accustomed to thinking twice about every ounce in their packs, trekking with a llama falls somewhere between luxury and decadence. You can stay light on your feet (you don't even carry a day pack!) yet still enjoy backcountry gourmet fare of the kind that canoeists typically gloat about.

Llama trekking has been a staple in the West for nearly two decades, but it's come fairly late to New England. While llamas can be spotted in paddocks from Connecticut to the Canadian border, only a handful of commercial packers offer their services in New England.

Frock got interested in llama packing because she "got tired of carrying a pack." After raising three boys in suburban Connecticut, she moved to the quiet village of Freedom, New Hampshire, 11 years ago to raise and train llamas. She now owns four of the South American ruminants, and she runs the only farm in New England breeding for classic athletic llamas (other farmers breed the animals for their wool or for show stock).

Frock offers llama-supported day hikes on about a dozen trails in the southern White Mountains — mostly in the rugged, knobby hills between the Kancamagus Highway, Route 113, and I-93. Trails run between two miles and six miles each way, and range from steep mountain ascents to untaxing valley rambles along dirt roads. You can request a specific hike, or let Frock suggest one based on your interests, physical capabilities, and hiking experience.

Trips typically begin at Frock's century-old farmhouse, where she loads up to four llamas in the back of her old 22-passenger school bus, which has been repainted with a llama scene and which she calls the "llama-mobile." (The llamas just hop in and lie down in the cargo area.) At the trailhead, she saddles up her llamas with ash baskets or nylon panniers (each llama can carry up to 100 pounds) then recruits willing hikers to lead them.

The first thing you learn is that llamas are very personable hiking companions. They don't kick or bite, so they shouldn't alarm either parents or children — or those leery of large mammals. While a llama has the bulk of a small horse, its gentle temperament more closely resembles that of a rabbit.

Frock also insists that — conventional wisdom notwithstanding — llamas don't "spit." OK, I'm willing to buy that. But I would still suggest staying alert when on the receiving end of a llama. They can "sneeze" or "cough" out whatever they last ate — grass, tender shoots of branches — at extremely high velocity.

The llamas on our trip, Avatar and Snowy, were both well trained and cooperative. Snowy followed along at the pace I set, walking a few steps behind most of the time and shoulder

*T*REKKING WITH A LLAMA FALLS SOMEWHERE BETWEEN LUXURY AND DECADENCE.

to shoulder at other times. Snowy stopped when I stopped. Demonstrating good backcountry etiquette, he would step off the trail to relieve himself. When annoyed for one reason or another (it was unseasonably hot the day we hiked), Snowy would let out a high-pitched hum to express displeasure. Snowy's one bit of unpredictable behavior was to sneak up and bump me with his head to shoo away the pesky flies that hovered around his eyes, a trick I might have appreciated even less in rugged terrain. For the most part, though, he was far easier to handle than my frenetic dog on a neighborhood walk.

Who should take a llama hike? They're great for parents with older children, especially kids who are reluctant hikers. Hikers who have bum knees or are otherwise unable to carry much weight are also good candidates. But anyone who is drawn to exploring the New England backcountry will find the trip all the more magical in the company of these animals.

ESSENTIALS

Llama Hikes of the White Mountains, 603-539-2865. Fairfield Llama Farm, 63 Elm St., Freedom, NH. Open June–November. Day hike for one to four people (including trailside lunch) $120, each additional person $20. Minimum age nine years; family hiking programs available; number of simultaneous groups limited to two.

Telemark Inn, 207-836-2703. King's Hwy., Bethel, ME. Steve Crone leads llama treks of six to ten people for one to three days in the White Mountains along the Maine-New Hampshire border. Day hike including lunch $85, children $65;

A llama ready for hiking.

three-day all-inclusive trek $475, children $350. (www.telemarkinn.com)

Northern Vermont Llama Company, 802-644-2257. 766 Lapland Rd., Waterville, VT. Geoff and Lindsay Chandler offer half- and full-day llama treks out of Smugglers' Notch ski resort. The trips follow cross-country ski trails to scenic Green Mountain overlooks. Half-day trips include a snack; full-day treks offer a full lunch, including fresh fruit and homemade baked goods. Half-day trip $30, children $15; full-day $60, children $30.

Remarkable Vistas in the Camden Hills

THE KNOBBY MOUNTAINS rising above Camden, Maine, at the western edge of Penobscot Bay are a dramatic backdrop for the village harbor. These ledgy hills won't challenge peak baggers and other humorless mountain marchers (the highest summit hereabouts is Mount Megunticook at only 1,380 feet, which barely ranks as a foothill by New Hampshire or Vermont standards), but they do offer enjoyable shorter hiking excursions and reward with remarkable views. From the hilltops, Camden becomes part of a dramatic tableau — one of ocean and islands and, below, a village of church spires and ship masts tucked around a tidy harbor.

Where to establish your base for an exploration of Camden's hills? One welcoming establishment, located on Route 1 between the village and Camden Hills State Park (where most hikes begin), is the Whitehall Inn, which first opened for business in 1901. The 50-room inn consists of a compound of three buildings. The original part was built for a sea captain in 1834, and it was later expanded with little harm to its architectural integrity. Now on the National Register of Historic Places, the inn is infused with old-world elegance and refine-

The Whitehall Inn was originally built for a sea captain in 1834.

ment — shuffleboard courts, tennis courts, gardens, wooden porch rockers, Persian carpets in the lobby — making a nice contrast with the rugged terrain of the nearby trails. The dining room serves traditional regional fare (such as haddock, shrimp, lobster, and in-season local produce) in an atmosphere that can be neatly defined in four words: linen, candles, classical music.

If you arrive after the Whitehall has been shuttered for the season (after the third weekend in October), the Edgecombe-Coles House, just north on Route 1, is another good option. This elegant bed-and-breakfast offers six nicely furnished rooms, spectacular vistas over Penobscot Bay (three rooms have ocean views), and a comfortable and homey atmosphere.

If you want to begin with a limbering walk, head back down Route 1 to explore the village. The side streets toward the harbor, lined with Colonial Revival and Victorian homes, invite quiet strolling. Be sure to visit the harborside park, which was designed by the celebrated landscape architects of Frederick Law Olmsted's firm. Or for a change of pace, the Edgecombe-Coles House has loaner bikes for guests; owner Terry Price, an avid cyclist, can suggest nice back-road routes, such as a ride into Rockport and a spin around its picturesque harbor.

Porch rockers await visitors at the Whitehall Inn.

For those with a horticultural bent, just south of town is Merryspring Nature Park — 66 acres dedicated to the preservation of Maine's flowers and shrubs. A series of intersecting paths traverses the grounds and makes for an hour's stroll; pick up a free map at the information kiosk near the entrance. Head south on Route 1, then turn right (west) on Conway Road; the preserve is one-third of a mile from the highway.

The real hiking begins just north of the lodgings at Camden Hills State Park, a 5,500-acre park capped by the region's most prominent hills and home to a well-marked network of trails linking peaks with ledges and vistas in and around the park.

Mount Battie's 800-foot summit can be reached by foot-path, but the auto road makes it the more crowded of the two peaks. Mount Megunticook separates the drivers from the hikers. Ledges on the southeast face, called Ocean Lookout (four-tenths of a mile below the wooded summit, which doesn't offer a view), can be reached via a 40-minute hike up a rocky one-mile trail from the auto road. From here you can look down at Penobscot Bay, the island of Vinalhaven, and the open ocean beyond.

Another perfect fall hike is to Maiden Cliffs, northwest of the state park. The cliffs rise dramatically above Megunticook Lake and provide exceptional views of the coastal interior area. Drive back to Camden, and head northwest on Route 52 for 2.9 miles. Look for the parking area on the right. Ascend the Maiden Cliff Trail for half a mile, then veer right on the Ridge Trail. After another third of a mile, head left on the Scenic Trail, which will take you for nearly a mile — past ledges with good views — to the top of Maiden Cliff. From here, pick up the Maiden Cliff Trail for a more direct descent to the parking area.

If the weather promises to hold and you can set up a shuttle with two cars, the region's best longish hike incorpo-rates all these trails in the Megunticook Traverse: Start by ascending Mount Battie, then follow the Tableland Trail to Megunticook. Descend the mountain's west side on the Ridge Trail to the Scenic Trail, then on to Maiden Cliff, and

ESSENTIALS

Whitehall Inn, 800-789-6565, 207-236-3391. 52 High St., Camden, ME 04843. Open Memorial Day weekend-Columbus Day weekend. 50 rooms. $75-$150, including breakfast; $110-$185, includ-ing breakfast and dinner. (www.whitehall-inn.com)

Edgecombe-Coles House, 800-528-2336, 207-236-2336. 64 High St., Camden, ME 04843. Open year-round. Six rooms. $140-$195, including breakfast and afternoon tea. (www.camdenbandb.com)

Merryspring Nature Park, 207-236-2239. Conway Road, Camden, ME. Open year-round daily dawn-dusk. Donation.

Camden Hills State Park, 207-236-3109. Rte. 1, Cam-den, ME 04843. Open May 15-October 15 for camping; year-round for day use. Camping $8-$16; day use $2, seniors older than 65 free, children 5-11 50¢, under 5 free. (www.state.me.us/doc/parks.htm)

finally down to Route 52. The whole traverse runs about 5.5 miles. Figure on four hours or so — more if the weather invites ledge lounging.

Gentle Ridges, Colorful Woods, and Picnics in the Litchfield Hills

THOSE WHO AREN'T entirely convinced that a hiking vacation suits their temperament might first consider stringing together a series of day hikes in Connecticut's Litchfield Hills. While the terrain doesn't present much of a challenge for veteran hikers seeking untrammeled, craggy peaks, it's hard to imagine a better place for a morning hike through a shady glen in search of songbirds, or for a lazy afternoon ramble through woodlands along a gentle ridge. By the end of a long weekend, you should know whether this kind of recreation leaves you enervated or energized.

Classic farms dot the landscape of the Litchfield Hills.

I'd suggest basing yourself at centrally located Lake Waramaug, just up the hill from New Preston. The lake, bordered with rolling hills, offers a pleasing sanctuary off the beaten path. The terrain is settled in that well-worn New England

courtesy Litchfield Hills Travel Council

kind of way — it's not wild, but neither are the homes along the shore stacked one upon the other. There's space, there's landscape, and there's a subtle sense of history.

For best value and down-home comfort, try the Hopkins Inn on a prominent bluff amid a cluster of other stately homes overlooking the lake. The inn, which first offered room and board to summer guests in 1847, has 11 simply and eclectically furnished guest rooms (best bet: number 17, an airy corner room with wonderful westerly lake vistas). Rooms are available with shared or private bath.

The inn has a lounge and a dining room, both of which have subtle touches of the European Alps; the restaurant specializes in Austrian meals. A trout tank hints (not very subtly) at the freshness of the fish; other entrées include filet mignon, lamb chops, and Viennese sweetbreads — food to fortify you for a day of walking. If the weather cooperates, eat on the terrace.

As for hiking, "it's one of my favorite topics," says Beth Schober. She runs the inn with her husband, Franz, who hails from Austria and is also the chef. She has a well-stocked library of local maps and hiking guides and gladly points hikers in the right direction.

If you arrive late in the day, ease into the right frame of mind with a walk along the lake road or through the adjoining 30-acre Hopkins Vineyard (the inn serves its wines). The lake road is posted to warn cars of pedestrians — a good sign, literally — and the road is narrow and winding enough that vehicles are hard-pressed to exceed 25 miles per hour.

My strategy for exploring the peaks and valleys of the Litchfield Hills goes like this: Arise and enjoy breakfast. Drive to a trailhead. Hike for an hour or two, looping back to the car. Head to a village to purchase a picnic lunch. Travel to another trailhead for a few hours' hike and picnic. Return to the inn for dinner. Sleep. Repeat.

A good place to start, says Beth, is about 20 minutes north of the inn, at Kent Falls State Park. "It's a very romantic place," she says. "Franz took me there when I was very young. I'll never forget it." Beyond a roadside rest area with an expanse of lawn and a herd of picnic tables, you'll see the base

LAKE WARAMAUG, BORDERED WITH ROLLING HILLS, OFFERS A PLEASING SANCTUARY OFF THE BEATEN PATH.

At the Federal-style Hopkins Inn, you'll enjoy great food and great views.

of an attractive cascade that tumbles 200 feet down a narrow valley cleft. A well-worn trail follows the falls to the top. There are good views of the cascades for a minimal investment of effort at this 295-acre park, located on the east side of Route 7, three miles north of Kent.

The village of Kent is a favored weekend hangout for celebrities and tycoons. You can pick up a sandwich on fresh-baked bread at the Stroble Baking Company; next door is the Kent Market for more prosaic supplies.

Across the Housatonic River from Kent, the Appalachian Trail descends from a ridge to follow the river. The lowland valley ramble makes a good hike of a few hours, particularly on days when high winds discourage treks to the ridgelines. To get to the trailhead, cross the river and turn right on Skiff Mountain Road. Follow for one mile, then bear right on River Road. Continue on this dirt road for about two miles until you arrive at a gate and parking area. The trail follows an abandoned town road through the river valley and past two red-pine plantations, one still alive but failing, the other a spooky forest of sun-bleached dead trees. Signs of long-ago habitation — a cellar hole here, stone walls there — pock the valley floor.

For more-challenging terrain, drive farther west on Route 341 to the Macedonia Brook State Park main entrance. Five major trails in the 2,300-acre park are color coded. The Macedonia Ridge Trail (Blue Trail), for instance, traverses a ridge that includes 1,350-foot Cobble Mountain and several other peaks. The views of the Catskills and the Taconics are excellent from the ridge. Park headquarters has free maps detailing the 15-plus miles of trails.

Return to the inn, and in the evening, leaf through their trail guides to track down other rambles for the following day. You've only begun to scratch the surface.

– Wayne Curtis

ESSENTIALS

The Hopkins Inn, 860-868-7295. 22 Hopkins Rd., New Preston, CT 06777. Open year-round. 11 rooms. $70-$85. Two-night minimum on weekends May-October and major holidays. ($$$) Restaurant open late March-January 1 daily for breakfast and dinner, Tuesday-Sunday for lunch.
(www.thehopkins inn.com)

Kent Brook Falls State Park, 860-927-3238. Rte. 7, North Kent, CT. Open year-round daily 8 A.M.-sunset. Parking fee May-October weekends and holidays: cars with Connecticut license plates $5, out-of-state plates $8.

Stroble Baking Company, 860-927-4073. 14 N. Main St., Kent, CT. ($) Open year-round daily 8-6.

Macedonia Brook State Park, 860-927-3238. Rte. 341, Kent, CT 06757. Open for day use year-round daily 8 A.M.-sunset; free. Camping mid-April to mid-September; 83 sites; $9-$13.

Every Which Way

BUT PAVEMENT

A S A TRAVEL EDITOR for *Yankee*, I am something of
a road warrior. Just this weekend I drove to Bar Harbor, Maine — five hours away — on Friday night and
made the return trip on Sunday. I enjoy driving New England's roadways, but in autumn, my favorite season, I try to
avoid my car like the plague. I just can't get a good, long look
at the leaves when I'm trying to navigate, and leaf-peeping
traffic can stress me out when I need to be somewhere
on time.

This year, I did my foliage viewing by water. I took an
afternoon cruise on Lake Champlain out of Burlington, Vermont, on a balmy Saturday afternoon during Columbus Day
weekend. Vermont's Green Mountains were more orange than
emerald, and the Adirondacks in New York were purple in the
light haze. I got to enjoy every inch of it with wind in my hair
to boot. The following day, I set out in a canoe on the peaceful
Lamoille River north of Stowe, Vermont, in Jeffersonville.
Lazy paddling was the perfect pace to enjoy the blue skies,
bright landscape, and farmland that drifted in and out of
view. When it was time to drive back home, I didn't mind
a bit.

In the spirit of leaving the pavement behind, here are
some of our favorite ways to see the foliage without driving
a car.

– *Carol Connare*

MAINE

Aroostook County Bike Trails, 888-216-2463 (Aroostook County Tourism). The crown of Maine is home to acres of potato fields — and rolling roads through pristine landscapes of the sort that have sprouted subdivisions elsewhere in New England. Bring your mountain bike and explore farm roads and a growing network of rail trails.

Grand Lake Outfitters, 207-796-5561. Grand Lake Stream. The area around the tiny outpost town of Grand Lake Stream in easternmost Maine is like a miniature Rangeley Lakes region — lots of deep lakes and old sporting camps tucked in the pines. Explore the big waters by canoe or sea kayak, with long-time residents Laura and Steve Schaefer. Trips run all summer and fall. Introductory tours from $25 per person; full-day tours $58.

Maine's Windjammers, 800-807-9463. Rockland, Rockport, and Camden. Maine's fleet of wondrously creaky windjammers offers visitors a way to experience the rugged coast the way the state is best seen: from the water looking inland. Excursions average around $110 per person per

night, including all meals. (www.sailmainecoast.com)

Rafting the Penobscot River, 800-723-8633, 207-824-3694. Millinocket. Outstanding views of Katahdin are just the icing on the cake during a daylong adventure on this turbulent river, complete with sudden drops, rocky gorges, and plenty of wildlife. Trips run mid-May to mid-September. Generally $85-$100 per person. (www.raftmaine.com)

NEW HAMPSHIRE

Mount Washington Sky Adventures, 888-353-2893, 603-466-5822. Rtes. 16 and 2, Gorham Airport. Grab your scarf and aviator cap for a skyline tour of the White Mountains in a vintage

Catch Maine's foliage from a windjammer.

three-seat Schweizer glider. $80-$120.

M/V *Mount Sunapee II,* 603-763-4030. Off Rte. 11, Sunapee Harbor. This port was once the destination for thousands of vacationers, ferried here by steamship from the railroad station in Newbury. Captain Dave Hargbol will tell you all about that plus much more on this 1½-hour narrated cruise. Mid-June to Labor Day ship sails daily 10 A.M., 2:30 P.M.; beginning mid-May, and in September and October, also weekends 2:30 P.M. $12, children 5-12 $7, under 5 free.

Monadnock Bicycle Touring, 603-827-3925. 797 Chesham Rd., Harrisville, NH 03450. For those who prefer two wheels to four, MBT's owners, Pat and Doug McCarthy, offer self-guided on- and off-road tours from picturesque village to picturesque village, even inn to inn. The company's home base, the Harrisville Squires' Inn, is a cheery one. It serves a breakfast hearty enough to

Canoeing is a great way to see fall color reflected in the water.

keep you pedaling all morning, and after a long day's bike tour, you can soak in the hot tub in the meditation garden and browse the fine arts and crafts in the inn's Hammersley Gallery and Studio. Customized two-day tours start at $50. Six rooms in the inn, each with private bath. $80-$90, including breakfast. Gallery and studio open Wednesday-Sunday 11-6.

North Star Canoes, 603-542-5802. Rte. 12A, Cornish. What better place to cruise down the river than on the placid expanse of the Connecticut River, between the rolling green hills of both New Hampshire and Vermont? Owners John and Linda Hammond will shuttle you upstream to a launch. The half- and full-day trips offer plenty of sights and include passage under the country's longest covered bridge. You can even make a night of it by camping at Wilgus State Park (802-674-5422). Trips late May to mid-October. Half day $12.50, children $5, under 5 free; full day $20, children $10, under 5 free. Prices include canoe rental, paddles, life jackets, and shuttle.

Sugar Shack Mountain Bike Park, 603-726-3867. Rte. 175,

Thornton, NH 03223. They call it mountain biking, but if your preference runs to rolling pasture, that's available, too. With more than 15 miles of trail on 240 acres to call your own, you'll find both gentle rides and technical terrain, all beginning at this working third-generation sugarhouse. Bike rentals and sales are available, and you can also camp here at primitive sites along the Pemigewasset River. Bike park open Saturday-Sunday 10-6. Trail pass full day $8, half day $6; camping $16.

Isles of Shoals Steamship Company, 800-441-4620, 603-431-5500. 315 Market St., Portsmouth. Nineteenth-century American Impressionist Childe Hassam found his muse on the isolated Isles of Shoals. Today you, too, can be inspired by one of the region's most informative boat tours. Choose from whale watches (five-hour deep-ocean expeditions), lighthouse cruises (see five lighthouses), a 2½-hour cruise around the historic isles and Portsmouth Harbor, or head to Star Island for an afternoon stopover. Wednesday mornings, you can go from Star Island to Appledore for a garden tour at the home of Hassam's former friend, poet Celia

Thaxter; call Shoals Marine Lab (607-255-3717) for arrangements. Cruises September 6-January 15 9-5. $16-$28. (www.islesofshoals.com)

Antique Speedboat Rides, 800-339-5257, 603-569-5257. Wolfeboro Trolley Company, 60 North Main St., Wolfeboro. John Hacker chimed in on the Roaring Twenties with his Gold Cup-winning race boats and a sleek line of runabouts. One of these Hacker-Craft, a 28-foot mahogany model named *Millie B,* is still making waves on Lake Winnipesaukee. Half-hour tours leave from the Wolfeboro town docks, weather permitting. July-August daily from 10 A.M.; only weekends spring and fall. $10, children 4-12 $5, under 4 free.

Attitash Bear Peak and Fields of Attitash, 603-374-2368. Rte. 302, Bartlett. One-stop shopping for a full day of family fun. Whether you prefer to ride a horse, a bike, a chairlift, an alpine slide, or a water slide, it's all here, surrounded by the spectacular setting of the White Mountains and the Saco River. Did we mention the driving range? Open mid-June to Labor Day daily 10-6; mid-May to mid-June and Labor Day-Columbus Day only

weekends 10-5. $21 value day-pass for unlimited use of slides and chairlift. (www.attitash.com)

VERMONT

Bike Shed Rentals, 802-928-3440. 1071 W. Shore Rd., Isle La Motte. Sure, you see a lot of people bicycling around Vermont ... problem is, a lot of those people are 17 years old and look like they live on granola bars and electrolyte drinks. For the rest of us, the solution is Isle La Motte, a mercifully flat, yet splendidly scenic, island at the northern end of Lake Champlain. Rent

courtesy Stowe Area Association

a road, mountain, or tandem bike (helmets, trailers, and maps available), and pedal serenely along the unspoiled waterfront, through pasture-land, and past the island's intriguing fossil reef formations. Open June, September,

and October only weekends 9-6, other days by appointment; July-August Thursday-Monday 9-6. $5 per hour, $15 per half day, $20 per day.

Craftsbury Outdoor Center, 800-729-7751, 802-586-2514. Lost Nation Rd., Craftsbury Common, VT 05827. Located on Hosmer Pond, just outside the postcard village of Craftsbury Common, the center offers cross-country skiing, mountain biking, canoeing, and even instruction in sculling ... in fact, Olympic sculling crews have trained here. Day use and equipment rental are available, but many guests stay overnight. Most

Vermont bikers enjoy climbing every mountain.

rooms share baths; there are also cottages available, however. The homestyle buffet meals are terrific, and the rates are extremely reasonable.

Open year-round. Rooms $118-$188; cottages with kitchenettes $195-$215; including breakfast, lunch, and dinner, also all sports facilities. (www.craftsbury.com)

Long Trail, 802-244-7037. Green Mountain Club, Rte. 100, Waterbury Center. Next to Lake Champlain and the Green Mountains themselves, the Long Trail is arguably Vermont's greatest outdoor asset. It runs some 270 miles from the Massachusetts line to the Canadian border and was designed — some say with exquisite cruelty — to take in just about every summit along the state's rugged spine. There are a variety of rustic accommodations, ranging from lean-tos to cabins with woodstoves, spaced a day's hike or less apart along the route; dozens of side trails make for interesting short excursions. The Green Mountain Club, which maintains the trail, has maps, guidebooks, and up-to-date reports on conditions. (www.greenmountainclub.org)

Smugglers' Notch Canoe Touring, 888-937-6266, 802-644-8321. Rte. 108, Jeffersonville. The Lamoille River meanders through some of northern Vermont's most scenic forest- and farmland,

and this is an ideal way to meander along with it. Three- to 12-mile trips, all on gentle stretches of river, including gourmet lunch tours. Canoes and kayaks available. Shuttles depart three times a day from Mannsview Inn, Jeffersonville. May-October daily. $50 for two people. (www.mannsview.com)

Reenactors aboard Lake Champlain Maritime Museum's gunboat Philadelphia II.

Vermont Fly Fishing School and Wilderness Trails, 800-235-3133, 802-295-7620. The Quechee Inn, Main St., Quechee. Signing up with a good instructor is the best way to penetrate the fly-fishing mystique; after that, it's all entomology 101 and a decent casting technique. If they aren't biting on the Ottauquechee or White rivers, Wilderness Trails rents out mountain bikes and arranges

courtesy Lake Champlain Maritime Museum

canoe and kayak excursions (offers fishing gear rentals, too). Trips May 1-October 31 daily by reservation; call about winter activities and prices.

Lake Champlain Maritime Museum, 802-475-2022. Basin Harbor Rd., Vergennes. Not just a museum but a major participant in headline-making underwater archaeology — a recent expedition located a vessel that sailed under Benedict Arnold's command. Vintage watercraft tell the story of military, commercial, and recreational navigation on Lake Champlain from sail through steam to motor vessels. A boat or two is usually under construction, and there's a working blacksmith shop. Board the full-size floating replica of the Revolutionary-era gunboat *Philadelphia II* for a taste of freshwater swashbuckling. Open early May to mid-October daily 10-5. $7, seniors over 55 $6, children 6-15 $3, under 6 free. (www.lcmm.org)

MASSACHUSETTS

Alert II, 508-992-1432. Pier 3/ Fisherman's Wharf, New Bedford. Operated by the Cuttyhunk Boat Lines, Inc., this 60-passenger, aluminum-hulled

ferry is the life and information line to the walkable, little-touristed island of Cuttyhunk. It's an hour's ride out through Buzzards Bay, and from Cuttyhunk's dock it's an easy walk to the observation platform overlooking the village, the harbor, and the small sandy beach on Copicut Neck. Bring a picnic. Runs Columbus Day to mid-June only Tuesday and Friday; mid-June to September daily. Day trip $17, children 1-11 $12. (www.cuttyhunk.com)

Essex River Basin Adventures, 800-529-2504, 978-768-3722. Essex Shipbuilding Museum Shipyard, Rte. 133, Essex. The Essex River Basin is protected and island-spotted, a perfect paddle for novice kayakers or beauty lovers. ERBA's three-hour guided tours frequently include a swim at Crane's

Beach or a walk on Hog Island. Open April-October. $45; two-hour sunset paddles $35. (www.erba.com)

Leaf peepers saddle up for prime foliage viewing.

Norwottuck Rail Trail, 413-586-8706 ext. 12. Elwell Recreation Area, Damon Rd., Northampton. Formerly a Boston & Maine Railroad right-of-way, this ten-mile paved bike path connects the college towns of Northampton and Amherst. It crosses the Connecticut River on a former rail bridge and threads Hadley's open farmland. Inquire about rental bikes. (www.state.ma.us/dem/parks/nwrt.htm)

Schooner *Thomas E. Lannon,* 978-281-6634. Seven Seas Wharf at the Gloucester *(continued on page 195)*

courtesy Vermont Tourism and Marketing

Foliage in Flight

My jumpmaster, Dave Strickland, told me that on a perfectly clear day you can see the foliage from Mount Snow, Vermont, to Block Island, Rhode Island, with the peaks of Mount Monadnock, Mount Greylock, the Mount Tom Range, the Catskills, and the Taconics aflame. I'd come to Airborne Adventures not just

altitude. But it didn't compare to having no barrier between the wind and me while under a billowing parachute. I had the widest smile ever on the entire way down, and for hours afterward. I wasn't sure if this was due to gravity's pull or the sheer joy of flying.

I was tethered to Dave, who has been skydiving for more

loop, and we turned to the right. Then I pulled the cord on the left side of the canopy, and we spun in the other direction so I could get a 360-degree view of the Pioneer Valley. Dave pointed out a farm with a large sugar maple dressed in yellow on the front lawn. He said it is always the first tree to turn in this area.

Below, brilliant yellow-and-orange maples lined South Hatfield's town center. A white church steeple peeked out above the treetops. I thought to myself, *This is what the birds see every autumn.*

We landed dead center on the target mark. The parachute fluttered down around me like elegant silk wings. In a week the leaves would be floating down, calling to be raked up before winter. In the meantime, I could say I had seen this year's foliage — from above.

Airborne Adventures, 800-444-5867, 413-586-1889. Northampton Airport, Old Ferry Rd., Northampton, Massachusetts. Tandem freefall skydive $195. (www.javanet.com/~skydive)

— Katrina Yeager

Marshall Elliott

Katrina Yeager gives the thumbs-up for a successful airborne adventure.

for the color, but also for the thrill of seeing the foliage from 10,500 feet.

The view from the plane was nice as we climbed to

than 25 years. We fell almost 6,000 feet in one minute. Then the parachute opened. My harness supported me as if I were sitting in a swing, and my body formed a Y, with my arms extended up and out holding the canopy control loops. I pulled down on one

Katrina Yeager

(continued from page 193) House Restaurant, Rogers St. (Rte. 127), Gloucester. Coast around Gloucester harbor on the 65-foot, two-masted schooner that Captain Tom Ellis helped build a few years ago to replicate the vessel that his grandfather (Thomas E. Lannon) fished on in the first decades of this century. Inquire about lobsterbake, music, and storytelling cruises. Two-hour sails $29, seniors $25, children 16 and under $20. (www.schooner.org)

Worthington Hot-Air Ballooning, 413-238-5514. Buffington Hill Rd., Worthington. Paul Sena will pick passengers up almost anywhere in the Berkshires — but he prefers to fly from Worthington and neighboring Cummington — to take them over the hills and down into

Get a bird's-eye view of foliage from a hot-air balloon.

the Connecticut River Valley. Request the multicolored "Thunderbuster" balloon: yellow, red, and orange on one side and blue and purple on the other. Champagne flights year-round. One-hour champagne flight $200 per person.

CONNECTICUT

Hartford's Rivers. Get to know the rivers that run through (and around and under) this city. Ride the Farmington River rapids in an inner tube, canoe the Farmington, or spookiest of all, take a canoe tour of Hartford's subterranean tunnels, all that remain of the "lost" Park River. **Farmington River Tubing,** 860-739-0791. Satan's Kingdom Recreation Area, Rte. 44, New Hartford.

Open Memorial Day weekend-Labor Day weekend daily 10-5. $12. **Huck Finn Adventures,** 860-693-0385. Various launch sites between Avon and Simsbury. Choose three-, five-, or nine-mile canoe or kayak trips on the Farmington River (April-November), or sign up for a three-hour guided tour in the underground Hartford tunnels (May-October). Call for canoe prices and launch areas.

Lee's Riding Stable, 860-567-0785. East Litchfield Rd., off Rte. 118. Trail riding on Lee's gentle horses through these hills is especially lovely during fall foliage. Ponies are available even for pint-size cowboys. Open year-round; call for an appointment. $25 per person per hour.

Mystic Seaport: The Museum of America and the Sea, 888-973-2767.

Mystic Seaport re-creates a 19th-century seafaring village.

Charles W. Morgan, the square-rigger *Joseph Conrad,* and the fishing schooner *L. A. Dunton.* Open summer daily 9-5, grounds open until 6. $16, seniors $15, children 6-12 $8. (www.mysticseaport.org)

***Sea Mist* Thimble Island Cruises,** 203-488-8905. Town dock, Stony Creek. Open June-Labor Day Wednesday-Monday, trips hourly 10-4. $8, seniors $7, children under 12 $4.

75 Greenmanville Ave., Mystic. This re-created 19th-century seafaring village is a living, breathing history lesson. Walk through the shops, homes, schoolhouse, and meetinghouse; watch guides demonstrate Colonial crafts; hear them tell their stories and sing their songs. Then check out the only remaining 19th-century whaler, the

SECTION IV:

For Poets and Painters

The Color Red

RED ENTERS our surroundings in a million ways, but wherever, however it occurs, it is never quite prosaic, never entirely innocuous, never completely without its pointed associations. All things that are truly red are exciting and cause excitement: cardinals, fire engines, certain roses, ripe tomatoes, and (by no coincidence at all) the flags of many, many states and nations. You don't ignore these things. Consider a village street where each house has a wash of laundry drying on the line. You'll pass down that street a hundred times and hardly notice where you are. But if you pass on a day when one line has a suit of red long underwear flapping in the breeze, your heart will be lifted up.

I think we are alert to red because in nature it's not that common a color, at least not in its most powerful, fire-engine manifestation. Understand, now, that the color I am celebrating is no equivocal, hesitant red. This is no ambitious pink, no overreaching orange, but scarlet — a true, unmixed red. In my neighborhood it is mainly the property of two songbirds, neither of them plentiful; two wildflowers (the scarlet bergamot and one of the lobelias); certain varieties of apple, well ripened; and — most abundantly — the dying leaves of hardwood trees. In this last guise, of course, the color has become famous, rising to the status of a regional institution. Every fall, people come to this little corner of the country from all over the world to see leaves, red and otherwise.

Even in composing the vast and complex spectacle of the autumn leaves, however, nature uses true red sparingly. The principal color maker in a Vermont valley is the sugar maple, and of these trees a hundred will turn lemon yellow and two hundred will turn some shade of orange for every one that turns scarlet. The leaves of blueberry bushes reliably turn an honest red (at least mine do) and so do the leaves and fruits of the sumac; but in the symphony of the fall colors these are soft and subtle tones. The colors that sell the tickets and fill the galleries are the oranges and yellows.

Nevertheless, if red is a color that autumn is apt to withhold, still it has its role there, an essential role — indeed an inevitable role, it seems to me, if you consider the meaning of red, its ring of warning. For I have, over many years, noticed how the very first leaves to turn, often before fall has properly arrived, are likely to turn red.

In the wooded fencerow near where I attempt to grow vegetables is a tree that turns early. It's not at all a big tree: 30 feet tall, no thicker than your leg. I think it's a swamp maple. It grows in a clump with three other trees of like kind and size and is remarkable in no way until around the middle of the last week in August. Each year at that same time the leaves of this little tree turn precisely that hard scarlet I have tried here to praise, the red of rubies. The tree seems to turn in a single night. In the morning I spot it at once. All around it, near at  hand and far off, the woods hold their midsummer green untroubled. They will hold it for another three weeks, maybe longer. Against their cool uniformity this sudden red is like a jar of paint dashed across a billiard table. It leaps out from the quiet morning like a shout, like a bugle note.

What warning could be more seasonable? By the time that little tree turns, we've all gotten pretty slack. We need to hear its universal admonition. The afternoons won't always last forever. Your ice cream won't always melt in the dish. The bees won't always buzz among the flowers. Look out — something's coming, that red slash says. You better get ready.

– *Castle Freeman Jr.*

Geese-Go-South
MOON

ARLY IN OCTOBER, in Geese-Go-South Moon, leaves rain down with a muffled sideslipping sound. Dust motes spin in sunlight like flour sifting in puffs onto the beginnings of batter. For the horses, this season is heavenly. We haven't had a killing frost yet. All our fields are open to them, and they wander like sleepwalkers from one area to another, grazing intermittently, sometimes standing for long, thoughtful moments silhouetted against the backdrop of forest or granite outcropping.

This is the season when tails at last become superfluous. The biting insects have fled. Except for small ectoplasms of gnats that still hover in the quiet air, all is benign and salving in the ether. Gone the vicious little trapezoidal deerflies that draw blood from animal and human. Vanished, too, the bot- and horseflies. The ubiquitous blackflies, that penance of the North Country, never quite disappear, but they are greatly diminished. And this summer's long tenure of mosquitoes appears to be over.

We are in the briefest and most beautiful moment of stasis. Along the perimeter of the pastures, fall-flowering asters, tiny blue florets with yellow centers, flourish. A few late blackberries go on ripening, pursued by the greedy broodmare, who rolls back her lips in order to nip them off, one or two at a time, without getting pricked by the thorns. Jerusalem artichokes, harbingers of frost, are in bud and threaten to open in today's sunlight. Toads have begun retreating to the woods after a long and profitable summer, deprived of their prey now in the vegetable garden. Mushrooms appear everywhere — two brain puffballs in the dressage ring, little pear-shaped lycoperdons dotting the pine duff like misplaced miniature golf balls, smoky hygrophorus clustering in the dark corners of the pine grove. Ripe honey mushrooms cluster at the bases of decaying oaks. Sometimes, traversing the woods on horseback, we spot a full bloom of oyster mushrooms swelling on the trunk of a dying tree.

Every day is more precious than the preceding. Daylight diminishes as the foliage flames with color. Dusk comes earlier in sharper air. The horses' winter coats thicken, blurring their summer-sleek outlines. Everything proclaims: We are reluctant. We are ready.

– Maxine Kumin

Once Upon a Time,

IN A FAR-OFF KINGDOM . . .

Denise Johnson

SOME YEARS AGO, I was checking into a hotel in downtown Detroit. It was October, and one of the young women at the desk, noticing my New Hampshire address, asked if the leaves had turned yet. I said they had and joked about being away from home at the worst possible time. Another young woman, overhearing us, asked what we meant by "the leaves turning."

"The leaves turning colors," said her co-worker.

"Colors?" She looked at us warily.

We became guarded as well. Could she truly not know? "You know, the autumn leaves turn different colors," I said.

"Like, *blue?*" she said in a tone heavy with sarcasm.

How do you explain fall color to one who's never seen it?

"Every year, the green leaves turn red, orange, yellow, brown, and sometimes even a kind of mottled polka-dot pattern . . ." I began, before trailing off when I saw the expression on her face. Of *course* she thought I was putting her on.

So then I tried the scientific approach. "Actually, it has to do with chemistry. The leaves contain these substances called anthocyanins," I started and watched her eyes glaze over.

Here's what I should have said: There is a little girl. She wears a red beret and a blue jumper. She comes every fall and paints each leaf a new color. They're very beautiful, but the paint makes the leaves heavier, so they fall on the ground, and the trees have to grow new ones in the spring.

Then we'd have understood each other. The language of myth, of fairy tales, of bedtime stories, is the best way — maybe the only way — to describe the indescribable.

– Tim Clark

Foliage Futures

MY MOTHER WAS born in the month of October, a fiery month. According to astrologers, she was a Scorpio: passionate, strong-willed, secretive, and with a tendency to enslave. The stock market crashed in the month of October. It happened on my mother's 13th birthday, an unlucky day. She says it was the quietest birthday she ever had. She remembers the silence at the dinner table and the ticking of the hallway clock. The stock market has fallen again and again in October, causing financial analysts to wonder why. What is there about the month of October that brings the markets down?

All I can think of is our world of green, green leaves turning and falling, not a crash but a gentle emptying of the pockets of summer.

October is my favorite month. It is the apocalypse of our year, the crescendo of all the heat and creativity of the summer months. The frost has come and brought rest to the weary gardener, but there is still the pageant ahead, the great color show we wait for all year. I am trying to think of a natural event so celebrated as the foliage, and I can't think of one. Here in New England it becomes the focus of our days. We talk about "peak," and the television weathermen give us percentages: When the color in the forests comes into its absolute fullness, it is 100 percent. But it is the approach we anticipate: In Burlington the foliage can be assessed at 75 percent while we remain at 35 percent, which means we have a lot more in store for us. And it is a movable feast: When our foliage deserts us, we can journey south and find more. Like starry-eyed lovers, we seem to forget the good times that have come before. We love the one we're with: "I don't remember a year when it was this good, do you?"

But of course, like the market, there are risks. Heavy rain can bring the leaves off the trees before their time. High winds can do that, too. And all the folks who have traveled so far to see this annual show return home to report that this business of the foliage is not all it's cracked up to be.

Oh, but it is! The thing is that you have to be here for the entire performance. Taking in a scene or two is just that: incomplete. A quote out of context. Living here, inside the drama, we watch the spectrum turn, a wide prism of the natural world that revolves at the pace of the turning of the earth. That tree that was tinted red yesterday is more intense today and then, gradually, like the flame turned up on a lamp, it's brilliant, unimaginably red.

If we speculate in foliage futures, we will lose. Our role is to stand back and observe. If the show disappoints, there is always next year. And, in the meantime, a small corner of foliage paradise can always be found, in a particular tree that outdoes all the rest or a small canvas of bittersweet and woodbine where the color outranks the disappointing browns that surround it.

It was predictable that my mother loved the fall. She looked on it as an opera performed just for her, and her exclamations of pleasure over a particularly fiery tree very nearly caused accidents. "Oh!" she would gasp as we drove along a back road, and my startled father would hastily apply his brakes, thinking she was trying to alert him to our imminent demise. But, no, it was only an oncoming tree in stunning hue.

As for my mother and the stock market and the shades of autumn, I think that all three were born under the sign of Scorpio: passionate, strong-willed, secretive, and with a tendency to enslave. Pretty dicey characteristics. Just the same, I'll put my money on October any day.

– Edie Clark

"And Remember TO LOOK UP AT the Hills"

S TARR KING, the admired 19th-century travel writer, thus opens his soliloquy on October in New England: "Nature seems to be carelessly running her hand over the notes, touching and indicating the great chords, before breaking into the full pomp of the autumn symphony." Warming to his theme, if not his metaphor, Mr. King asks, "Whence have these hues been distilled that surpass the richness of the Orient and the flames that are reflected in the Amazon? Whence has overflowed upon the prosaic air of New England this luxurious sweetness through which the light transudes upon a pageant such as no poet has ascribed to the hillsides of Arcadia? How near to us are the fountains of miracle! How close the processes and magic of the Infinite art!"

He meant the place where I live. My early view was simpler: Winter was white, spring was light green, summer was dark green, and fall was red. This made sense: It was a large example of my father's explanation of how the white fur of an ermine comes out from under the brown of a weasel; it was the same animal, adjusted for the season.

Later I'd hear the headmaster of the school where my father taught. The students gathered at 7:00 every evening, and as the headmaster ended some of the October meetings, he'd say, "And remember to look up at the hills." Most of the students came from other parts of the country, and that was when it came home to me that autumn in New England is different from autumn in other places.

Forty years farther on, I realized that those of us who live here don't always look up at the hills in the way the headmaster meant; we see the leaves change color, but it's just what happens in the fall, and we're more apt to talk about how it was rainy and foggy all through the week of October 12 and how the people on the tour buses from Texas still pointed their camcorders into the damp gray void.

Then, last October, I was walking up the long meadow path that leads to my cabin. It was full dark, and I was making my way by foot memory, when suddenly I was aware of a sort of lamp ahead of me, a large red glow. It was the color that took me by surprise, because another of the things that we see without really seeing is the monochrome of night. Our eyes require a certain level of illumination to register color, and as the light fades in the evening, the world goes to black and white. But now it was dark, and I was seeing a red maple tree in my meadow.

That's how bright the color was last October. The sun was many hours gone, but the day that went with it over the horizon had turned the leaves of my maple so brilliantly red that the tiny glow of the stars and the gibbous moon were enough to rekindle the color in my eyes, and I saw a midnight torch beside the path where none had been before. How near to us are the fountains of miracle. How close the processes and magic of the Infinite art.

– Nicolas Howe

Down-Leaf Time

SOMETIME ON the chilly end of the fall, say a week or so either side of Halloween, a dry, pensive little segment of the year interposes itself between autumn and winter, a brown patch the color of a fox: Down-Leaf Time. It's the period when all the leaves that are going to fall have fallen but before they have disappeared. In that stretch of time — a week or two, not more — the country is visited with a flood, a tidal wave of dead leaves.

Not along the highways, where trees are few, but beside the lesser roads and lanes, and in the woods, the fallen leaves lie deep. They blanket the ground. They advance upon the countryside irresistibly, like high water. The leaves fill the hollows, drift knee-deep against the stone walls, overflow the roadside ditches. They heap up behind stumps and fallen trees, then bury them. With a dry rustle they mount higher. The wind blows the leaves in dry brown shoals over the land. For a few days, the lanes that run through the woods become rivers of leaves.

In this interval that belongs to the fallen leaves, leaves by ones and twos get into odd places, like mice or lost sparrows. Leaves are found in the parlor; perhaps they blew down the chimney. They fly in the windows on a warm afternoon. They fill the corners of the woodshed and float on the coffee left in cups on the porch.

Down-Leaf Time has its own sights and sounds. There is a hard new light in the woods when the leaves are gone, like the unexpected light that comes into a house whose roof has been blown off. The down leaves also have a voice. Stirred by the wind or by your passage through them, they protest with a shuffling rattle. On a damp day, especially, the fallen leaves fill the air with a peculiar smell, not unpleasant, a little like a spice you seldom have a use for: saffron or cardamom.

The brown floor of the woods, inundated with down leaves, lies beneath the gray and white of the bare trees above and gives the wooded hillsides seen from a distance the dun color of a landscape on which snow will soon be falling. Down-Leaf Time is a transition, in part. It takes the year into winter, but it is also a season by itself, a season in miniature.

What is a season, after all? Except in the strictest calendrical sense, in which they are quarters of the year bound by the fixed dates of the equinoxes and solstices, the seasons would seem to be variable and subject to interpretation. Off the calendar, then, a season is a stretch of time with a beginning and an end, both indistinct, that has its characteristic events and tasks and that has very often something to do with vegetation. So we have lilac time, maple-sugar time, apple-blossom time, Indian summer, mud time — not true seasons on the calendar, but seasons nonetheless, known to all and calling up familiar responses that we may hardly be aware of.

Down-Leaf Time is that kind of little season. You won't see it begin. The bright autumn leaves start to fall heavily — when? — sometime after Columbus Day. The hard frosts arrive. Wild geese in their clamorous echelons pass overhead all day long — and then do not. The World Series comes and goes, likewise Election Day. Then Down-Leaf Time is over. You won't see it end. The back roads are no longer full of leaves, the lawns no longer covered with leaves, the woods no longer flooded with leaves.

Where do they go? The tale of Down-Leaf Time is quickly told, but what happens to the leaves? They don't go back where they came from, like the floodwaters they resemble. They can't all be burned, or raked, or stuffed into those clever orange bags made to look like enormous pumpkins. They blow into the woods, and there they darken. The cold rains fall on them, and they darken more. Then the snow covers them over for good, and they are gone for another year. Down-Leaf Time is not a beautiful season. Certainly it's not a famous one. It has neither press nor poet, but still it has its friends.

– *Castle Freeman Jr.*

SECTION V:
Fall Fun

Meet Me AT THE *Fair*

A T THE FIRST SIGN of fall we anticipate the best of the agricultural fairs and harvest festivals. This is the season of giant pumpkins, scarecrow contests, cider pressing, tractor pulls, 4-H livestock exhibits, candied apples, and many other fun family activities. We don't have room for a comprehensive list, but here are some of our favorites.

MAINE

Windsor Fair, 207-549-7121. Fairgrounds, Rte. 32, Windsor. Starts on a Sunday, always ends on Labor Day Monday, runs for a total of nine days in late August/early September; 8 A.M.-midnight. $5, seniors on Thursday and children under 16 free. (www.windsorfair.com)

Oxford County Fair, 207-743-6723. Fairgrounds off Rte. 26, Oxford. Second Wednesday after Labor Day through Saturday for a total of four days in September; 9 A.M.-10 P.M., midway opens noon. $5, seniors on Thursday $3, children under 3 free.

Franklin County Fair, 207-778-4215 or 207-778-2684 (after 6 P.M. only). Farmington Fairgrounds, High St., Farmington. Third full week in September; weekdays 9-9, weekends 9 A.M-11 P.M. $5, children 8-11 $2, under 8 free.

Common Ground Fair, 207-568-4142. Crosby Brook Rd., Unity. Third weekend after Labor Day for a total of three days in September; Friday and Saturday 9-7, Sunday 9-5. $6, seniors and children $2. (www.mofga.org)

*T*HIS IS THE SEASON OF GIANT PUMPKINS.

Fryeburg Fair, 207-935-3268. Fairgrounds, Rte. 5 north of Fryeburg. Sunday through Sunday for a total of eight days, always includes the first Wednesday in October; 7 A.M.-9 P.M. Friday-Sunday $5, Monday-Thursday $4, seniors on Tuesday free. (www.fryeburgfair.com)

Annual Blue Hill Fair, 207-374-3701. Mountain Park, Rte. 172, Blue Hill. Labor Day weekend in September; Thursday 4 P.M.-close, Saturday-Monday 8 A.M.-close. $6, children 12 and under free.

Annual Litchfield Fair, 207-683-2487. Fairgrounds, Plains Rd., Litchfield. Weekend after Labor Day for a total of three days; Friday-Saturday 7 A.M.-11 P.M., Sunday 7 A.M.-8 P.M. $4, senior citizens and students ages 12-18 $2, children under 12 free.

NEW HAMPSHIRE

Hopkinton State Fair, 603-746-4191. Fairgrounds, 392 Kearsage Ave., Contoocook. Ends Labor Day, runs for a total of five days in September; 8 A.M.-11 P.M. $8, seniors $7, children 6-12 $5; parking $3 per car. (www.hsfair.org)

Rochester Fair, 603-332-6585. 72 Lafayette St., Rochester. Starts second Friday after Labor Day for a total of nine days in September; daily 10-10. $6, seniors $5, children under 10 free; parking $2. (www.rochesterfair.com)

Deerfield Fair, 603-463-7421. Fairgrounds, Rte. 43, Deerfield. Starts 24 days after Labor Day for a total of four days in September/early October; Thursday-Saturday 8 A.M.-10 P.M., Sunday 8-7. $6, seniors $4, children 12 and under free. (www.deerfieldfair.com)

Harvest Day at Canterbury Shaker Village, 603-783-9511. Shaker Rd., Canterbury. First Saturday in October, except when it falls on Columbus Day weekend; 10-5. $10, children 6-15 $5. (www.shakers.org)

Sandwich Fair, 603-284-7062. Rtes. 109 and 113, Squam Lakes Rd., Center Sandwich. Columbus Day weekend in October; 8 A.M.-dusk. $7, seniors $4, children 8-12 $3, under 8 free.

VERMONT

Annual Orleans County Fair, 802-525-3555 or 802-525-6210. Orleans County Fairgrounds, Roaring Brook Pk., Barton. Third weekend in August; 8 A.M.-10 P.M. General admission $6.

Bondville Fair, 802-297-1882. Rte. 30, Bondville. Fourth weekend in August; Friday noon-10, Saturday 10-10, Sunday 10-5. $3, children 12 and under free.

Annual Champlain Valley Fair, 802-878-5545. Champlain Valley Fairgrounds, Rte. 15, Essex Junction. Ends Labor Day, runs for a total of ten days in late August/early September; 9 A.M.-midnight, concessions 10-10. $7, children 4-12 $3, under 4 free; parking $2. (www.cvfair.com)

Vermont State Fair, 802-775-5200. Fairgrounds, Rte. 7, Rutland. Starts the Friday of Labor Day weekend and runs for a total of ten days in September; 8 A.M.-midnight. $7.

World's Fair, 802-889-5555. Fairgrounds, Rte. 110, Tunbridge. Second weekend after Labor Day for a total of four days in September; Thursday 8 A.M.-11 P.M., Friday and Saturday 8 A.M.-midnight, Sunday 8-8. $3-$8, children 12 and under free; parking $2. (www.tunbridgefair.com)

Fairbanks Festival Weekend, 802-748-2372. Fairbanks Museum and Planetarium, Main St., St. Johnsbury. Next to

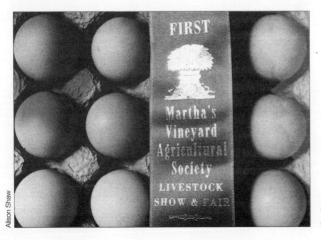

Award-winning eggs on Martha's Vineyard.

last full weekend in September; Saturday 10-4, Sunday 11-4.
$1. (www.fairbanksmuseum.org)

MASSACHUSETTS

**Martha's Vineyard Agricultural Society Livestock Show
and Fair,** 508-693-4343. West Tisbury. Third weekend in
August; 9 A.M.-11 P.M. $6, seniors $5, children $4.

Cummington Fair, 413-238-7724. Fairgrounds Rd., Cummington. Fourth weekend in August; Thursday-Friday 4-
midnight, Saturday 8:30 A.M.-midnight, Sunday 8:30 A.M.-
11 P.M. $6, children 10-16 $3, under 10 free. (www.mafa.org)

Franklin County Agricultural Fair, 413-774-4282. Wisdom
Way, Greenfield. First Thursday after Labor Day, through
Sunday, for a total of four days in September. $6, seniors $3,
children 9-17 $4, under 9 free. (www.fcas.com)

The Big E, 413-737-2443. 1305 Memorial Ave., West Springfield. Starts second Friday after Labor Day, runs for 17 days in
September; 8 A.M.-10 P.M. $11, children 6-12 $7, two-day pass
$17. (www.thebige.com)

Early Nineteenth Century Agricultural Fair, 800-SEE-1830
or 508-347-3362, ext. 325. Rte. 20, Old Sturbridge Village. Last
weekend in September; 9-5. $18, seniors $17, children $9,
under 6 free. (www.osv.org)

Topsfield Fair, 978-887-5000. Rte. 1, Topsfield. Ten days in October, closing on Columbus Day; 10-10. Weekends and holidays $9, weekdays $8. (www.topsfieldfair.org)

Annual Bolton Fair, 978-779-6253. Bolton Fairgrounds, Main St., exit 27 off I-495, Bolton. Last full weekend in September; 9-6. $6, children $1; parking $2. (www.boltonfair.org)

CONNECTICUT

Brooklyn Fair, 860-779-0012. Brooklyn Fairgrounds, ½ mile south of jct. rtes. 169 and 6, Brooklyn. Weekend before Labor Day for a total of four days in late August or early September; Thursday noon-11, Friday-Sunday 10 A.M.-11 P.M. $5, children under 12 free. (www.brooklynfair.org)

Woodstock Fair, 860-928-3246. Jct. rtes. 169 and 171, South Woodstock. Labor Day weekend for a total of four days in September; Friday-Sunday 9-9, Monday 9-8. $8, seniors $7 Saturday-Sunday only, children 12 and under free. (www.woodstockfair.com)

Goshen Fair, 860-491-3655. Fairgrounds, Rte. 63 south of town center, Goshen. Labor Day weekend for a total of three days in September; Saturday-Monday 8 A.M.-dusk. $6, seniors $4.50 Saturday only, children under 12 free.

Norwalk Seaport Association's Oyster Festival, 888-701-7785 or 203-838-9444. Veterans Memorial Park, East Norwalk. First weekend after Labor Day in September; Friday 5-11, Saturday 10 A.M.-11 P.M., Sunday 10-9. $7, seniors $5, children 6-12 $3, under 6 free. (www.seaport.org)

Pumpkin Festival, 203-925-4981. French Memorial Park, jct. rtes. 8 and 67, Seymour. Third Sunday in September; 10-5. Free. Shuttle-bus service available from free parking areas at Chatfield School and Silvermine Industrial Park.

Durham Fair, 860-349-9495. Fairgrounds, jct. rtes. 68, 17, and 79, Durham. Last full weekend in September; Friday-Saturday 9 A.M.-11 P.M., Sunday 9-7. $8, seniors $6, children under 12 free; three-day pass $20. (www.durhamfair.com)

Berlin Fair, 860-828-3935. Fairgrounds, Beckley Rd. off Rte. 372, East Berlin. First weekend in October; Friday 11-10:30, Saturday 9 A.M.-10:30 P.M., Sunday 10-6:30. $6, seniors $2, under 12 free.

Annual Apple Harvest Festival, 860-628-8036. Town green, Southington. Last weekend in September and first two weekends in October. Free.

Annual Hebron Harvest Fair, 860-228-9403. Lion's Park, Rte. 85, Hebron. Thursday-Sunday after Labor Day in September; Thursday 6-10 P.M., Friday noon-11, Saturday 9 A.M.-11 P.M., Sunday 9 A.M.-10 P.M. Thursday-Friday $5, Saturday-Sunday $6; seniors $3, children 12 and under free; parking $2 per car.

Annual North Haven Fair, 203-239-2668 or 203-239-3700. Washington Ave. (Rte. 5), North Haven. Thursday-Sunday after Labor Day in September; Thursday 5-11 P.M., Friday 3-11 P.M., Saturday 9 A.M.-11 P.M., Sunday 10-8; $7, children under 12 free when accompanied by an adult. (www.northhaven-fair.com)

RHODE ISLAND

Annual Hopkinton Colonial Crafts Festival, 401-377-7795. Crandall Field, Rte. 3, Ashaway. Third weekend in September; 10-4. Free.

Oktoberfest, 800-976-5122 or 401-845-9123. Newport Yachting Center, 4 Commercial Wharf, Newport. Columbus Day weekend for a total of three days; Saturday noon-10, Sunday noon-8, Monday noon-6. $3. (www.gonewport.com)

Harvest Fair, 401-846-2577. Norman Bird Sanctuary, 583 Third Beach Rd., Middletown. First full weekend in October; Saturday-Sunday 10-5. $4, children $1. (www.normanbird sanctuary.org)

More Fall Fun!

MAINE

Annual Septemberfest. *This weeklong festival always starts on Labor Day Monday and ends on the following Sunday.* It features seminars on fishing first aid, wilderness training, outdoor taxidermists' organizations, and craftspeople making snowshoes and moccasins. Saturday events include fly-fishing, face painting, pony rides, and seminars on wilderness first aid for children. Road race held on

Children's muster at Norlands Living History Center.

Sunday. Monday-Saturday 9-9, Sunday 10-6; Free. Kittery Trading Post, Rte. 1, Kittery. 888-587-6246. (www.kitterytradingpost.com)

Eastport Salmon Festival. *Always held the Sunday after Labor Day.* A ticket includes a seaside meal, a boat ride out to salmon pens, and a bagpipe serenade. Back on dry land, grab a plate piled high with fresh Maine spuds, corn on the cob, and salmon grilled to perfection. Crafts vendors, sushi chefs, and sea farmers show and tell their secrets. Dinner 11-3; other events all

day; $10. Peavey Memorial Library lawn, Water St., Eastport. 207-853-4644.

Norlands Autumn Celebration & Civil War Reenactment. *Always the fourth weekend (Saturday-Sunday) in September.* This festival combines the celebration of the rites of autumn with an exploration of the area's Civil War history. Amid rumbling hay- and wagon rides, the hooting of woodsmen's team competitions, fragrant cider pressing, and the clatter of country meals, you can learn more about the Civil War by speaking with living history interpreters, enjoying era-appropriate fashion shows,

and observing battle scenarios. Saturday 10-8, Sunday 10-4. $2, ages 10 and under $1. Norlands Living History Center, Norlands Rd. off Rte. 108, Livermore. 207-897-4366. (www.norlands.org)

Kraut's Ready! *Every year in mid-September, locals keep their eye out for a one-inch ad in area newspapers announcing, "Kraut's ready!"* It's the signal that Morse's crunchy, perfectly tart sauerkraut is set to eat. While buying your supply ($2.15 a pound), try it fresh out of the barrel, heaped on a hot dog. These days the company store is open September through mid-May, and after nearly 80 years, the shelves hold a new taste sensation — mouthwatering Black Dog Salsa. Monday-Friday 8-4, Saturday 10-4 (hot dogs 10-2). Kraut can be shipped late September-late April. Morse's Sauerkraut, Rte. 220, Washington Rd., Waldoboro. 207-832-5569.

Annual Fall Festival Arts and Crafts Show. *Always the Saturday and Sunday preceding Columbus Day.* Overlooking Camden Harbor, this show brings together approximately 85 selected artists and craftspeople from Maine, New England, and the East Coast to show and sell their work.

Saturday 9-5, Sunday 10-4. Free. Camden Amphitheater, Harbor Park, Camden. 207-236-4404.

NEW HAMPSHIRE

Dublin Crafts Fair. *Always the second Saturday in September.* Eighty craftspeople offer a variety of fine hand-crafted items for sale. Refreshments are for sale all day, and there is plenty of parking nearby. 10-3:30. Free. Townsend Field, Rte. 101, Dublin. 603-563-8111.

Grand Old Brewers Festival. *Usually the Saturday and Sunday of Columbus Day weekend.* In the 1880s, Frank Jones was the largest producer of ale in the world: 500 workers turned out 250,000 barrels of golden suds a year from his Portsmouth brewery. Jones threw an annual picnic to boost morale, and Strawbery Banke Museum has adopted — and adapted — his idea. Old-style games of keg rolling and tug-of-war are played on the lawn beside a microbrew tent, featuring the best modern-day recipes from around New England. Also on display are early brewing artifacts and state-of-the-art home-brew systems. There's also live

entertainment, a children's tent, home-brewing demonstrations, and Victorian victuals. 10-5. $5 festival only, admission to the festival and Strawbery Banke Museum $12. Marcy Street, Portsmouth. 603-433-1100. (www.strawberybanke.org)

Annual New Hampshire Highland Games. *Always the second weekend (Friday-Sunday) after Labor Day.* The largest gathering of Scots in the East is right at home in the lush greenery of Loon Mountain. For over 20 years, the sounds of fiddles, harps, and bagpipes have floated through the air over the 70 clans and thousands of others who attend. In between dancing, golf, strongman competitions, and sheepdog trials, many gather under tents to share histories. Workshops, which include whiskey-tasting and genealogical research, strengthen bonds. Shortbread, meat pies, and fish-and-chips help fill out kilts worn by contenders in the best-dressed Highlander competition. Competitions are held in piping, drumming, athletics, pipe bands, Scottish fiddle, and Celtic harp. 9-5. Call for tickets and prices. Loon Mountain Recreation Area, Lincoln. 800-358-SCOT. (www.nhscot.org)

Apple Harvest Day. *Always the first Saturday in October.* This New England harvest celebration features an outdoor crafts fair with more than 100 crafters, entertainment, pancake breakfast, apple-pie baking contest, and games. 9-4. Free. Downtown and Henry Law Park along Central Ave., Dover. 603-742-2218.

Shaker Harvest Festival. *Always the first Saturday in October.* This event features harvest foods; hands-on activities such as cider pressing and butter churning; horse-drawn hayrides; children's activities; and demonstrations of crafts, sheepherding, and ox handling. 11-4. $5, youths $2. Enfield Shaker Museum, Rte. 4A, Enfield. 603-632-4346.

Annual Wool Arts Tour. *Always held the Saturday and Sunday of Columbus Day weekend.* Winding country roads and gentle mountains make the Monadnock region the perfect place for a weekend drive, especially during the height of fall foliage. The self-guided tour lets you meander the region's back roads while peeking in on several farms. Watch wool shearing, spinning, and dyeing — and ask questions

along the way. Children especially seem to enjoy the tour: They meet sheep, play with angora rabbits, and receive one-on-one knitting instruction. It's a good time to stock up on homemade socks and hats or gather material for your own woolly projects, for winter is just around the corner. 9-4. Free. Antrim, Hillsboro, Washington, Henniker. 603-588-6637.

Fall Foliage Festival. *Always the Satuday and Sunday of Columbus Day weekend.* A celebration of autumn with country breakfasts, a chicken barbecue, lobster dinners, a five-mile road race, a farmers' market, and arts and crafts; also ox pulling and woodsmen's competitions. Saturday 7 A.M.- 8 P.M., Sunday 7-6. Free; parking $3. Center of town, Warner. 603-456-9775.

Keene Pumpkin Festival. *Usually held the Saturday before Halloween.* Keene earned the Guinness World Record for displaying the most carved pumpkins, and in years past, the fiery array of more than 17,000 illuminated jack-o'-lanterns has included gourds from England, Ecuador, Denmark, and the Balkan Peninsula, as well as many from local fields. Costumed children parade and

courtesy Old Sturbridge Village

Apples being prepared for old-fashioned cider pressing.

collect treats on what is reputed to be the widest Main Street in America. Bring a pumpkin and a votive candle, and enjoy music and events all day and into the night. 10-10; final pumpkin count at 8 P.M. Free. Main St., Keene. 603-358-5344.

Metcalf Farm Halloween Weekend. *Pumpkin lighting takes place the two days preceding Halloween, and Halloween Day itself.* With help from friends and neighbors, and sometimes even strangers, the Metcalf family carves hundreds of pumpkins to light the fields of their 200-year-old farm for Halloween. Starting in mid-September, they sell over 10,000 orange cucurbits; then, as a thank-you to the customers, they adorn their barn, roofs, bankings, and greenhouses with glowing grimaces. Follow a ghost trail into the back field, if you dare. Free. Rte. 25, Piermont. 603-272-4372.

VERMONT

Hawk Walk. *September to November.* The 20-minute hike up Putney Mountain is what we call a bargain-basement price for a million-dollar view. And from September through late fall there's a bonus: Thousands of migrating hawks fly within sight of its rocky summit.

Stop at the Putney General Store for a sandwich and directions to the trailhead. Once on top, you'll be lifting your binoculars in the company of hard-core hawk watchers who can spot sharpies and broadwings by the mere flap of their feathers. Over a thousand have been known to fly by in a single morning. Trailhead off Putney Mountain Rd., Putney General Store, Rte. 5, Putney. 802-387-5842.

Southern Vermont Garlic & Herb Festival. *Always the Saturday of Labor Day weekend.* Enjoy samples of all sorts of garlic-inflected foods provided by local restaurants; take weed walks; participate in games such as garlic golf and the garlic toss; and join other brave souls in the garlic-eating contest. 10-5. $3. Jct. rtes. 9 and 100 South, Wilmington. 802-368-7147.

Bennington's Annual Antique and Classic Car Show and Swap Meet. *Always the second weekend (Friday-Sunday) after Labor Day.* This three-day show attracts over 700 vintage autos and more than 400 vendors of auto-related paraphernalia each year, but we're partial to the tractors. After ogling meticulously restored woodies and all those gleam-

Pumpkin harvest at Old Sturbridge Village.

courtesy Old Sturbridge Village

ing fenders, we find the old farm-equipment nuts. They're in the field playing tractor games like weight pulling, "dunk the dog," and blind man's race. Over 75 dated machines (some rusty, others handsome) turn out, including a few doodlebugs — modified Model T's cobbled together for farm use, proof that frugality is the true mother of invention. 9-4. $5, children under 12 free. Willow Park, Kocher Dr., off Rte. 7, Bennington. 802-447-3311. (www.bennington.com)

Annual Shelburne Farms Harvest Festival. *Always the third Saturday in September.* The emphasis here is on the environment, as is much of Shelburne Farms' work. The Green Mountain Audubon Society is on hand with workshops. There's also a children's farm yard, lots of exhibits, and demonstrations from Vermont quilters, broommakers, and other crafters. Vermont performers such as storytellers and singers entertain throughout the day. There are free hayrides on the grounds designed by Olmsted, and there's even a puppet workshop for the kids. 10-4. $5, children $3, under 3 free. Shelburne Farms, Harbor Rd., Shelburne. 802-985-8686. (www.shelburnefarms.org)

Northeast Kingdom Fall Foliage Festival. *Always starts on Sunday of the last weekend in September and runs though the first Saturday in October.* One day in each town. Bazaars, exhibits, nature and village tours, and church suppers celebrate Vermont's fall foliage in eight neighboring towns. Some towns offer bus tours. Times vary. Free; fee for bus tours. Marshfield, Walden, Cabot, Plainfield, Peacham, Barnet, Groton, and St. Johnsbury. 802-563-2472.

Weston Antiques Show. *Always held the first weekend that has an October date in it, and runs Thursday-Sunday.* Thirty-six outstanding exhibitors from around the country present their wares. Attendance: 2,000. Thursday preview party 5-7 P.M., Friday-Saturday 10-5, Sunday 10-4; $25 for the party, $5 for the show. Weston Playhouse, Rte. 100, Weston. 802-824-4100.

Annual Stowe Foliage Art and Fine Craft Festival. *Always the second weekend (Friday-Sunday) in October.* 180 artists and craftspeople. 10-5. $6; free parking. Top Notch Field, Rte. 108, Stowe. 802-253-7321.

Foliage Fest and Tree Tag. *Begins the Saturday of Columbus Day weekend, plus the next two weekends. (Three weekends, all told.)* If you're the type who finishes holiday shopping in July, why not tag your tannenbaum in October? Elysian Hills Tree Farm combines a family foliage frolic with a chance to choose your Christmas tree. Wander through 100-acre woods, hop on a hayride, buy pumpkins for your porch, learn of old-fashioned organic rhubarb and heirloom turnips (both grown on-property), and refresh with cider and doughnuts. Best of all, you can arrange for all your greenery — wreaths, garlands, and trees — to deck your December door. Weekends noon-4. Free. Elysian Hills Tree Farm, I-91 to Rte. 5 to Middle Rd., Dummerston. 802-257-0233.

Time Line. *Always held the Saturday and Sunday of Columbus Day Weekend.* The hills are alive with the sound of war on Hogback Mountain this Columbus Day weekend. Authentic battle encampments span nearly 2,000 years of history. Meet Roman, Revolutionary, and Civil War soldiers outfitted with real and reproduction garb and weaponry. Peacetime is portrayed, too; reenactors are "in character" and eager to chat about period cooking, crafts, and camp life, as well as the action they've seen. On a clear day you'll be treated to a 100-mile view that's just as good for the soul as it is for spotting the enemy. Saturday 10-5, Sunday 10-3. Donation. Living History Museum, Rte. 9, four miles east of Wilmington. 802-464-5569.

MASSACHUSETTS

Gloucester Schooner Festival. *Always held Labor Day weekend.* This weekend includes the Mayor's Race for 100-foot schooners, races for other classes, a parade of sail, deck tours, public sails, a Saturday night fish fry, a boat-light parade (4th), and fireworks (4th, 9:30 P.M.). Times vary; free. Harbor Loop, Gloucester Harbor, Gloucester. 978-283-1601. (www.cape-ann.com/cacc)

Family Fun Days. *Always falls on the Sunday and Monday of Labor Day weekend.* Entertainment and hands-on activities for all ages. Enjoy toy hot-air balloon flights, 19th-century games on the Common; music, storytelling, puppets, and other amusements, especially for families. 9-5. Free with general admis-

sion to the Village. Old Sturbridge Village, 1 Old Sturbridge Village Rd., Sturbridge. 508-347-3362. (www.osv.org)

King Richard's Faire. *Starts Labor Day weekend and runs for the next eight weekends.* Have a Renaissance romp with roving minstrels, winsome wenches, swordsmen, and soothsayers, when hundreds of actors re-create a 16th-century marketplace at festival time. King Richard and Queen Katherine encourage merrymaking, from jousting and jesting to juggling and mime. Wash down a spit-roasted slice of pig with a yard of beer, join in the royal parade, and shop for crafts in the bazaar. Some visitors dress for the occasion, and you can, too; faire wear is available for rent. 10:30-6. $18, children ages 5-12 $9, under 5 free. Rte. 58, South Carver. 508-866-2311, 508-866-5391.

Outdoor Antiques & Collectibles Show. *Always starts the Tuesday after Labor Day, and runs until the following Sunday.* The largest flea market in New England features more than 4,000 dealers. If there's something you're looking for, it's probably here. You just have to find it. Here are some tips: the best day to

shop is the first day a show opens, and be there early; expect to barter; if you see something you like, buy it — don't expect it to still be there when you circle back in 30 minutes. And dress for the outdoors. We speak from experience: Even if the skies look clear, wear sturdy shoes and bring the umbrella. Generally open daybreak-6 P.M. Some show lots charge a small admission fee; others do not. Rte. 20, Brimfield. 413-283-6149 or 283-2418.

Essex Clamfest. *Always the Saturday after Labor Day.* Restaurants compete for the title of best chowder in town (tastings $3); there is also an arts and crafts fair as well as games, pony rides, and entertainment. 11-3. Free. Memorial Park, Rte. 22, Essex. 978-283-1601.

Banjo & Fiddle Contest. *Always held the second Saturday of September.* Watch or participate in this amazing banjo and fiddle contest. Contestants will compete for $2,500 in cash, trophies, and ribbons. Contest categories include old-time banjo, fiddle, bluegrass banjo, bluegrass fiddle, banjo-other styles, twin fiddle, ethnic fiddle, and the very popular banjo and fiddle-any style. Free work-

Families enjoy the oxen during a celebration of farm life.

shops taught by the experts! Food, drink, and a helpful music store will be there as well. Register early to guarantee a spot. 10-6. Free. Boarding House Park, 40 French St., Lowell. 978-970-5000. (www.nps.gov/lowe)

Annual Harwich Cranberry Festival. *Held the first and second weekends after Labor Day.* Billed as the "biggest small-town celebration in the country," starts with a kid's day on the 9th, with a sand-sculpture contest and other beach fun at Bank Street Beach (10-4; free; Bank St., Harwich Port). The second weekend includes a professional arts and crafts show, including 300 juried exhibitors, a Cranberry Expo (home/trade show), a midway, and fireworks (16th, 8 P.M.). Saturday the 16th 10-8, Sunday 10-5. $4, children 12 and under free; free parking, free shuttle-bus service on the second weekend. Harwich High School, Oak St., Harwich. 508-430-2811.

Annual Bourne Scallop Festival. *Always held the second weekend (Friday-Sunday) of September.* This is the largest scallop festival on the East Coast — a marketplace for crafts, gifts, and specialty foods amid a background of continuous stage entertainment and children's rides and games. Friday-Saturday 11-10, Sunday 11-8. $1; additional fee for dinner; free parking. Buzzards Bay Park, Main St., base of the railroad bridge, Buzzards Bay. 508-759-6000.

Farm City Festival. *Always the weekend after Labor Day.* No needles in these haystacks, but you may find candy or a gewgaw during a treasure hunt in the timothy down on Prowse Farm just south of Boston. This 44-acre farm was once J. Malcolm Forbes's renowned breeding stable; now it's an emerald oasis in suburbia. Spend the day shopping for fresh food and flowers, sip wine, sample cheese, meet miniature horses and Clydesdales, and bump into a llama or an emu. There will be wool spinning and log sawing, horse- and tractor-drawn hayrides, magic shows, 4-H exhibits and antique tractors, native song and country dance, and also the Raptor Project (the largest traveling exhibit of birds of prey in North America), equestrian demonstrations, and a climbing wall. This year's featured attraction is the Fernald Lumber Yankee Hitch. 10-5. Free; parking $5. Historic Prowse Farm, exit 2B off Rte. 128 (Rte. 138 to Milton). Right at light, farm on right, Canton. 781-828-FARM.

Gloucester Seafood Festival. *Held the third weekend in September.* A celebration of this old seaport and its principal product, featuring a food pavilion, harbor and boat tours, marine arts and crafts, entertainment, and fishing contests and demonstrations.

Fall is the best time to visit our living-history museums.

Friday 4-8 P.M., Saturday 11-8, Sunday noon-7. Free. St. Peter's Park, Waterfront, Gloucester. 978-283-1601. (www.cape-ann.com/cacc)

Old Deerfield Fall Craft Fair.

Held the fourth weekend of September. More than 260 crafters gather on the lawn of Memorial Hall Museum under the foliage for this two-day juried show, which attracts traditional folk artists and contemporary hand-crafters, from Shaker furniture makers and rug hookers to potters and fiber artists. Find New England favorites like clam chowder and Wind-sor chairs alongside wooden toy carvers and basket weavers. Bring the family — there's a special game-and-toy area just for kids. 10-5. $6, children 12 and under $1. On the lawn of Memorial Hall Museum, exit 24 off I-91, six miles north on rtes. 5 and 10, Old Deerfield. 413-774-7476. (www.deerfield-craft.org)

Harvest Festival.

Generally the Saturday before the Topsfield Fair. A celebration of a bountiful harvest at the centuries-old picturesque farm. Artisans demonstrate and sell crafts, and there is pumpkin decorating, a children's craft table, horse-drawn hayrides, house tours, and old-time fiddlers. 11-5. $4, children $3. Spencer-Pierce-Little Farm, 5 Little's Ln., Newbury. 978-462-2634.

Annual Waters Farm Days.

Always the first weekend with an October date in it. Free horse-drawn hay-wagon rides, lumberjack demonstrations, a Yankee heritage craft show, displays of gas engines and tractors, Revolutionary War encampments, antique farm equipment, house tours, petting zoo, games and activities, live music, and much, much more! Food and refreshments available along with Waters Farm's specialty hot apple crisp topped with ice cream! 10-4. $3, under 12 $1; free to those in historic costumes or antique clothes. Follow signs from Rte. 395, exit 4A or Rte. 146 to Central Tpk., Oxford exit, Waters Rd., Sutton. 508-883-3839.

Haunted Happenings.

Always starts the Friday of Columbus Day weekend and runs through October 31. When you're thinking of Halloween, witches come to mind. When you're thinking of witches, Salem comes to mind. We can think of few better places to celebrate Halloween, because the whole town participates in the more than 80 events — officially the largest Halloween festival in the entire world. Review the lives of the so-called witches of Salem's past, then visit spell-casting workshops, a psychic fair, candlelight walks, and fiendish feasts. In addition to parades, fireworks, and kids' days, there are loads of macabre happenings — haunted houses, ghost-story telling, and other wicked events leading up to Halloween night itself. Town-wide, Rte. 1A, Salem. 978-744-0013. (www.salemhaunted happenings.com)

Apple Festival.

Always the Saturday of Columbus Day

weekend. Festival preparations begin when four local orchards donate "drops" and families gather 40 bushels of crisp Cortlands. Members of a local congregation peel, pare, core, and slice the apples, then follow with a two-day "bake-in" to prepare 500 pies with handmade crusts. The pastries are the star of the festival, offered fresh, frozen, or by the slice with a scoop of ice cream or cheddar cheese. Press a glass of refreshing cider before picking up a small sugar pumpkin of your very own. 10-3. Free. Town common, and the grounds of the Harvard Evangelical Congregational Church, Harvard. 978-453-8788.

Annual Cranberry Harvest Festival. *Always Columbus Day weekend, Saturday through Monday.* Visitors can take helicopter tours over the autumnal splendor or get down to earth by tasting a fresh berry and talking to growers. Cranberry-related cooking demonstrations and contests, farmers' markets, and a food court round out the activities. 10-4. Free; parking $2. Edaville Cranberry Bog, Rochester Rd. (off Rte. 58), South Carver. 508-295-5799. (www.cranberries.org)

Paradise City Arts Festival. *Always Columbus Day weekend, Saturday through Monday.* A festival of juried contemporary crafts and fine art from more then 200 American artists, including custom-made furniture, paintings, ceramics, art glass, metalwork, fashion, photography, jewelry, and sculpture; festival dining tent features chefs from the area's most popular restaurants; children's entertainment, live jazz performances, and continuous demonstrations. Saturday-Sunday 10-6, Monday 10-5. $8, seniors $5, children $2; free parking. Tri-County Fairgrounds, Rte. 9, Northampton. 413-586-6324. (www.paradise-city.com)

Shades of Autumn. *Always the Saturday through Monday of Columbus Day weekend.* Why eat just one kind of apple when you can have 119? That's how many varieties Stearns Lothrop Davenport cultivated by collecting cuttings from old orchards. Now his trees are in the care of Tower Hill Botanic Garden. Take a tour of the antique apple orchard and sample several varieties of pre-20th-century apples. On a guided walking tour, you'll learn about differences in taste and texture. Bring home a sample of your favorites. 10-5. $7, seniors $5, children $3. Tower Hill Botanic Garden, 11 French Dr., Boylston. 508-869-6111. (www.towerhillbg.org)

Vineyard Craftsmen Arts & Crafts Fair. *Always Saturday and Sunday of Columbus Day weekend.* Over 60 artists and crafters, including both local artisans and off-island crafters, display wares ranging from woodworking and jewelry to ceramics, clothing, and skin care. Proceeds benefit art scholarship fund. 10-4. Free. Edgartown Elementary School, Robinson Rd., Edgartown, Martha's Vineyard. 508-693-7927.

Columbus Day Parade. *Always the Sunday of Columbus Day weekend.* Starts at Springfield Technical Community College on Federal Street to State Street, winds down to Main Street, and ends at Columbus's statue at the corner of Main and Mill streets. Parade includes 24 bands, ten floats, and a replica of the *Santa Maria.* There are vendors, too. 1 P.M. Free. Downtown, Springfield. 413-732-7449.

Ashfield Fall Festival. *Always the Saturday and Sunday of Columbus Day weekend.* The center of this small

Massachusetts town is transformed during this community celebration. There are quality crafts for sale, as well as art, food, games, exhibits, and continuous entertainment. Festival favorites include maple fried dough from Gray's Sugarhouse, craft demonstrations at Ashfield's historic town hall, and tag sales running the length of Main Street. 10-5. Free. Main St. (Rte. 116), Ashfield. 413-585-5253.

Great Jack-o'-Lantern Fest. *Starts during the middle of October and runs for eight nights.* Thousands of creatively carved pumpkins transform a woodland park into an incandescent art gallery. Spooky tunes, special effects, and theme-carved gourds create over a dozen scenes, from a science fiction shrine with caricatures of Spock and Captain Kirk to a den of steaming volcanoes, howling dinosaurs, and lava, all of it rendered in rind. Over 40 carvers work to create the gourd-scapes, using 50 giant pumpkins (each over 100 pounds) and truckloads of smaller ones. 6-10 P.M.; $9, children 10 and under $5. Carbuncle Park, Rte. 12, Oxford. 508-987-8272 or 508-987-5681.

Harvest Weekend. *Generally the third weekend in October.* Come help farmers dig potatoes, husk corn, shell beans, and thresh oats. Find out how gardeners generations ago saved seed, dried herbs, and stored vegetables in root cellars and storage pits. Stroll the common to enjoy New England's stunning fall colors. 9-5. Free with general admission to the Village. Old Sturbridge Village, 1 Old Sturbridge Village Rd., Sturbridge. 800-SEE-1830. (www.osv.org)

CONNECTICUT

Booth Library Book Sale. *Always held Saturday-Tuesday over Labor Day weekend.* One of New England's largest book sales will feature 100,000 books and recordings. This annual fund-raising event has something for everyone. Books will be offered in more than 60 categories, plus computer software, records, rare books, and puzzles will be available. Saturday-Sunday 10-5, Monday 9-4. $5 on Saturday only. Shelton House, Newtown. 203-426-4533.

Guilford Fair. *Always the weekend preceding the Durham Fair — usually the third weekend in September.* This annual fair features a cir-

cus (all three days), a nationally known country music act (Saturday night), home arts, agricultural exhibits, flowers, a giant pumpkin contest, and entertainment each day. Friday 1-11 P.M., Saturday 9 A.M.-11 P.M., Sunday 9-8. Admission charged; free shuttle buses from free commuter lots. Guilford Fairgrounds, Stonehouse Ln., Guilford. 203-421-3110.

Annual Orange Country Fair. *Always the third weekend in September.* Old-fashioned country fair with Doodlebugs (old-fashioned farm trucks modified to drag heavy weights), tractor pulls, farm animals, a pigeon tent (homing pigeons released every hour), arts and crafts, rides for small children, and an antique show with 25 vendors. Saturday 10-6, Sunday 10-5. $5. Orange Country Fairgrounds, Rte. 152, Orange Center Rd., Orange. 203-795-2800.

Annual Outdoor Antiques Show. *Always the last Saturday in September.* At this show 100-plus dealers display and sell furniture and small collectibles. The show is held outdoors, rain or shine. Sponsored by the Lebanon Historical Society. 10-4. $3; free parking and refreshments.

Town green, rtes. 87 and 207, Lebanon. 860-642-7247.

Annual Chowderfest. *Always Columbus Day weekend.* Chowder, water, foliage. Seaport open 9-5, food served from 11-3. $16, children 6-12 $8, 5 and under free; plus cost of food. Mystic Seaport, 75 Greenmanville Ave., Mystic. 860-572-5315, 888-9-SEAPORT.

Head of the Connecticut Regatta. *Always the Sunday of Columbus Day weekend.* "The Connecticut River is a natural race course with a 90-degree bend at Middletown," says regatta administrator Pat Callahan. More than 600 rowing shells run the second-largest such contest in the United States. Single, double, four-man, and eight-seat shells slip off the launch in Cromwell, pass under bridges, and slice silently through sheltered riverine woods — and past the boisterous crowd at Harbor Park — before crossing the finish line 3.5 miles later. More than 3,000 competitors vie for top times, from high school and university crews to masters teams and rowers from Canada, Ireland, and England. 9-5. Spectators free. Connecticut River, off Rte. 9, Middletown. 860-346-1042. (www.hctr.org)

Fall Foliage Festival. *Always the Saturday after Columbus Day.* Artisans, crafters, furniture-makers, food vendors, and a wide variety of activities for everyone young and old. There's also live entertainment, an antique auto show, and a small locomotive ride for kids. 10-4. Free. Shuttle-bus service available from free parking areas. Main St. (Rte. 44), Winsted. 860-379-1652.

Children enjoy a Civil War reenactment.

RHODE ISLAND

Rhode Island Labor and Ethnic Heritage Festival. *Always held the Sunday immediately preceding Labor Day.* Events and exhibits at this family event include folk, ethnic, and children's music on three stages; dancing; labor exhibits; children's activities; traditional folk arts and crafts; ethnic foods; and photography. Noon-6 P.M.; free. Slater Mill Historic Site, 67 Roosevelt St., Pawtucket. 401-725-8638.

Annual Classic Yacht Regatta, Classic Yacht Parade, Nautical Bazaar, and Vintage Automobile Rendezvous. *Always held the Friday through Sunday of Labor Day weekend.* Join the excitement at this event and view more than 100 wooden classic yachts racing through Newport Harbor on Saturday. Sunday's festivities include a nautical bazaar, Dixie band, parade (Sunday 2 P.M.), vintage automobile rendezvous, children's activities, refreshments, and more. All day. Free; free parking. Grounds of the Museum of Yachting, Fort Adams State Park, Newport. 401-847-1018. (www.moy.org)

French Farmers Market. *Always held the second Saturday of September.* French-Canadian food, music, and dance. Arts and crafts, open-air market, free historic trolley tours, apple pie contest, pony rides, and much more. 9-3. Free. River Island Park, Woonsocket. 401-769-9846.

Annual Burrillville Arts Festival. *Always the weekend after Labor Day.* One of northern Rhode Island's biggest and best outdoor arts festivals. See a wide display of paintings, crafts, handmade works, and much more, set in historic Harrisville village. Festival also features fireworks, a chicken barbecue, and a band concert. 10-5. Free. Ample parking; shuttle-bus service provided. Assembly grounds, Harrisville Village. 401-568-4345.

Fall Foliage in the Blackstone River Valley. *September-October.* Enjoy the beautiful colors of fall in many different ways: by riverboat, train, trolley, airplane or helicopter, canoe, bicycle, or a walk with llamas! Times and dates vary, so call for a schedule and more information. Various locations in and around Pawtucket. 401-724-2200.

Pasta Challenge. *Always held the Sunday following Labor Day.* Dozens of Rhode Island restaurants cook up six tons of pasta and 800 gallons of sauce for 5,000 pastaphiles. Noon-4. $10, children 10 and under $3. Davol Sq., Providence. 401-351-6440.

International Boat Show. *Always the third full weekend in September, Thursday-Sunday.* The largest boat show in the Northeast, spanning ten acres along the historic waterfront. Features hundreds of new boats in the water, sailboats, powerboats, and equipment from over 600 exhibitors. 10-6. $12-$30. Newport Yachting Center, Old Port Marine, and Bannister's Wharf, all along America's Cup Ave., Newport. 401-846-1115. (www.newportexhibition.com)

Run Around the Block. *Always the Saturday after Labor Day.* 15K run around the island on rolling blacktop roads. Starts at 1:30 P.M. Free to watch. Isaac's Corner, Block Island. 800-383-2474.

Block Island Birding Weekend. *Always the first weekend with an October date in it.* Bird with members of the Audubon Society of Rhode Island from dawn until 4 P.M. at one of the best sites on the East Coast to observe migrant species. Birding followed by lectures and guided walks focusing on fall migration. All lodging and meals are included; call for prices. Block Island. 401-949-5454.

Annual Oktoberfest. *Always Columbus Day weekend.* German entertainment, food, and musicians from Bavaria. Saturday noon-10, Sunday noon-8, Monday noon-6; $8, children 12 and under free. Newport Yachting Center, America's Cup Ave., Newport. 401-846-1600.

Blackstone River Valley Fall Train Excursion. *Always the Saturday after Columbus Day.* During the four-hour round-trip ride, travel along the railways of the Blackstone River Valley, view peak foliage, and learn about both the history of the region and about the Providence & Worcester Railroad. 10-2. Call for reservations and prices. Cumberland, Rhode Island, to Worcester, Massachusetts. 401-724-2200.

Final Advice:

DOS AND DON'TS OF

Fall Foliage

With over 60 years of travel editorial under our belts, we know a thing or two about how best to enjoy foliage in New England. Here are some tips for being a savvy leaf watcher.

1 **DO** get lost. Carry a good map (we like the detailed atlas and gazetteer by DeLorme mapmakers in Yarmouth, Maine; 207-846-7000), and get a little lost. With 7,401 miles of unpaved roads in Vermont alone, there's ample opportunity to find adventure.

2 **DO** observe proper foliage etiquette. Locals use the back roads to get from here to there as promptly as possible. If you're oohing and ahhing at five miles per hour, pull over when someone's behind you. And **DO** ask a landowner's permission before tramping into the fields.

3 **DO** get out of your car, and walk, and smell, and listen. Foliage is the most sensual of New England seasons, from the sweet aromas of our apple orchards to the swirling of leaves and wind, from that first whiff of wood smoke on a frosty fall day to the crunch of dry foliage underfoot. *Seeing* foliage is only *half* the fun. Many of us remember our parents shoving us into the car when we were young and driving for hours with out-of-town relatives. We hated it.

How TO BE A SAAVY LEAF WATCHER.

4 **DO** visit New Hampshire's Franconia Notch and see the Old Man of the Mountain. But **DON'T** slow the car down to a crawl on I-93 to see him. Pull into the viewing area, get out of your car, and go for a walk down the historic and scenic paths.

5 **DO** pick up a parking pass for New Hampshire's White Mountain National Forest to avoid a parking ticket. Funds go to protecting the forest habitat. Your best bet is to phone ahead (603-466-2713) for the pass or write: Fee Demo Program, White Mountain National Forest, 300 Glen Rd., Gorham, NH 03581. 12-month pass $20, $25 for two vehicles in the same family; one- to seven-day pass $5; seniors half price.

6 **DO** as professional foliage photographers do when composing photos. A single crimson maple in the foreground with a white church behind and a little blue sky showing will translate better than a 40-mile-distant panoramic view. **DON'T** forget your polarizing filter; the filter enhances the vivid colors. **DO** bring lots of film.

7 **DO** look for changing views. Search out roads with hills and curves, roads that meander through changing vistas of woods and farms and small villages. If there is a better combination than water and stone (stone walls, stone bridges) and autumn leaves, we don't know it.

8 **DON'T** be a hit-and-run leaf watcher. **DON'T** rush. A picnic by a waterfall beats dashing all about, hoping to see just one more place before dark.

9 **DON'T** panic that "peak" is passing you by. Peak color is a continuum, not a moment fixed in time. Within a few miles you'll see different stages, depending on types of trees and elevation. "Seeking peak is missing the point," says Kit Anderson, a Vermont cultural geographer. "It's like condensing the entire season and the entire experience into this one moment, like a sound byte, and people miss it."

10 **DO** respect "Moose Crossing" signs. Northern New England is moose country. Cars and passengers do not always survive collisions with 1,000-pound moose.

11 **DO** wake early. The colors will be most vivid with the morning dew and morning light. Watching the dawn mist rise off our forest-ringed lakes and rivers may be the best treat of all.

12 **DO** linger to enjoy the late-afternoon light. The deep shadows late in the day set off all colors against areas of darkness.

13 **DO** have lodging reservations during the prime leaf-watching period of late September to mid-October. **DON'T** expect to stay for just one night. Most places require a two-night minimum during foliage.

14 **DON'T** let your lack of lodging stop your visit. Local Vermont chambers of commerce, for instance, keep a quiet list of hospitable locals who open up that spare room in their homes for intrepid leaf watchers. If possible, **DO** come midweek.

15 **DO** look skyward, especially if you're hiking. Mid- to late September is when thousands of broad-winged hawks ride the thermals south. The raptor migration is worthy of a trip in itself.

16 **DON'T** be a color snob and ignore everything except bright reds. Trees exhibit an astonishing range of colors. Foliage season means subtle shadings of peach and corals and apricot, the delicate yellows of beech and birch, the soft browns and purples. **DON'T** let rain keep you indoors. Wet weather brings out the most vivid colors.

17 **DO** go beyond where most people go. Vermonters have a saying: When good people die, they go to

Vermont. When good Vermonters die, they go to the North-east Kingdom — but relatively few tourists do.

18 **DO** visit northern Maine for wondrous color with few crowded roads. But **DON'T** ever think you have the right-of-way when approaching a logging truck on the narrow roads.

19 **DO** let New Englanders help you find the prime local foliage spots. Best bet for advice: district forest rangers. Many of them are "leaf spotters," asked by the state to report daily and weekly on foliage conditions in their area. Their pride in their home vistas spills over if you stop in at their headquarters and ask where *they* would go.

20 **DO** include valleys and the seacoast in your travels. Though most people head to the mountains, in fact the lowland areas boast the brightest and earliest colors. Look for the swamp maples surrounding the marshes.

21 **DO** use technology to help your foliage viewing. *Yankee*'s "Foliage Central" on our Web site, NewEngland.com, gives one-stop viewing of foliage around New England. Here you will find our favorite driving and walking tours, a leaf-identification chart, foliage hot-line phone numbers, and links to all the New England states' foliage sites.

FROM A *Quaking Aspen*

ED MAPLE

RED MAPLE

SUGAR MAPLE

ECKLED ALDER

TAMARACK

TUPELO

AMERICAN MOUNTAIN ASH

QUAKING ASPEN

Illustration by Erick Ingraham

NAME	COLORS, FEATURES & CHANGES
AMERICAN MOUNTAIN ASH	Bright red berries and red leaves; prominent on high ridges in early fall.
YELLOW BIRCH	White and mountain birch, colors the high slop bright yellow in early October.
TAMARACK	The only local conifer that sheds all its needles; yellow needles stand out in swamps.
WHITE ASH	Yellow, purple. Stands out in October; leaves fall with first heavy frost after changing color.
NORTHERN RED OAK	Leaves turn deep red and orange, then a warm dark brown.
PIN CHERRY	Purple, green leaves, changing to yellow.
SUMAC	Dark red or purple leaves; fuzzy twigs resemble antlers "in velvet."
SUGAR MAPLE	Yellow, orange, and sometimes red; mid-Octob most prominent colors.
RED MAPLE	Stands out early; bright red with yellow, orang bare by mid-October; also called swamp map
STRIPED MAPLE	Its huge leaves turn bright yellow or a cream co stands out in mid-October.
QUAKING ASPEN	Leaves stay green until late in the season, then turn yellow, often after other trees are bare.
BASSWOOD	These large leaves turn pale yellow; basswood also known as linden.
AMERICAN BEECH	Yellow leaves fade to bronze and often stay on tree through the winter.
WITCH HAZEL	Yellow leaves camouflage small yellow flowers.
SPECKLED ALDER	Doesn't change color, so stands out in swamps green leaves brown a little and fall in Novembe
LARGE-TOOTHED ASPEN	Has larger leaves than quaking aspen, but has same color changes.
WHITE BIRCH	With yellow and mountain birch, colors the hi slopes bright yellow in early October.
TUPELO	Commonly found near swamps; leaves turn re

The color bars show color changes from month to month. Colors shown from top to bottom within a ba
Color changes are given as a guide only. Leaves in the northern part of the state will change sooner, those

| SEPTEMBER | OCTOBER | NOVEMBER |

present at the same time. Color changes from left to right within a bar are changes over that time period.
the southern part, later.

HOW TO TELL A *Speckled Alde*

AMERICAN BEECH

PIN CHERRY

YELLOW BIRCH

WITCH HAZEL

WHITE ASH

ST▮

BASSWOOD

NORTHERN RED OAK

WHITE BIRCH

SUMAC

LARGE-TOOTHED ASPEN